SO-BEA-711

CORPORATE SOCIETY AND EDUCATION

CORPORATE

SOCIETY

and EDUCATION

The Philosophy of Elijah Jordan

by **GEORGE BARNETT** (and **JACK OTIS**)

FOREWORD BY MAX FISCH

Ann Arbor: The University of Michigan Press

FOREWORD

In recent decades the social sciences have flourished in the United States beyond anything imagined in other countries and times. They have enjoyed a support from government, industry, and the foundations which has been second only to that of the natural sciences essential to industry, warfare, and rocketry.

Despite this flourishing, however, the literature of social sciences on the whole has been intellectually thin and anemic. The opening gambits of radical, progressive, liberal, and conservative argument on a wide range of issues have become commonplaces. There is frequent and premature recourse to principles of philosophic generality and to universal human sentiments beyond which, it would seem, there is no appeal except to force. Rare is the attempt, and rarer the success, at working out the middle connections between the principles and sentiments on the one hand and the particular measures on the other, in behalf of which the appeals are made.

There is in fact only one social philosophy of even moderate complexity that is at all widely known, and it cannot be found in the work of any single philosopher, but is variously pieced together from the ethics sketched in James's "The Moral Philosopher and the Moral Life," the metaphysics of Dewey's *Experience and Nature,* the social psychology of G. H. Mead, and the political theory of A. F. Bentley's *The Process of Government.*

We have produced, however, one other social philosophy, of comparable scope and power. It is in my judgment the only one that has sufficient strength to stand up in a strong wind. It is the work of a single philosopher, Elijah Jordan. His central works are *Forms of Individuality* (1927) and *Theory of Legislation* (1930). Among his supporting works, the nearest to these is *The Good Life* (1949).

Jordan did not give separate and extended development, as Dewey did, to the application of his social philosophy to education. There are ample indications in his writings, however, from which such an application can be worked out. This is what Professors Barnett and Otis undertook to do. In the absence, however, of any adequate exposition and interpretation of Jordan's social philosophy itself, Professors Barnett and Otis were obliged to supply that also. It has come about in this way that the first substantial interpretation of Jordan's work appears in a book addressed primarily to students of educational theory.

Both Jordan's philosophy and Professor Barnett and Otis's statement of it deserve to be studied and criticized. If the outcome of such study and criticism is a more democratic philosophy that knows its way through Jordan and beyond—a democratic philosophy with a Jordanian strengthening—so much the better.

Max Fisch

PREFACE

Some years ago we were fortunate enough to participate in an extracurricular seminar in sociology conducted by Erich Ahrens of the University of Illinois. His critical examination of fundamental concepts of sociology, such as the individual, society, human relations, and others, resulted in our conviction that something was basically at fault with the science. Professor Ahrens led us to see that the aversion of social science to philosophy was self-defeating and that for the science to progress it must turn to the philosophy of culture. He excited our interest in Elijah Jordan by making us aware that here was a thinker, almost completely neglected, whose philosophy of culture was a most significant contribution, theoretically and practically, to modern life. It is to Erich Ahrens that we owe our introduction to and understanding of Jordan.

To Archibald W. Anderson of the University of Illinois goes our thanks for the original suggestion and encouragement to undertake this book. Several persons have read the manuscript in its original form and have offered counsel and encouragement which greatly contributed to the improvement of the work and to its completion. For such help we are indebted to James K. Feibleman of Tulane University, Herbert W. Schneider of Columbia University, Lawrence Haworth of Purdue University, and Darnell Rucker of Colorado College. The aid we received from the study of Jordan's legal philosophy by Thomas M. Haynes of Lehigh University goes far beyond that indicated in the text. We are particularly grateful for the efforts of Max Fisch of the University of Illinois, who gave of his time and wisdom throughout the period of preparation. We are, of course, solely responsible for any shortcomings that remain in the book.

Our appreciation for grants-in-aid goes to the All-University Research Committee of Michigan State University, and to the University Research Board of the University of Illinois.

George Barnett
Jack Otis

CONTENTS

INTRODUCTION

Elijah Jordan, American Philosopher

Elijah Jordan (1875–1953) is a little-known American philosopher who, in the view of the writers, has much to say of a practical and theoretical nature about education. His philosophic position, moreover, is flatly opposed to many powerful trends found in modern life, and this may, at the very least, serve the positions which his thought fundamentally contradicts by helping them to sharpen their defense. His theory of the corporate person has been chosen as the object of analysis, for it seems to offer the most direct means by which to comprehend Jordan's implicit or explicit opposition to other positions, as well as the way into the core of his own philosophy, from which one can infer his significance for education. With respect to educational theory, the underlying assumption of this investigation is that educational programing is inevitably based upon a theory of the nature of cultural reality, of that which is assumed to be of ultimate value in the world, and that the adequacy of educational theory is crucially related to the soundness of its foundations in a theory of culture.

Jordan's central importance, perhaps, is as a philosopher of culture, for no matter how abstruse or apparently abstract his speculations are, a point upon which many professional philosophers are agreed, Jordan always has in mind the ongoing activities of man. As he understood it, the philosophic task was to understand the complicated realm of human action. The fact that his thought contradicts many intellectual trends in contemporary life has made for difficulties not only in communication but in being heard at all, and a certain degree of intemperateness of expression found in some of his works is, to a minor extent, a reflection of his solitary struggle to swim against the tide. Much more importantly, the bitterness with which his work is salted is a concomitant of his philosophic insight into the nature of modern civilization and into the failure of theory to come to grips with it effectively. To this task of comprehending the practical activities of man was given every energy that the philosopher could muster, an endeavor that was no mere academic exercise; for implicit throughout the whole of his work is the message: "Civilization is here at stake."

Elijah Jordan lived in a world already interdependent, a world whose development was overwhelmingly in the direction of increased integration. The rapid object development which has occurred in the past century and a half had, in terms of man's mastery of space-time relationships, reduced the world to a size considerably smaller than the area represented by the Greek city-states of classical civilization. Jordan looked out upon a world in which no nation stood alone; none could do so without impairing its own growth and development. The increasing integration of societies throughout the world and their greater objective dependence upon one another are for Jordan irrepressible tendencies as long as civilization continues, although he is far from convinced that civilization will continue at all. Objectively, the isolated society is nonexistent, except in the minds of men whose patriotic exhortations move each nation-state closer to its tomb. Jordan was struck by this unrelatedness of mind to objective fact, and when asked shortly before his death about the evolution of his thought, he replied:

I suppose the greatest challenge came from reflecting on the impact of the first world war. One would have to recall the period of prosperity and optimism preceding the war to understand the shock which came with the deluge of suffering—physically, economically, and socially—which was brought about in the first great world conflagration of our century. My own reflective reaction and my own particular problem was: how is one to explain the objective situation which brought home so powerfully the moral bankruptcy of our so-called culture at the very moment when people's subjective states of mind were running in a completely opposite direction. Almost everyone —except those behind the locked chamber doors—those who really knew—expected humanity to be reaching soon the mecca of prosperity which science from the 18th century French Enlightenment on has promised us; instead came the most fearful rain of blood that the modern world had ever known, the god of progress crumbled—and you as well as I know what the result was. Man asked for a drink of cool spring water and received a cup of warm blood. After the war came the lost generation—the Hemingways and all the rest; fatuous optimism soured into self-pitying pessimism (just as it has done after this war, witness the nauseated, nauseating existentialisms), and the flight into the illusory epicureanism of the roaring twenties soon followed, only to have the bottom drop out with the depression.

This then was the background against which my thinking at the time took place—why did the war happen? What were its real causes? Why should it have come as such a surprise to everyone, to prick the bubble of progress just as it was to reflect myriad beauty and prosperity? [1]

Herein lies the heart of contemporary cultural disorder—the tragic gap between man's mind and the objective realities of his world; therefore, Jordan said, the fundamental problem before man is to develop a mode of thinking consistent with cultural reality. If this is not done, man's thinking will inevitably tend to be empty and abstract, concerned with its own shadowy inner processes or enthralled by a scholasticism of signs and other vain endeavors, while the culture stumbles on like a blinded monster. The development of a logically valid cultural theory is the ultimate desideratum, a development predicated upon a valid metaphysics.

Antimetaphysical Tendencies of Current Philosophy

In Jordan's view the denigration of metaphysics in modern thought is a serious problem. It means that men have come unreflectively to adopt a false metaphysics, for a metaphysics there must be. The sole issue is whether or not it is adequate. The prevalent metaphysics holds that the real has its status as such through becoming an experience, whether that of an individual or a collectivity, so that reality has come to be identified with a state of mind, and the analysis of culture has consequently become psychological or social-psychological. The psychological analysis of cultural reality leads to a failure in man's comprehension of culture and to a correlative inability to develop objective principles for the ordering of life. The whole notion of objective principle, in fact, is lost in attempting to find it through psychological analysis. As Hume effectively demonstrated, when scientific law is defined as the simultaneity or succession of the impressions of an experiencing subject, then all that one may validly speak about are psychological expectancies. The latter constitute the only "law" that man may achieve, since impressions from external objects are all that man may "know." What is true for the natural sciences, empirically or psychologically interpreted, strikes even harder at the attempt to understand the cultural life of man. In the realm of values the position of modern thought is that opinions are galore and everyone is entitled to his own, but objective principles for the evaluation of culture are sought after by deluded fools, religionists, metaphysicians, authoritarians, or simple victims of "common sense" ways of thinking. However, Jordan locates the failure in the psychological approach, which he rejects completely as a source of principle; principle is not to be found in the states of mind of men. If what is real is real by virtue of its relationship to an experiencing subject—individual or collectivity—the world of culture is submerged, and culture is then only a name attached to anything and everything and therefore meaningless.

Jordan's view of culture stands, then, in fundamental opposition to many of the cherished beliefs and firmly held assumptions of modern life. These beliefs and assumptions have taken on institutional form and threaten the continuance of that life itself. A faulty theory of cultural reality underlies the breakdown of contemporary society. An unsound metaphysics rules the day, while the importance of all metaphysics is denied. In contrast to preceding periods in the history of American philosophy, this is an age in which metaphysics, hitherto considered the very heart of philosophy, has been largely discarded as worthless or, worse than that, positively destructive. Formerly, however divergent philosophies may have been, they were largely agreed on the importance of metaphysics, and their differences lay within that province. Now, however, the philosophic issue in part exists, not between one metaphysical doctrine and another—although to some degree this is yet the case— but rather between metaphysical and antimetaphysical positions. Werkmeister believes that by the time of World War II the faith in metaphysics had been replaced by criticism. Surveying recent developments in the history of philosophy in the United States, he says:

. . . anti-metaphysical tendencies now prevail in most philosophic discussions. This is not to say that there is at present no interest in metaphysics in the United States, for there is. . . . But the most stimulating and most significant discussions are now carried on essentially on a nonmetaphysical level and, most often, with a distinctly anti-metaphysical bias.[2]

Morton White, in seeking to characterize the philosophy of the twentieth century, chose finally to call this "The Age of Analysis." He qualifies this definition by calling attention to other movements in the period, but nevertheless believes that the dominant trend has been toward analysis, whereas preceding eras have been characterized by synthesis and the construction of large systems.[3] Positivism has been notably influential in the social sciences, which generally have been based upon it, although, to be sure, many social scientists are quite unconscious of their underlying philosophic position. Nevertheless, these sciences have prided themselves on their freedom from theology and metaphysics, and on the replacement of theological and metaphysical questions by scientific, empirical ones. The influence of positivism has not, however, been confined to these sciences, but has been extended to culture as a whole.

Despite the dominance of positivism in contemporary thought, a number of philosophies continue to sustain themselves and to combat this influence. Philosophers as divergent as Mortimer Adler and Kenneth Benne have depicted the disastrous consequences of positivism for culture generally and for education in particular. Adler has stated that the choice is either God or the professors, theology or positivism, and has chosen the former alternatives.[4] Everett Hall, however, has indicated that this may not exhaust all the possibilities and affirms metaphysics as supplying the ground.[5] Hutchins also, although closely associated with Adler as a leading exponent of rational or classical humanism, suggests that for a skeptical age, theology will be unacceptable and proposes metaphysics as the choice.[6] Sidney Hook, on the other hand, condemns all of the foregoing proposals as false choices. He rejects positivism but also theology and metaphysics. Although he once wrote a book on the metaphysics of pragmatism, and although noted experimentalists such as Childs and Stanley have developed the metaphysics of that position, Hook now rejects metaphysics as an option. The choice for him lies between theology and/or metaphysics on the one hand and experimentalism on the other. Of politics he has said, for example, that quite opposite conclusions may be drawn from the same metaphysical position, or that the same conclusions may be drawn from different metaphysical positions. The same holds true of education.[7] Brubacher, however, concludes that the issue has been stated falsely, and that the question does not involve a choice between metaphysics and antimetaphysics, but between one metaphysical position and another. He maintains that it takes a metaphysics to negate one.[8] To this might be added the frequent observation that positivism, despite its antimetaphysical position, inevitably affirms certain metaphysical assumptions. Hook himself in his earlier writings indicated the ways in which method itself is inescapably bound up in such assumptions. It may be, then, that the either/or choice Hook presents is not adequate; there is ample ground for believing that even his general philosophic position, experimentalism, has an implied metaphysics also.

Jordan's corporatism is overtly metaphysical, but he finds his own position neither with the "metaphysicians" nor the positivists. We need not choose, Jordan says, to ally ourselves with metaphysics, when this is understood to mean the creation of fictitious entities, nor with a positivism that is crudely empirical. He has given considerable attention to the positivistic tendencies of modern thought in general, particularly with reference to politics and law as evidenced in positivistic jurisprudence. While he is generally critical of that thought as based upon naïve empiricism, he nevertheless believes that a significant idea is contained in it. Similarly, he cautions against excessive rationalism as instanced in American and French constitutionalism, which attempted to write the constitution of the state out of the head of man and ignored the environing facts. Nevertheless, metaphysics is essential, even if it is not to be identified with this type of rationalism. Jordan wishes to avoid the abstractions of both the particularism of empiricism and the universalism of rationalism. Jordan's position combines the two approaches in what he himself has called metaphysical positivism, which is a negation of any inherent antithesis between metaphysics and experimentalism. It might be said either that his philosophy is a metaphysical experimentalism or that it is an experimental metaphysics. Yet if the experimentalism of Dewey is identified with or is itself a metaphysical position, Jordan's philosophy is to be distinguished from it. Jordan affirms a metaphysical politics and education which are distinct from those of Dewey, and while the purpose of this study is not comparative, the suggestion here is that Jordan's thought constitutes an original formulation, whatever its likenesses in certain generic terms to other philosophies. As a philosophy which is continuous with idealism yet experimental in nature, which is metaphysical and also positivistic, which is rationalistic and empirical, Jordan's corporatism is worthy of careful attention. It is a distinctive formulation in a period which generally maintains the necessity of choosing either one or the other of the pairs, and which has tended with much self-congratulation to choose for itself the empirical-experimental as either nonmetaphysical or antimetaphysical. Although Jordan was fearful of the danger of system-building as a development of closed, dogmatic positions, nevertheless his philosophy represents an effort to construct an inclusive whole, a task which he did not complete. His effort was expended in the direction of synthesis, and had Jordan had his way, this would not be "The Age of Analysis" but "The Age of Synthesis," provided large formulations could be kept open and growing. If, as Whitehead suggests, fundamental progress depends upon the reinterpretation of basic ideas, then Jordan's philosophy represents a lifelong effort in that direction. His position is a further development and restatement of the political and ethical thinking of Socrates, Plato, and Aristotle. In modern terms it represents a reformulation of objective idealism as expressed, for example, in the work of Bernard Bosanquet and James Edwin Creighton. Some have identified Jordan with the thought and language of Hegel. The effort to catalogue Jordan's philosophy, however, may lead to misinterpretation of his position. As Max Fisch says,

It would be easy to dismiss Jordan's metaphysics as a variant in some respects of Hegelianism, in others of Aristotelianism: his analogical identity is the concrete universal; his Quality-Relation is matter-form; etc. Similarly, it would be possible by some violence, to read into him the Crocean theory of the relations between aesthetic, logic, economic, and ethic. If we are to bring his metaphysics under one or another of Stephen C. Pepper's 'root metaphors,' it will have to be that of the 'organic whole.' But if this be Hegelianism, it is Hegelianism without the dialectic and without optimism; and the differences between this and every other 'organic whole' metaphysics will be found to be as significant as the resemblances. In the end, it must be judged on its own merits, not on those of its antecedents; and there are no helpful labels.[9]

Although, then, the philosophy of Jordan is by no means discontinuous with certain other developments in the history of philosophy, his formulation is novel. Its originality as a theory of cultural reality has great import for education.

Confusion in Ideas of the Corporate

To characterize contemporary society as corporate has become a commonplace. What is implied and often expressed is that previous societies were differently constituted or based upon a different principle, presumably individualistic—at least much more so than the principle of society today. While proponents of divergent philosophies may agree on the fact, at least as far as the descriptive term "corporate" is concerned, their interpretations of the nature and significance of that fact vary. From the point of view of laissez-faire individualism, of course, corporate development has been tragic, and salvation lies in a return to earlier atomistic principles. Even such a dominant factor in culture as the modern corporation, whose existence and development are a flat contradiction of atomism in social and economic theory, is taken to be a private person with private interests—interests not to be contravened by the intrusion of the public controls which are characteristic of interdependent society. The social planning that increasingly marks present societies, here and abroad, is seen as the road to serfdom. Apart from these classical liberal doctrines, however, there have been a number of theories, alike in their rejection of atomism, which affirm corporatism in social theory but nevertheless differ crucially among themselves as to its meaning. Golob would go even further in extending the range of corporatisms by including an extreme form of individualism. He states that corporatism has been associated with theories extending from anarchism or anarchic democracy to nationalistic totalitarianism.[10] Generally, however, the category has not been extended so broadly, and if the range is indeed as great as he indicates, categorization may be lost altogether, for the term may then be too inclusive to have much meaning. Granted, however, a common opposition to individualism, corporate theories manifest significant differences as statements of positive doctrine, even within certain national developments. Bowen, for example, in writing on German corporative theories of the state, found it difficult to clarify this tradition.[11] Within Germany there have been great variations on what he takes to be a common theme, and while there have been some theorists identified with the general corporatist position who were markedly antistatist and advocates of federalism and the decentralization of authority and control, there have been others who advocated a thoroughgoing statism. Of some interest is his description of the attacks made by the German corporatists on Marxism during the nineteenth century. They argued that the collectivism associated with Marxist thought was not a corporate but ultimately an individualistic, atomistic position, because in the end there was to be a classless society in which absolute individual freedom or anarchy would prevail. Even the rather common allegiance of German corporatists of the nineteenth century to organic social theory was distinguished by different interpretations, with correspondingly greater or lesser degrees of autonomy granted to various organs. One view tended toward monism and centralization, another toward pluralism and decentralization. The general view, however, was an "organic" one.

Developing as they did . . . under the continuous influence of one form or another of the 'organic' conception, German corporatist doctrines have typically expressed antipathy to the individualism of the Enlightenment, to the egalitarianism of the French Revolution and to the Marxian theory of class conflict. Furthermore, Manchester liberalism, Jacobin democracy, and revolutionary socialism have as a rule been subsumed under a single rubric and then rejected as products of the same spirit of 'mechanical' or 'atomistic' individualism. Most German corporatists have held this spirit to be the antithesis of a truly 'social' outlook, and in place of individual rights, interests, and values they have stressed the binding ties of the community. . . . [A]ccording to the general corporatist conception the nation is an 'organic' union of many lesser communities or 'estates' rather than a simple aggregation of interchangeable human 'atoms.' [12]

Even within this single tradition, then, there is difficulty in defining the central character of corporatism, and when the attempt is made to include other of the various forms, the difficulty becomes even greater. Some identify the corporate with the social and the organic, as Bowen has indicated, although his placing "social" and "organic" in quotation marks itself points to some difficulty of definition. The social may, for example, simply be synonymous with collective, but collectivism, although usually interpreted as anti-individualistic, may in fact be individualistic in at least either of two senses. Either society may be conceived as a collectivity of individuals, that is, atomistically, or, as already indicated, collectivism may have as its goal the ultimate establishment of absolute individual freedom. Collectivism is, however, more frequently taken to be opposed to individualism and allied with a "social" conception. Dewey, however, in attempting to find an appropriate term to describe the character of modern society, eliminates both "socialistic" and "collectivistic" and says that "corporate" is the key word.[13] In an illuminating chapter entitled "The United States, Incorporated" he depicts the changes that have transformed American society. Rejecting the terms "socialistic" and "collectivistic" because of their partisan connotations, he finds the clue in the ever-increasing importance of the role of the corporation when corporation is freed from its narrow, technical, legal meaning. "We may then say that the United States has steadily moved from an earlier pioneer individualism to a condition of dominant corporateness." [14] Despite the fact that he discards "socialistic" and "collectivistic" at the beginning of the chapter, he later uses these words and even the term "organic" as synonymous with "corporate." For example, he says that regardless of their desirability or undesirability, certain changes which have come about are indications of the extent to which society "is formed and directed by corporate and collective factors toward collective ends." [15] Again, he emphasizes in this mood that the facts he has cited are neither to be deplored nor celebrated, but are used to show "the decline of an individualistic philosophy of life, and the formation of a collectivistic scheme of interdependence, which finds its way into every cranny of life, personal, intellectual, emotional, affecting leisure as well as work, morals as well as economics." [16] He speaks of the need to expand "social corporateness to include the average consumer or else [have] economic suffering on a vast scale." [17] He also uses the word "socialization" as a neutral term, at one point to mark the integration which has everywhere been taking place but (now evaluating this fact) which unfortunately has been mechanical, quantitative, and external, and which thus needs to be based upon a new individuality that will be corporate.

When the corporateness becomes internal, when, that is, it is realized in thought and purpose, it will become qualitative. In this change, law will be realized not as a rule arbitrarily imposed from without but as the relations which held individuals together. The balance of the individual and the social will be organic.[18]

Thus Dewey has to all intents and purposes used synonymously "social," "collective," "organic," and "corporate" within a single brief chapter.

Corporatism has usually been associated with organicism as totalitarian political theory, and the corporative state of Italian fascism has often been cited as a notable example. Bowen as well as many others have noted, however, that corporate development has not been confined to undemocratic countries, but has occurred in democratic countries as well. A democratic theory of corporatism has developed, perhaps best exemplified by modern liberalism. Dewey, as a modern liberal, distinguished his own position sharply from either atomism or organicism, and although he employs the term "organic," he makes it clear that democratic social theory must be dissociated from organicism. When it is said by some liberals that the choice for democracy is not between individualism and collectivism but between collectivisms, the meaning is evidently similar. While collectivism has often been associated with totalitarianism, modern liberals insist that a distinction must and can be made between democratic and totalitarian collectivism. In affirming the necessity of transforming or reinterpreting American social theory so that individualistic democracy is superseded by social democracy, the modern liberals often identify the latter with collective or corporate theory. Thus the terms "organic," "social," "collective," and "corporate" have all been associated both with organicist theory and with democratic theory. Two sharply opposed philosophies, the democratic theory of modern liberalism and the totalitarian theory of organicism, fall by their own definition within the category of corporate theory and often make use of the same language to describe their positions. Perhaps what is indicated by this brief survey of the uses of the term "corporatism" by opposed theorists is the necessity of learning more about its meaning. It is questionable whether theories that are so directly opposed to one another as democracy and totalitarianism should both go forth under the banner of corporatism. If they do, then the term may be so broad as to be meaningless. The need for amplification here, however, must not be interpreted as a problem confined to semantics, simply a question of language. The language difficulty is ever present no doubt, but a much more significant problem is involved, no less than the meaning or nature of cultural reality itself. A metaphysical problem is clearly involved here, for these different conceptions of the nature of society as corporate are based upon fundamentally different metaphysical premises.

In Jordan's view, corporatism is neither democratic nor totalitarian, and the corporate is dissociated from the social, the collectivistic, and the organic. The choice for him does not lie with any of the theories identified as atomism, organicism, or modern liberalism, and hence there is the need for the formulation of a philosophy distinguished from these. His effort to develop a positive statement also leads in some degree to a criticism of the metaphysical positions allied with the politics of other philosophies. His theory is a deliberate attempt to set out the metaphysical foundations of corporatism, to develop a corporate theory of individuality as the basis of the corporate state.[19]

Corporate Society: Politics and Education

The close relationship between politics and education has long been recognized by philosophers, who have often conceived of their own social theory as at once educational theory also. At least this has been the case with those philosophies which affirm a positive role for the state in human affairs. On the other hand, in such a philosophy as classical liberalism, for example, in which the state is conceived as essentially evil and the role of government limited to a minimum, negative function, the relationship between the state and education is viewed as negative. Classical liberalism would "keep politics out of education and education out of politics" and would generally separate the various institutions of society, such as the church from the state. Opposed to this general conception are those philosophies which have been earlier discussed as corporate and which generally assert a positive relationship between the state and other institutions, including educational institutions. While these positions differ in their interpretation of that relationship in crucial respects, they are alike in affirming a constructive function for the state. Modern liberalism is an instance of this general philosophy which, while fearful and ever watchful of the state, is critical of its predecessor, classical liberalism, for taking the state to be inherently evil. It consigns a distinctly positive function to the state, although those holding to this theory disagree as to the extent of that function. If democratic political theory is identified with modern liberalism rather than laissez-faire individualism, then both democratic and totalitarian theories have a positive view of the state, in contrast to the negative view of classical liberalism. The distinctions between democratic and totalitarian conceptions of politics are, of course, many and of great significance, and with respect to the state, totalitarianism is willing to assert a completely positive view, while modern liberalism is exceedingly hesitant about going all the way. Correspondingly, there are different implications for education: the totalitarians hold that all schools are state schools, whatever their nominal auspices, while modern liberals would generally maintain a place for private as well as public institutions and would conceive of spheres of action, educationally and otherwise, at least partially free from the state. In fact, according to the latter theory such a qualification is essential for freedom. While no inevitable opposition is said to exist between individual or institution and the state, neither is the relationship conceived as inherently one of perfect identity, as is the case with organicist theory. This attitude may be illustrated by Hook's reaction to the proposals of two prominent educational philosophers. To Brameld's suggestion that education become the copartner of politics,[20] Hook says that in such a partnership we know which partner will dominate the other.[21] There is little doubt in his mind that education would be reduced to a servile condition as the mere agent of the state. His response to Meiklejohn's assertion of the identity between man, education, and the state, indicated in part by the latter's statement that "all the activities which give a man dignity are done 'for the state,' "[22] is that it constitutes a state worship which must be condemned. Neither man nor education is one with the state as such. According to Hook, Meiklejohn's conception of the state is not of this earth, and the relationship of perfect identity which he maintains blinds man to the reality of conflict which may exist between man and the state, and education and the state. The result is subjugation by the state. Modern liberalism is critical of any theory which fails to distinguish "between existing states on earth and the perfect state in heaven"

or which overlooks the reality of existing relationships in favor
of a theoretical conception of relationships. Hook is fearful that
existing states will be identified with ideal states, that existing
statesmen will be identified with ideal statesmen, in short, that
the empirical fact will be sacrificed to an abstract idea.[23]

The politics of modern liberalism falls somewhere between a
negation of the do-nothing or do-little state of atomism and a full
affirmation of the positive state. On the other hand, we find
Jordan affording a wholly positive conception of politics and
law, with the state a fully responsible "partner" in the cultural
enterprise, whatever its nature, educational or otherwise, while
at the same time he rejects the social absolutism demanded in
organic political theory. Corporatism, as he defines it, is clearly
positive in its approach to the state, as much so as totalitarianism
and more so than modern liberalism, yet it is to be markedly distinguished from either of these. Correspondingly, its conception
of education in relation to politics is different from either. Corporatism, as conceived by Jordan, is a distinctive political philosophy with significantly original implications for education. In
the view of the authors his theory represents an important contribution, at once political and educational or political-educational, a philosophy appropriate for modern society.

The current insistence that educational philosophy and practice be consistent with contemporary cultural reality is perhaps
a reversion to the wisdom of Aristotle and his affirmation of the
need for education to be in accord with the constitution; as such,
it demands that we comprehend the constitution and construct a
political or cultural foundation for education. The assertion that
society is now corporate and that education must be consistent
with that reality calls for a more definitive corporate social theory.
Education is in need of a philosophy which will make modern
life intelligible and the educational "product," or citizen, intelligent. Perhaps, then, the fundamental problem with which education is faced in contemplating a "new" society, one that is
here and yet in the making also, is the need to create a theory that
will be at one with cultural reality, not merely to describe what
is but also to suggest what might be. Such definitions of the corporate life, as we have seen, are numerous. Jordan's corporatism,
which differs from any of these, makes its basic contribution
through a re-examination and reinterpretation of the nature of

action and individuality. He finds most political theories fallacious because they are founded on subjective theories of action and individuality which, when applied consistently, yield subjective theories of politics. These in turn become progenitors of subjective theories of education. The need is for an objective or corporate theory of action and individuality, and this Jordan proposes as the foundational concept for the understanding of culture as a whole, as well as for the understanding of education.

The Scope and Plan

A theory of society is always a theory of education, if not explicitly, then implicitly. The classic example of a deliberate attempt to combine both was made by Plato in *The Republic*. While a number of political philosophers have developed the educational aspect of their theories at length, Jordan has not done so. He has written much on politics, little directly on education; consequently, the educational implications of his social theory need to be made explicit. The main effort of this essay will be an attempt to state and to appraise the political-educational significance of Jordan's work. Emphasis is necessarily placed upon the political as indispensable to the understanding of the educational theory.

Although this is not a comparative study, the educational counterpart of the politics of modern liberalism, social reconstructionism,[24] is given considerable attention for several reasons. Public policy has moved greatly in the direction of realizing its tenets, and the social view has taken hold even among those who are traditionally individualistic, often despite their protests to the contrary. The Republicans, for example, while disavowing the welfare statism of the Democrats, have in fact often gone beyond their opponents in both policy and practice. While there are still many hortatory remains of individualism, the concrete directions actually taken by our politicians and political institutions depart further and further from that theory. Furthermore, social reconstructionism has had a considerable degree of success in combating traditionalism as well as the laissez-faire individualism that marked the newer education in its earlier years. Its influence has, however, not been primarily that of negation, for as

a positive theory it is increasingly embodied in educational practice. If special consideration is to be given to any theory, the
importance of social reconstructionism for society as a whole
and for education warrants singling it out for interpretation and
appraisal. In addition, its use affords an opportunity to clarify
the significance of Jordan's philosophy both as criticism and as
affirmation. For these reasons the social-reconstructionist position is employed here in describing and evaluating Jordan's
theory.[25]

As our discussion of the confusion in the ideas of the corporate
reality suggested, Jordan found it necessary to redefine that concept and corporate theory itself. The problem created by the
confusion is essentially more than one of obtaining agreement
as to how "corporate" is to be used; ultimately the problem concerns the whole nature of cultural reality. Such a problem involves a reconstruction of the basic concepts of cultural theory.
To develop a consistent philosophy which would make sense of
modern society, it was necessary for Jordan to revise many fundamental concepts in social thought, such as action, individuality,
institution, society, property, contract, etc. Departing as it does
from commonly accepted meanings, the vocabulary of Jordan's
philosophy presents difficulty for both the reader who seeks to
understand and appraise and for the writer who seeks to explain
and interpret. To overcome this difficulty as far as possible in
this essay, Jordan's conceptions in most cases have been contrasted with definitions from opposing positions, and the differences have been further investigated in applications to policy and
practice.

It will be necessary to describe the corporate theory of Jordan
in some detail in order to draw inferences from it for education,
and this will be done in Part One, "Corporate Society." Part Two,
"Corporate Education," presents the implications of Jordan's political theory for a philosophy of education.

Part One CORPORATE SOCIETY

CHAPTER 1
CORPORATE THEORY OF ACTION

Jordan and Other Action Theories

If concepts have objective reference, if they designate some order of fact, then faulty conceptualizing leads to a failure in the practical management of affairs. In this connection the failure to define clearly the meaning of action has caused much difficulty in the study of ethics and in the social sciences as a whole. What, then, is action? Is action the resignation or withdrawal from the world (inaction) of the mystic? Is action to be equated with the reactions studied by the psychologist?—or with sheer movement and energy expenditure, as action is typically defined by the technologist? Is action made intelligible by locating it in a causal source, such as the individual, group, society, or God, a mover who originates action and from whom action gets its status in the world? A careful consideration of the nature of the act will suggest the answers to these questions.

Briefly stated, an act issues into an object, which then sustains or advances the world in which it takes its place. As a result of the object's constructive import to a world, further action is made possible. That an act objectifies and adds something constructive to some overt, existential state of affairs is central to Jordan's corporate theory of action.[1] From this rather simple statement a great many important implications follow. On its negative side, nothing which does not issue into an object deserves the name of action. Action always changes something in the real external world; therefore thought, while a stage of action, is not yet action. What the relationship of thought to action is will be taken up later, but in the meantime a clear distinction between the two should be noted in

the fact that the act presupposes a real, that is, an objective, overt, public relation, while thought contemplates a relation that is ideal and exists only in the symbols by which it is represented. It is true that thought objectifies its relations and conditions in the 'act' of thinking, but it objectifies them on a basis of ideal possibilities and in abstractly logical and universal terms. Its significance for us lies merely in leading us to see that, logically, there is a fundamental difference between thinking and action and that the one cannot be reduced to the other.[2]

The manipulation of mental states, the shifting about and re-arrangement of ideational furniture in the mind, is not yet an act and cannot become so until it has embodied itself in some designatable objective structure. Unless the thought incorporates itself in the world, it is but empty and formal or abstractly log-ical from the point of view of action.

Nor is movement, mere energy expenditure, action. The utiliza-tion of physical energies in moving about in space and time is not an act, since no object is realized in the process. War is not action, but simply motion and commotion, because its issue is object destruction, and if it be insisted that it is an act because "objects" of war come out of it, then it is an act that contradicts itself, since it is patently destructive of the object basis upon which acts, even the "act" of war itself, depend. Movement, which like thought is necessary to an act, is not sufficient for an act, and this "distinction of action from movement," Jordan states, "involves all the real differences in the world."[3] The act not only realizes itself in an object, but the object itself must be of such a nature that it is "a factor of the stability of the external world in order that action may always have a solid ground on which to proceed."[4] Viewed in this way action is cumulative; it grows.

Similarly, it is necessary to distinguish action from reaction. An act, as the bringing forth of an object, is dependent upon, and is intended to have an effect in, the environing world through the presentation therein of a new fact.[5] The development of a school or a road, for example, is dependent upon existing material conditions, and when objectified makes a difference to the com-plex of facts in which it is situated. It is in this sense that action is objective in nature, *issuing out of and into a world.* Reaction is subjective in origin and import, since it issues out of the phys-ical and/or mental state of the organism and ends in the satisfac-tion or need reduction of the organism: i.e., the biopsychological organism feels tense or perhaps hungry, smashes a vase or eats, and hence is relieved, internally at rest again with itself. The "end" of the reaction is inaction, not an object. Thus reaction is homeostatic; it maintains an equilibrium, but it does not build a culture, and the psychologism which endlessly describes it provides no insight into the world-building nature of man. Therefore action is not a function of the individual so far as he is a cause or so far as he is, in terms of need reduction or need satisfaction, an issue or effect.

An act has no cause; it is free and spontaneous. This is true because while an act is related to an incomplete state of affairs in the world, the state of affairs depends upon thought for its recognition and diagnosis. The status of the objective fact situation is the ground for the building of the new school or road. The structure of the world, the condition of reality, is the ground for the act, and is also the existential complex into which the act issues as a new fact, a new piece of reality, that qualifies or modifies the world. Action then issues from a world and objectifies into a world, so that its comprehension depends upon logic, not upon the assumption of a spiritual power independent of this world or upon psychology, whether individual or social. Said in another way, the unit of the act is the object, and the act is not complete until the object has been realized. It is the school, the road, or the skyscraper which is the completion of the act, and not the cessation of individual or social energies; hence it is the object in its meaning, that is, its place in an order of environing facts, which requires understanding if the act is to be understood.

Finally, action is not to be identified as technical accomplishment. Knowing how to make a technically sound object does not mean that one can make an object which has fitness in the furtherance of action. A road technically sound is not right if built in the wrong place, nor is the invention of a hydrogen bomb an act because it represents a tremendous technical achievement. Characteristic of technical "action" is the isolation of the object from its environing ground, so that all that is considered needful is the formal correctness of the object as such; but the object cannot in *fact* be separated from its conditions and consequences, as Jordan illustrates:

Five dollars is the correct price to pay for a pair of shoes. But it may very well be wrong that the price of shoes is five dollars. Shoes that can be sold for five dollars because they represent sweated or child labor may be technically correct, good shoes, 'worth the money'; all contractual obligations involved in the process of their production may be scrupulously met; yet five dollars is a wrong price for the shoes. The total shoe situation is not fit to enter into a moral world;

it ought not to exist. The reply that we must have shoes, or cheap shoes, that men must be rewarded for their labor, skill, risk, etc., misses the point entirely. We must have shoes, cheap, good (technically), promptly, etc., but all these are subordinate to the demand that shoes be right; meaning by this that the whole shoe situation, production, distribution, consumption, must be appropriate to the total cultural world which defines the shoe and creates the need for it.[6]

The act stands in relation to a whole no matter what may be the state of mind of the technician, and anything entering into the act or consequent upon the act which negates the world in which the act stands, falsifies its status as action. Thus action for Jordan is identified with the moral because it maintains a world in which action may go on, and the moral in this sense is identified with the practical. No act is practical which is self-contradictory and in its total import destroys the conditions upon which it rests; thus colonialism, the product of hardheaded "practical" interests and "men of action," is reaping its reward of blood and hatred. However, it never was more than a partial act at best.

To state the action theory of Jordan in more positive terms, if action is of such a nature as to issue into an object which is its end and has its place in furthering the conditions of action, then there are two constituent ingredients of anything having the status of an act, viz., concrete, logical thought and a solid, material world.

Thought and Action

The very basis upon which thought proceeds is the assumption that there is a world beyond the individual mentality with which ideas connect and in which they may attain substantiality, and that in the external world ideas may thus make real differences in the nature of things. If this assumption is correct, then thought is concrete and practical in nature, for it is simply a stage in an object's development; it is that stage of an object in which it is prevised in ideal form. It is the planning stage of action in which what the object is to be is projected into a future state of affairs; [7] the object is designed in thought, whose relationship to action is exemplified by the architect's function in the building of a home. Thought is the birth of an object; said another way, the object is the idea brought to completion. Therefore, according to Jordan, it is only thought which can embody itself in an object.

Thought is to be distinguished from subjective feeling, which does not *objectify* but *materializes* as when, in a fit of anger, we smash a vase or do injury to a loved one. In no case can feeling be an originator of action since, unlike thought, it possesses no designing capacity.

[Feeling] possesses command of forces, as is illustrated in impulse, but it cannot direct them to the production of any definite form. It can move, but it cannot act. You may get results from the force of feeling; but you will never get a formed object or any shape that expresses design, and the result will have no intelligible relation to the feeling which it follows. Its force is, like all forces, irrational. Feeling and its forces are the material out of which intelligence may shape ends for conscious and sentient beings; but it is not such an end.[8]

Viewed *objectively*, feeling, as "the total of organic receptivity," [9] is largely passive in nature and is the original primal background or medium in which thought takes place. Feelings as existent qualities, as the "feel" of things in the world, are a material of life rather than its active energizer. Feeling is substance to be shaped by the active agency of thought into an object of value, and its highest form is in an aesthetic object. Viewed *subjectively*, the feelings may move, but they do not create. Feelings may move the individual to kick the boards lying before him or to weep; thought designs them into a bookcase or lays out the structure of a sonata. Feelings per se can never originate an act, assume the role of "springs to action," since they are indiscriminate as to the objects with which they relate.[10] Feelings may attach to anything—to "soap operas" or to the plays of William Shakespeare, to comic books or poetry. Thought, on the other hand, makes distinctions between objects and objectives, and thus makes possible the act. It is thought, then, which, as ingredient to the make-up of objects, is constitutive of the world built by action. It is through a thought-relationship to the world that action becomes spontaneous and free. States of mind, feelings, may be causally manipulated through the variation of physiological and/or other conditions, but thought, when conceived as a phase of action, cannot be a caused event, for it is dependent upon the logical conception of something of meaning to be realized in the world, something which is not present in fact at the time of its imaged formulation.

However, the relationship of thought to action is not without a significant difficulty: namely, that control of the act is possible only while it is in ideal form,[11] while the objective consequences of the act do not exist until the act has been realized in an object.

This gives the awkward situation: We cannot know whether an act is right or wrong until after it is done; but our responsibility for its rightness or wrongness must be determined before we act.[12]

It is this thought-object relationship which gives to the life of man its character of adventure and which is the logical ground of experimentation in the realm of action. Man is obliged to think as hard as he can in order to act and while he is engaged in action; and after the act has ended in an object, he must re-examine his thinking on the basis of the facts of action.

World and Action

Since without things of all kinds culture has no more status than a dream, a material world is presupposed in every act. The material world, for the purpose of this analysis, may be distinguished as two realms, that of nature and that of culture.

NATURE

Inevitably involved in man's action life, to one degree or another, is the world of nature. This is the framework of substantial things without which an act cannot be conceived as existent in the most literal sense of the term.[13] The world of nature, of concrete, substantial, relatively fixed conditions in which objects have relations, is logically necessitated for thought, action, and experience to have a ground. There are substantial, existent relations between animals and plants, plants and the soil, the soil and rain, the seasons and plant and animal growth and development, the sun and plant and animal life, etc., and action utilizes this substantial world in the bringing forth of an object. "The world of nature is . . . a great storehouse of materials awaiting action to give them the form of value objects, and it is the presence of this world of materials as 'resources' that constitutes the strongest stimulus to action." [14] The world of nature makes it possible to develop special objects called tools which are extremely important for the action life of man, and with the development of tools nature has become modified and man has increased many fold his capacity for action.

Nature is a realm whose phenomena modify one another causally. This is significant for action, because causal relations, as contrasted with a world of sheer flux, suggest that the objective world is capable of change and control, and the human purpose or idea may then amount to something more substantial than a mental phenomenon.[15] The orderliness of the changes found in nature, where plant and animal life maintain a relatively fixed structure despite variations of environmental circumstance, means that life and growth are elements of nature, and the fact of life and growth suggests for action purposes that nature is something to be worked with, since there are energies or dynamic tendencies internal to it. The truck farmer does not create the tomato; he develops a tomato through the ordering of natural circumstance. The elements involved in growth depend upon chance circumstances and chance looms large in nature,[16] e.g., an acorn on a sunny hillside will develop differently from one on the shady side of the same hill. However, this implies that the very indeterminacy of the environment, the peculiar collocation of objective possibilities open to the actor, is the ground of the spontaneity or freedom central to an act.

This infinity of possibilities is just the objective world that is implied in any act. The objective fact of freedom we are to recognize as the real opportunity given in the objective world implied by an act, and it is upon the presence of this world of objects in the agent's environment that his moral destiny will depend.[17]

Nature, while it is the realm of cause and of relatively fixed and stable material conditions, is not to be interpreted as the "cause" of action. Nature is the material ground of action, but action is always spontaneous or free; in its thought phase, as we have seen, an act is dependent upon the envisagement of significant possibilities present but not yet realized in the world, and in its overt phase its realization will alter the structure of that world as well as that of the actor. The development of steel is grounded in its significance for industry, which it in turn modifies in countless ways. Thus an act not only has a ground but modifies its own ground, while a caused event is an inevitable, repetitive process. Nevertheless, the living, growing, substantial structure which nature is contains the warning that freedom, so far as it is real in action, can never be absolute. Nature compels fantasy to become the logical imagination if she is to play a co-operative part in action.

Man's earliest world is the world of nature. With nature he must co-operate or he will perish, since without its energy and order his own puny physique would be inadequate to the task of bringing forth an object. He works with the design and order found in nature to bring forth an object, an object which represents the fusion of his mental-physical energies with the stuff of nature. *An object of culture is always the synthesis of the energies of man with the energies of nature,* but the world which primitive man celebrates is largely the world of nature as he comes to see its significance. He acts in terms of it, as in food gathering or hunting; he celebrates its content that he has found to be of meaning and value—the rice crop, the sun, the buffalo, the camel, the fish, and the men who stand in a meaningful relationship to the world of nature (so the hunter is esteemed by the Indian and the Eskimo). Man asserts the nature-world which he has in common with his fellows by means of language; he defines its meaning and beauty in dance and painting and other art forms; he holds the materials of nature to be sacred and ritualizes its content so that all may know these are ends of action. In his art forms he copies the rhythms of nature, the fluttering of leaves; in his dance he imitates the posturing of birds; the sounds of animals are given permanence in song.

To act effectively upon this common world of nature—to build canoes, hunt, harvest—men have need of their fellows. Thus the bond which naturally develops between men is objectively necessitated by nature, for the achievement of an object requires men's co-operative efforts if the act is to come to fruition. The object development of primitive man is small, and so also the world in which he acts; therefore he is at the mercy of nature, and his culture, having a limited object system, disappears with the disappearance of the group. However, even the most primitive group has its body of objects upon and through which it acts and which mediates the social relations of the group.

As men come to follow out their purposes with greater effectiveness, the realm of nature recedes and the realm of culture, the object world created by action and the furthering of action, looms larger in the affairs of men. Through the development of objects characteristic of the permanent activities of man, his experience creates "for itself a body in which it takes permanent lodgment and abode." [18] Then if Jordan on the one hand is referring to the world of nature in which action takes place, on the other hand his reference is to the world of culture, the body of objects man has created in following out his purposes.

By the world of culture we mean the structure that has resulted from man's efforts, throughout his entire historic career, to control nature in the interests of his own purposes. It is the system of nature as modified by human purpose. This structure is called 'culture' or 'civilization' to distinguish it, as the work of man, from the original nature. . . . It is the work of man as a type, of men in their corporate capacity, and of men as individuals only as they function as elements of agency within the corporate body. [19]

Since the stuff of culture consists of objects, culture is not something to be conceived as distinct and separate from or opposed to nature, but more properly, since it has its roots in a material basis, as an outgrowth of nature. *Culture is nature's growth in meaning and value.* The object world is not split into nature *and* culture, but is more adequately expressed as the nature-culture world, though for the sake of brevity hereafter we shall simply designate the nature-culture world as the world of culture, bearing in mind that it is a further development of nature's potentialities as a result of man's work in and upon it.

CULTURE

Man's new object world is of central importance to his life. There are three major senses in which it is of utmost significance to him: (1) as the stage for action and the medium in which life is lived, (2) as the instrument of action and life itself, and (3) as the objective end or corporate whole of action.

Stage for Action

The object world is the stage for action. Action necessarily presumes a world external and objective to the actor as the relatively fixed place in which action occurs; an act would be meaningless or lack a rationale unless it could be assumed that the world will remain essentially what it is while the act is in process. [20] The building of a bookcase depends upon the relatively fixed qualities of the wood, the books, the library in which the bookcase is to have its place, the income which is to main-

tain all these objects, etc. Without the presupposition of a relatively stable world in which the act takes place an act would not
be worth the effort.

The object world is the medium in which life is lived, for what
man is and does connects with objects at every point. Superficially viewed, this medium may seem to be merely "out there"
as something external to his nature, but it is inevitably part of
his life. Whether he is primitive man, agricultural man, man the
hunter, or modern man, the content and form of his life is largely
determined by the nature of the objective world in which he
has his being. Through object development a world very different from that of the state of nature is achieved, and the life that
is led by man is necessarily different as a result; a world whose
objective constituents are museums, railroads, airplanes, automobiles, radio, television, universities, cities, hotels, apartment
houses, suburban homes, theaters, movie houses, streets, and
daily newspapers, signifies that life has become qualitatively
different from the life lived only a short time ago. The nature of
human life cannot be understood apart from the objective medium in which it is lived.

Instrument of Action

The object world is the instrument of action since through it
action is accomplished. Through General Motors cars are produced; through schools men are educated; through hospitals
health is restored. As things are organized in the world, they become effective as opportunities for the realization of purposes; [21]
phrased more strongly, without the instruments the purposes
themselves might not exist, or if they did they would have mere
psychological existence.

Objects are the means to life itself in the sense of maintaining both man's physical and mental existence. The comfort and
security to be found in life, indeed physical existence itself, are
absolutely dependent upon objects of all sorts being available
to man. For example, the objective world as transformed by
developments in agriculture, industry, medical science, sanitary
engineering, dams, efficient methods for the preservation of food,
etc., has doubled the life expectancy of white Americans in little
more than a century.

Mind is equally dependent upon objects. In the elementary

sense intellectual life obviously depends upon physical well-being, but beyond that it demands that certain types of objects be available. The maintenance and development of the mind is literally dependent upon writing materials, books, chairs and desks, adequate lighting, schools, etc. Today advances in scientific theory require a multiplicity of extraordinarily expensive and complicated kinds of equipment; for example, the betatron is already obsolete for the advanced student of physics, and the synchrotron, which no single university can afford, is now required if scientific theory is to go forward. Lacking the necessary objects, intellectual development is seriously handicapped, whether the point of view is that of the individual or the corpus of science. Objects are also important to the life of the mind in that they enter into the process of thought and thus are basic in the modification and formulation of ideas. Plaster and its qualities may mean a wall, or a cast for a broken limb, or a piece of sculpture. The very purposes men have are inextricably intertwined with objects, and it is through this interdependence that they become the objectives of life.

Corporate Whole or End of Action

The object world is the corporate whole or end of action since every act has bearing upon the objective world in which it takes place. This does not mean that the individual necessarily aims at such a consequence, since in most cases he probably does not; but it does mean that the very production of an object inevitably tends to constitute the world for better or worse, that it makes real differences within the total world.[22] Thus whether a school or a tavern is built in a neighborhood has a significance for that neighborhood, for the city, ultimately for the whole state, regardless of the psychological motives or intentions involved, whether they be generous or mean. Logical analysis of the way in which facts are ordered in the world, rather than supernatural speculation or psychological probing, is the method through which the meaning of the act is understood. Jordan is most insistent that

acts are objective dynamic relations within the structure of the world and not states of mind of individuals. And it is this objective character, this relation of an act and its appropriate object to the world the act tends to constitute, the cosmic relation, that is the basis of the moral quality of the act.[23]

In the practical activities of their ongoing existence men organize their lives about objects. The objects which are not yet present in fact become the objectives of life, or what Jordan calls "purposes" in his special use of the term.

We speak of our objects when we have in mind the things we want some day to see done and made effective in the life of men. And such a question as 'What object does he have in view?' is intended to ask about the kind of a world the individual's thought and activities tend to create. It may be that his object is fame or riches or what not. But in any case, whatever is the answer to the question, it indicates a kind of world, the kind of world characteristically in mind as the medium and condition of his life or action. In this sense, 'object' is equivalent to purpose, and although we often, perhaps generally, think of purpose in subjective terms as if our purposes meant merely the ways we have of feeling about things, we really know when we come down to it that purposes are always combinations of systems of objects. This we know because when we reflect we see that purposes are essentially objective because they can be held in common by many people, while states of mind cannot be shared. The word object then means purpose, a system of objects which shows the effects of elements of order which have been put into it by thought and action. If my object is a home, it means bricks and stones and lumber and concrete, *ordered* into form by thought and action, and as I see the house now in my mind there is not only forms and colors of materials in my mind, but I am also conscious of raising the bricks up on the wall or of sitting on the porch. It is in this way that subjective elements become *parts* of objects.[24]

As an objective or end or purpose, the object-to-be-realized is organizing of activity since it calls forth certain specific movement patterns for its accomplishment. In building a home, obtaining an education, rearing a family, etc., the physical-mental energies brought into play mean that not only is the individual's nature being formed in a certain direction, but that it is forming in a direction common to all others who aspire toward the same end. The object as end is designer of the movement-patterns necessary for the act and thus shapes the minds of all who are engaged in the achievement of the objective. Through the maintenance of common objects men maintain their own lives as well as the lives of others whom they will never "experience" through primary relationships, such as future generations. Moreover, through the acknowledgment of a common objective, such as a clean neighborhood, for example, men attain unity of mind. Common ends or objectives are the actual basis upon which the unity of men depends, not propaganda, mentalistic appeals, exhortations of fear or love for supernatural powers, or psychological manipulation of any kind.

The achievement of the object as end, the attainment of purposes, is the fulfillment of the practical activities of man, and as such is an experience of the greatest significance. It is the objective completion which action seeks.

. . . such objects [as ends] appear as realities in every experience that is fully intelligible, in which we know there is a reality that completes and fulfils our thought and our act. It is for this reason that perhaps the highest form of experience is that which embodies the skill of the workman in forms of the ideas, such, for example, as may be observed in the creations of a competent cabinetmaker or mechanic or sculptor, or in the 'makings' of the poet. There is in such an experience all there can be anywhere within the whole scheme of reality, for within the experience there is no requirement of anything beyond. All the thought of life has been or is being incorporated in the substance of reality by the adequate performance of the activities which that thought adumbrates in advance. Thought and act are one. It is the end because there is nothing beyond. It is thus perfect satisfaction, complete fulness, life as thought made real in itself as act, as end.[25]

Since objects of any consequence are achieved by men who are co-operatively organized in object systems of various types, this implies that the most satisfying intercourse with one's fellows occurs in the pursuit of a common life objective, and support for this inference is found in the songs of work gangs, the communal dances of harvesters celebrating the earth's yield, and the joys of family life.

RELATION

When Jordan argues that objects are the medium of life (and below it will be shown that this is the institutional medium), he means that therefore they are not mere external things. Indeed, objects are the common content of our life, and this conception gives special import to action and the category *relation*. Action results in objects standing in a different relation to one another from that in which they stood prior to the act, and thus makes a difference in the qualities of the objects themselves. The type of garage, or its positioning with respect to a house, makes a real difference to the qualities the house will have, as well as to those of the garage itself, and to the appearance of the neighborhood.

But this is a very different conception of relation from the one most commonly, if unconsciously, accepted, for according to traditional individualistic theory things exist as separate, independent, self-contained reals, and such relations as may exist between these entities are categories separate and distinct from the entity itself. The entities themselves are not affected in any way by their relations, whether in them or out of them, so that the relation becomes some unsubstantial or unreal thing or else a third thing between the two entities. If the latter, then the insoluble problem arises as to the nature of the relation to the relation, and one enters into an infinite regress. If the former, then the concept of growth, as well as of action, has no meaning, since both growth and action assume that things as a result of their relations may be favorably or adversely qualified and to that extent have their natures modified. For classical, atomistic individualism things are what they are unto eternity.

Jordan's solution is to posit that relations are themselves substantial and real, i.e., a thing is what it is by virtue of its relations, is indeed constituted by its relations. Thus, in the natural world, the stunted tree is a manifestation of inadequate relations to sun, water, and soil and is made up of these relations. Relations, far from being external, or causal, impactive, billiard-ball relations, in which entities remain forever what they are, are internal, qualifying the character of the individual in relation. The relation to a child qualifies and in a sense becomes the character of the parent. The child is of his substance; its joys and sorrows are his. The same is true of all the elements of culture to which the individual is related. To the religious man a crucifix thrown in the mud is not a mere piece of metal lying there in space and time; it is something that strikes at the very character and sensibilities of the individual.

The object has at one and the same time both public reference to a world of meaning and value in which it stands, and internal reference as incorporated within the personality of the individual. To take the instance of the cross, the relations in which it stands constitute its reality; the relations of the crucifix to the church, and ultimately of the church to the world, are what provide it with its meaning. Then to view the crucifix as an isolate entity is to lose its reality as crucifix. Relations also constitute the reality of the individual's personality. The order of fact constituting the church is the relational medium for the individual and becomes the content and principle of the individual's life. It is in this sense that the relation between the individual and objects is one of identity, not a homogeneous identity in which the individual as a distinguishable real is lost, but what Jordan calls "analogical identity." The relation is of part to whole with each implying the other. It is the principle of analogical identity which supports the work of anthropologists when they study individuals or families in order to attain insight into the whole society, or when they study the society at large in order to attain understanding of its members. The individual as related to an order of objects, in this case the church, stands for it as a type. The Roman Catholic is an individuation of his relations to the church; in other words, he is analogically identical with it. On the other hand, the Catholic church is the public order of fact announcing what its types, through their relations with it, are to be, and in this way *it is a type of mind made objective and objectifying in the world*. Similarly, the relations organized within the business system, democracy, feudalism, etc., are instanced in the businessman, democratic man, feudal man, for the man is analogically identical with, or constituted by, the object world with which he is unavoidably in relation. He is the particular individuation of the type American, Protestant, Republican, Elk, businessman, husband and father, etc. His human nature is the complex of objective relations in which he is located.

Thus these objects . . . get worked into the very tissue of thought and feeling, so intimately connected with mind, in fact, that it is no longer possible completely to distinguish 'mind' from its 'object.' This intimacy grows so close in many cases, and it is especially true of the immediate objects of culture, that the very best you can do when you want to describe the essence of mind is to describe it in terms of *a certain order of objects*. That is, the mind, as the basis of the personality or the self, is literally *made up* of objects ordered in peculiar ways, so that we can now repeat without fear of ridicule the proposition that culture is essentially a matter of objects and not of states of mind, and that culture is self-culture and the function of the personality. And we can do so now because the self or personality is itself made up of systems of objects ordered in definite and peculiar ways. Then the life of culture, even the life of self-culture, is a matter of the most significant handling and arrangement of objects that intelligence can make possible.[26]

Four important inferences may be made from Jordan's concept of relation as constitutive of individuality:

1. As noted above, when Jordan insists that man acts in terms of his world, neighborhood, family, nation, science, etc., he also means that man is acting for himself, since self and world are analogically identical. The object world is the content of the individual in terms of which he acts, for he has incorporated it into his character. To act for one's biological self is not yet an act, in the sense in which action is a feature of human life, for all that acting in terms of the organism can mean is the maintenance of an equilibrium. Therefore, it is through maintaining and developing the external world that the individual maintains and develops what is internal to his selfhood. It is the principle of such self as he has. Through a creative mental-physical relationship with the world, through incorporating it and acting upon it, the individual develops his self or "soul," to use the religious term. In this sense the soul is not given as ready made but represents an achievement reflecting one's active relations to the world.

2. From the point of view of their potentialities for developing an active, creative relation to life, it is absolutely imperative that men have free access to the objects of life. What men are to be is dependent upon what they can do, and this is laid out as potentiality in the objective structure of things; therefore, to put any artificial restriction in the way of establishing relations with the requisite materials is to frustrate men's efforts to realize themselves, and concomitantly to prevent them from making the best contribution of which they may be capable. The point is that self-realization, self-expression, or self-culture is not effected out of one's innards, since they necessarily involve the relation to or utilization of materials external to the self.

3. It is through their relation to common objects that individuals develop a common mind and character. As related to the Catholic church they become Catholics, and the significance of this inner unity developed between men is that it does not develop through the purely psychological relations or interactions of men in themselves but through their relation to a common system of objects. That is to say, their inner relations with one another depend upon their relations with an order of fact. Where the religious institution is subdivided into more or less opposed orders of fact, as in Catholicism, Protestantism, Judaism, etc., the inner relations of persons may be strained or broken as a re-

sult. The terrible bitterness and violence between cattlemen and "squatters" during the settling of the West is best understood as the result of the conflicting relations in which their respective objects stood, the unordered and antagonistic object relations becoming internal to the men involved. Similarly, the division in the structure of industry, the conflicting objectives incorporated within it, are destructive of cordial inner relations between individuals despite the modern psychological ministrations of management and the new era of "union statesmanship." A point that cannot be insisted upon too strongly is that at no time do men have direct, unmediated relations with each other. They have their relations through their object world—their culture—and the goodness or badness of their interpersonal relations is a derivative of the objective order or disorder which they have built into their public life.

4. The substantial individual made up of relations is also the superindividual or Person. The relations which make it up give it new capacities and powers that it did not possess before these relations came into existence. To use Jordan's illustrations,[27] both sodium and chlorine independently have unique properties, capacities for relation different from each other, but when they are combined to form salt a new entity appears in which many of the properties of sodium and chlorine have disappeared and new qualities have emerged, qualities which were not present in the constituent parts when they were isolated from each other. The new qualities are properties of salt and nothing else. Similarly, a man and a woman possessing certain specific and unique qualities, marry, and as a result of this combination each develops characteristics not present, or present in attenuated form, before the marriage. The state of marriage brings forth new qualities in each because it is a new type of relation. When children are born, still other qualities appear in the adults, never present before, and the relational complex of parents and children is itself something new, marked by its own characteristic qualities. The Jones family is a new individuality or unity, and as a distinguishable entity having individual characteristics may be regarded as a person.

Now this new thing we see in the family seems to have its nature and substance in the *relations* that hold among the individual persons who constitute it. The complex whole of these relations becomes itself a person. This group of persons, so united in a new personality and embedded in a system of property objects which constitute for it a *home,* and assuming relations to other family-persons so as to constitute the school, the church, and other social personalities, then becomes a person who can act, can hold property, can 'sue and be sued' and in every way be treated as an independent entity—a corporate person.

Again when Jones, Smith, Brown, etc., get their job relations mixed up in certain ways, suggesting that the whole complex of their relations could be organized into such an entity as would be profitable to all of them when it enters into practical affairs, the *thing* their relations constitute becomes a grocery 'firm' or a bank, or perhaps a labor union. And this bank or union turns out to have qualities and characteristics and powers of action that the persons who have incorporated it do not have. When it is firmly entrenched in a system of property objects it becomes a person with extraordinary capacities for action in the business and industrial field—a powerful corporate person.[28]

The institution or corporate person is a new individuality, a more comprehensive person, with qualities all its own by virtue of the type of relational complex that it is, and within which interpersonal relations take their form. This multiplication and creation of objects and their ordering into new and more comprehensive wholes means the creation and growth of new qualities in life.

QUALITY

The quality of a thing is then the Fact of a situation when the facts are perceived in *their* organic relation to one another. While a painting may be analyzed into its component colors, tones, lines, masses, forms, brush strokes, etc., its quality is not any one of these facts but rather the synthetic whole they form in their mutual implications. This means that there is no substance behind quality. Quality is not superimposed upon things through the peculiar mental capacities of a perceiving subject, but rather quality is what is itself substantial about a situation; it is the substance of the facts in their relations. The "ugly neighborhood" is just the relational whole of unpaved, muddy streets; unpainted, ramshackle houses; refuse strewn about; unkempt, pasty-faced children; and shabbily dressed, beaten, or malevolent adults. The quality of the neighborhood, of life, expresses itself not as an equation or quantitative judgment of the natural sciences, but as feeling, in this case the feeling of vague fear, repulsion, and pity unavoidably associated with the relational system which is this neighborhood.

It is frequently argued that when making a judgment of quality one may say whatever one pleases about an object or situation, since it is assumed that quality is not objective. Facts are objective but qualities are attributes of the mind of the perceiver. To be sure, such is the case if the qualitative judgment represents something imposed upon the materials from the mind of the knower. However, if the mere use of concepts or standards worked out by the knowing mind is held to be the ground of the irrationality of the qualitative judgment, then all of the sciences are equally irrational since all conceptualize in order to perceive and judge. What is required of any standard or concept that amounts to more than a phantasm is that it refer to something external to mind. The concepts virus, molecule, atom, ugly, sublime, red are in a perceiving mind, it is true; but the rationality of these concepts depends upon their reference to realities external to the perceiving mind. Existential status in the world is the logical ground for conceptual formulation in mind, and alone enables man to distinguish between phantasy and idea.[29] The objects of action, the facts of culture, are qualities and can be made intelligible only by the concepts which characterize their relational order.

To comprehend the quality of an object (the neighborhood, the concentration camp, the painting of a child, a blade of grass) is to see it whole, that is, in its design or system of internal relations, through which we are enabled to grasp its idea or larger implication—in this neglected neighborhood, the pathetic, unrealized quality of a business civilization; in the concentration camp, the horror of a world fascism has built; in the careless strength of a child, the health of a civilization; in the blade of grass, the miracle of the green life and steadfast growth of nature upon which culture is founded. That is to say, to adequately "get" the quality of anything is to grasp its relational feel, e.g., the tragic quality of the great play, the sickening nature of the pointless sex and brutality of the cheap novel or movie, etc. Then it may be said that *quality is objective feeling*, and this means nothing beyond the design of an object or the relations of an order of objects and what they imply as a result.

Then what Jordan is arguing, in essence, is that action is objectified in culture, and culture is objective feeling or quality, the raising to a higher level of raw nature (primitive feeling). Thus insight into culture is one and the same with insight into the qualitative nature of life, and such insight is possible because man is at one with the world through feeling.

. . . I should suggest that all we know about our minds and their modes of procedure in perception or elsewhere we have learned from objects that are known and known to be real before we discover our minds or their methods. Objects are known through the identity of their substantial quality with the substantial quality that is immediate in the individual mind as feeling; i.e., the quality of the universe is continuous with and so identical with the quality in us as the basic feeling. So that the how of their relation is an idle question, since a relation of identity does not submit to a how. The presence or 'existence' of objects is the original fact, and these objects are the knowledge that we have of the world; and in their qualities and relations they are the source and origin of the knowledge we have of ourselves. What is original is the system of objects; and it is a spurious and unnatural question to ask *how* or *why* they are 'given' to us. This 'given' cannot be made to mean anything, for it presupposes that the mind is 'there' complete from the start and that the objects are 'there' and known in full before the 'giveness' can be made intelligible. . . . The continuity of the essential quality of mind with the essential quality of objects is thus a necessary presupposition, so that the unity of mind with its object guarantees the possibility of knowledge as a necessary postulate. That I can know and know the real in the sense that I identify myself with real objects in a community of quality is the ground postulate of metaphysics.[30]

Action, in building a world, in bringing forth new objects and ordering them appropriately, is concomitantly the growth of intelligibility in the world and of quality.

However, what we are more concerned with here is that action, in building new qualities into life, at the same time incorporates within that life a different feel, such as may be instanced in the marked difference between the felt qualities of life in nomadic and agricultural societies, or in agricultural and urban life. These objective qualities of the culture, of what has been built into life through the creation and ordering of things in the world, take form in the feelings of the individual as he lives and acts in that world. If the dominant quality of the life as organized is acquisitive, or competitive, or militaristic, or co-operative, or peaceable, etc., this dominant quality will become internalized in the feelings of the mass of men, and for this reason, as has been often noted, the profoundest educational influence upon the child is the total nature of the world which he experiences. However, the objective order of life is not to be thought of as *causing* the individual to be what he is, since an active relation to life is required (the library per se does not cause the individual to become learned). Moreover, the act of thought can always free the individual from being "determined" by his environment; rather, the objective order is better understood as the ground upon which he builds his feeling life and the organization of his mind, or as the cultural medium which he ingests into his mental-physical substance in the process of growth. The individual is, then, an individuation of the qualities ordered in life: he is the songs he sings, the religious services he attends, the job he works at, the recreational life in which he participates, the family of which he is a member, etc. That is, through his relations to it culture becomes internalized within him, so that culture is personal and he "takes it personally" since the qualities of his personality have developed out of it and issue into it. His feeling, thinking, and doing have the objective order of life as content, and that is why they are of his substance. As it prospers or fails, so does his life. It is therefore the breakdown of the concrete systems of relations, or the qualities which a society has built into the world, which the chief of the Digger Indians has in mind when he speaks of the broken spirit of his people:

In the beginning . . . God gave to every people a cup, a cup of clay, and from this cup they drank their life. . . . They all dipped in the water . . . but their cups were different. Our cup is broken now. It has passed away.[31]

But the objects into which action issues, and the relational order they exhibit, comprise the system of property. The property order conveys—is—the quality or objective "feel" of a culture. Viewed in this way, property has meaning of great significance.

PROPERTY

It is through property, then, as the total complex of objects, that human life is lived; from property life takes on its special qualitative character. As the means, the medium, the content and ends of life, it is the "elementary good" to which thought, feeling, and will attach, and it is in this sense that property is the essence of the person. But, as has been implied in the discussion on quality, the reference which property has to the person is not at all to ownership, for the mere ownership of property is perhaps the least important of its relations, or at best is pertinent to objects so individualized, such as small tools, clothing, and that which is appropriate for the adequate sustenance of the individual—the Aristotelian indispensables—as to be of little consequence to the larger life in which man has his being. However, even with respect to the indispensables it is not ownership that provides the principle, but the nature of the particular individuality, which in order to further its active relations to the world, must have certain objects close at hand. Property as disposed with reference to its satisfaction of needs and wants is property at its lowest term, for as appropriated to the sheer self-preservation of organismic life it does not yet have a role in action. The order of property, when it is an order and not chaos, is its disposition not with reference to individual centers of control but with reference to the furtherance of action, and the right of the natural individual to the control of indispensables is at bottom based upon his use of them in the conduct of an active life. Moreover, action is objectively necessitated since without it man in his object world—culture—cannot be sustained.

The relation of property to the isolate individual in capitalist theory, or to the elite group in feudal theory, or to a collective sum of individuals in socialist and communist theory, falsifies the nature of property. Property as mere possession to be owned, controlled, and enjoyed by some one person, a group, or many people typically means little more than that through the "right" of possession the owner is enabled to prevent its possession or use by anyone else.[32] Then defining property as "private," i.e., through the possessive relation or as a source of subjective satisfactions, may merely permit the owner to do with objects as he pleases, e.g., to withhold them from functioning, as in production restrictions, the food storage "problem," the hanging of original art masterpieces in private homes, etc.; but since the very nature of the object is public as the issue of action and as necessary to the furtherance of action, private property is really a contradiction in terms. The private property notion is a low stage in the growth of civilization since it "hinders the development of cooperation between men" and serves "to isolate the individual and to set his purposes against all other purposes." [33] Then private property, with its backward reference to the individual, group, or nation, is a perversion of the true meaning of property, for the significance of property is disclosed through its intent or portent to the world; its meaning inheres in its forward reference to or function within the public life man has built. The Suez Canal, for example, must be so operated as to promote the transportation of goods, in which its role is of worldwide significance, and the entire question as to the "right" of ownership by a private company, one nation or many, is irrational. So far as the question is one of control, in the sense of furtherance of function, it is the nature of the property that determines the nature of the control, and in the instance of the Suez Canal it is necessarily international. However, control here does not refer to the legalistic establishment of a sovereign power, but to the principle of the appropriation of property to its public function. The use of property for individual, group, or national advantage means that property has been expropriated from its public and universal function. No owner, whether an individual, a collectivity, or a nation, has the right to prevent property from performing its public function, e.g., to shut down United States Steel, General Electric, the Ford Motor Company, etc. From the point of view of historical development, current function, and future portent, these properties are not the exclusive domain of anyone. They are the common wealth, the qualitative orders of life erected through action. As individual ends synthesized in public form they are Persons, and Persons are inviolate.[34]

The central difficulty with the theory of property as possession is its dual assumption that property is related only to individuals or groups and that it is related to them on an exclusive one-at-a-time basis, so that what one individual or group now has cannot at the same time be an object for others. However, in actuality this is true only of indispensables—food, clothing, bed, domicile, toothbrush—since objects of any advanced nature are patently related to more than one individual at a time and to other objects as well as to individuals. A school, a department store, a utility, are at one and the same time shared by many people and are not consumed or destroyed in the process of entering into the lives of many individuals and groups. In view of the fact that they are shared objects, the objects of a common life, their breakdown necessarily involves a breakdown in the interpersonal relations which men have through them; men are not particularly congenial when they are hungry or cold, and some of our choicest epithets are reserved for the local utility when there is a break in water or electric service. Objects are related to objects: the supply of electricity depends upon coal mines and the system of transport, a department store is related to the whole of industry, the beauty of a lawn depends in part on what the neighbor does with his. The layout, disposition, and accessibility of property are tremendously influential in man-to-man relations since the latter always occur in a property medium, and it is therefore no exaggeration to say that the property order structures the order of interpersonal relations. The property order is the concrete quality of life, the silent, omnipresent medium in which the feeling tone of social life grows and is made stable. The feudal organization of objects—their unlimited accessibility to some despite incompetence, and the impossibility of their attainment for many others despite competence—means the feudal organization of interpersonal relations. In spite of the special psychology of the individuals involved, the relation of noble to serf, of rich man to poor man, of boss to worker is fixed hard in the institutional system, and it is this latter which is dominant in human relations. It is through property that human life attains its "permanence and solidarity and continuity" [35] when rightly ordered, or interminable strife when wrongly ordered. In the last analysis, "Property is the skeletal basis of all the personal and other relations which in social usage are summed up in what is called public life." [36]

In so far as possession, in this case common ownership, is also the principle of socialism and communism, it is equally false and impractical. The meaning of property is far from exhausted by its reference to the subjective satisfactions of individuals or collectivities, although, to be sure, there is such a relation. Property, as the qualitative structure of culture developed by life through action, takes on its meaning with reference to an act; therefore individuals or collectivities are not principle for property, but are themselves disposed with reference to the end in which the act issues. Although the individual physician or group (A.M.A.) is best qualified to make the decision about the location of doctors and the equipment they need, this decision, when principled, has in view what is needful for health viewed as universal end. Health is objective law for the physician, not his own special advantage over other individuals or groups, which is an interest but not an end. Then when Jordan says that the essence of property is public, he is not referring to people but to the ends made objective in life, ends that are common and stand for universal functions that must be perpetuated and developed if human life is to be what it is and to become what it is not yet. Health, family, industry, religion, recreation, education, etc., objectively predicate the objects and persons proper to the ends they comprehend and perpetuate, so that the disposition of property and persons need make no reference to an individual or a group. Individuals or groups as such have nothing of principle in them for the ordering of property; thus all they can do when they make themselves *the* end is to expropriate property to themselves. But property is *proper* only when appropriate to an end.

CONTRACT

Property as disposed toward the achievement of public ends, the furtherance of man's action life, cannot be that which separates individuals and nations from one another into private worlds and opposes them to each other, though this is the present consequence of the sovereignty of interest over property. Similarly, contract, if it is to be constructive of cultural order, cannot be construed as the guarantee of the sanctity of private property and thus the agent of divisiveness which shatters that order to bits, though this too is the common interpretation. The contract that is a function of superior force or guile, enabling the greater or more cunning power legally to shackle an individual, group, or nation in order to pick its pockets, ultimately contradicts the attainment of ends; nor is there anything sacred about such a conception of contract. Indeed, men commonly see it as a fraud and have to be often and piously reminded of the "sanctity of contract."

Traditional legal theory makes two fundamental errors about the nature of contract. One of its basic assumptions, more often violated than observed in contemporary affairs, is that contract has legal consequences only for the two parties named in it, or at least primarily for these two and only incidentally for third parties. Jordan maintains, however, that an analysis of the facts shows this assumption to be false. It is easy to show the public significance of even so private and personal a contract as marriage, and when, for example, the relations between such a corporation as United States Steel and such a union as the AFL–CIO are considered, the unreality of viewing these as a private affair is even more readily seen. It is clear that the public interest is involved, and the courts have increasingly recognized the public bearings of supposedly private agreements. The continued expansion of the police power is further recognition that the "parties at interest" are more than two and so must be conceived in a way that our prevailing legal conception of contract fails to do. The public is a party to all contracts, and where the rights of the public have been usurped or negated, where action is blocked or prevented from realizing its proper end (as in the restriction of patent rights), the contract is illegal.

A second basic assumption of traditional theory is that contract involves only the consent or assent of natural persons, while property or the system of objects is considered only of subsidiary importance. It is fallacious, however, to assume that will and object are separate, independent existences, since how the object could be taken by an external force and applied to the will or how the will could be taken and forced to adapt itself to the object are meaningless questions and contradictory. What is willed is an objective; the object is will realized. Furthermore, on the assumption that will is independent of object, there is no inherent necessity in the relationship, and contract, as mere convention or artifice, may be made or destroyed, accepted or rejected, "at will" as the natural persons see fit. Contract then becomes purely a matter of the subjective wills of natural persons as the inherent subjects of rights, whose relations to one another are reduced to scheming for advantage. Yet contract, Jordan argues, is not artificial but natural, and is to be found in the active complex of fact moving to completion in an end, a complex which incorporates persons and things in its growth. It is not based upon compulsion or caprice, nor upon any mere psychological meeting of minds, but is a function of a complex of fact ordered with respect to an end. This—the complex of fact—is the ground of obligation and of the sanctity of contract.

The object contracted for is not something to be created out of the blue, nor is it a new fact, because it is inherent in the complex that has come "into existence" as the unity of the facts when they have taken on a certain degree of order.[37]

By way of illustration, the contract between the school board and the building contractor for a new high school has nothing to do with the school board or the contractor as natural persons, but inheres rather in their function as cultural agents. The school board is the agent of the educational act, as the contractor is of a certain type of industrial act, and when the objective facts of life (population growth in this instance) require it, industry co-operates with education in order that the educational act may be sustained or developed. Moreover, regardless of the formal, legal "rights" of the contractor, the contract has been violated if the building is of shoddy construction, since the result is the weakening of the educational act. Likewise, the ultimate legality of the automobile sale inheres in the place the automobile is to fulfill in the recreational, professional, or family ends of the individual, the complex of fact serving as the objective ground for contracting the automobile. Again, despite what the formal sales document might say, if the automobile is a "lemon," or the terms such that the consumer is inhibited in carrying out the varied activities of life, then the contract is a fraud. The contract as a lawful document has nothing to do with anyone's advantage over anyone else, but is a statement of what new facts must be brought to realization in order for action to continue and achievement to grow.

What binds the wills of men together in a unity is an end, ultimately the End, culture as value objectified or realized in property objects. The binding power between labor and management is industry and the objects in which, as a typical human act, it issues. Neither labor nor management work for themselves nor for others; the principle here is neither selfishness nor altruism. Men have no bosses and do not work for one another in any case. Rather they work with each other for things. When Jordan says this, he is indicating the natural union of men's efforts in culture as common end. The common will inheres in that end, and contract is an expression of this meeting or unity of wills, the law of bodied persons organizing them into more comprehensive or larger or higher individualities. The real social

contract is an agreement of wills, but it is not a meeting of subjective wills. Real will is common will as intending a common
object and is a function of the public body.

Contract is . . . the law of obligation not only among persons considered distributively but also in the person. Obligation is then the
bond of unity between the person and his end. But the end is the
whole of persons. The contractual obligation is the principle of order
in organized life and must be looked upon as dynamic and constitutive.[38]

Property is the embodiment of personality, the system of instruments appropriate to all personal purposes; contract provides the
principle of property allocation and the law which controls the
organization of propertied persons into higher personalities.[39]
The organization and order of life are provided by property and
contract: life is organized through property as material means,
and contract is its principle. Order is achieved through property
operating as public function and contract as public law.[40]

A functional organization of society is indicated, in other
words, in which the acts of each individual as a natural person
are joined in a relationship that is objectively grounded in an
end. The end is the justification for, as well as the principle of,
the relationship. The reason that men ought to behave in certain
ways toward each other is to be found in the necessity imposed
by the end to be attained. The end as an objective to be attained
through action is the ultimate authority.

Institution, to use the term that is inclusive of different types
of corporate persons, is the end as objective fact whose stable
basis is its body of property and whose active tendency to effect
its end is contract. Institution is the unity or synthesis of property and contract in observable and statable form.

INSTITUTION

The institution, as the relatively stable organized means to
an objective, is the end made public. It is the common purpose,
not as a quantitative sum, but as a qualitative synthesis. It is the
public end in which individual and group activities are synthesized and made whole, and as such, institution is the typic
order incorporating an end stabilized in a property system that
is the product of action. That is, human action objectifies itself
in a concrete body of property, and each form stands for a typic
human act and product, so that the institution, as objective order,

is the principle of life and the key fact of culture. The institutional complex is the world as qualified by action, and men working to maintain and develop health, education, family, industry, religion, recreation, etc., are men with human qualities, or men of culture, or men of principle. As the order of objects which tends toward a common life purpose, institution is objective principle.

The import of this definition of institution as objective end is that the individual, whether the reference is to an object or a person, is not comprehensible as a unit separate and distinct from all the world, but is characterized by *unity* with and *continuity* with the objective end which constitutes him and to which he refers. The books, the classrooms and laboratories, the scholars, the buildings and their layout, are the objective order of what is proper to the end of the reproduction and advancement of knowledge. The end is their constitutive principle. It constitutes them an order. Action, as governed by this end, has literally brought them into being. In turn, the college has its special function in the common End of action that sustains itself, i.e., it makes a special contribution to the whole good. The principle for institutions is the whole world of culture that action has built. Then to view objects and individuals as separate and distinct, to isolate them from their objective relations with each other and with the end that principles them and is in *deed* their binding unity, is to make them unreal.

Due to the fact that man has a continuing action life, objects are created and organized into even larger or more comprehensive forms. The previously simple if primitive act of cleansing one's body in rain water or at the nearest pond becomes institutionalized in the harnessing of huge reservoirs of water which are aerified, filtered, chemically treated, and piped into residences, so that the act of cleansing one's body may continue in more effective modes. The efforts of the individual are no longer directed toward the collecting of rain water as best he can or the seeking out of nearby water sources for bathing, but toward the maintenance and development of the organized means—the water corporation—through which he achieves his purpose. In similar fashion, walking on foot or riding on animal-drawn vehicles gives way to organized systems of transportation. The lack of selection or haphazard selection of religious leaders develops through action into the organized church. Efforts of work which were applied directly to nature become organized within industry. Thus, as a result of action and without man's conscious intent, he has built himself into an institutional world which mediates both his interpersonal relations and his relations to nature, and these institutions are the products of no single person or group—they are the objective structures precipitated within history.

If the connection between man and nature has become highly institutionalized, then man today acts chiefly toward or within his culture rather than upon nature.[41] It is within and toward structured orders of objects and persons, such as the family, the church, industry, education, etc., that he acts. They are the organized means through which he acts and the ends of his acts. As the public forms which typic human activities have taken, institutions, once they are developed, organize and guide his action. Culture in its typic form as institution, as the objective quality of human life, is the principle of the individual's life, and by maintaining and developing it he maintains and develops his own life. Through industry, objects for the fulfillment of human purposes are created; at the same time, industry is what man maintains as the end of his act. By maintaining and developing the order of objects and persons known as the family, the property of home, furniture, clothing, lawn, etc., and the wife, children, and parents, the institution is maintained, and the individual's capacities and qualities as parent or child are developed and brought to fruition. By participating in the world as it is organized toward common life ends, the individual attains his unity and continuity—his true individuality—with that world. As the content of his feeling, willing, and thinking, the qualities of the organized world become the qualities of the individual, for the institutional world prescribes the form his life is to follow and the purposes of his life, often without his conscious awareness or assent.

Unwittingly erected in the course of action, themselves the means and ends of action, institutions are the more comprehensive ("higher") individualities in which man's life is incorporated. The part man has played in action has been constructive of realities the like of which he never anticipated and whose nature he yet fails to grasp, and failing to understand the corporate reality, he has lost control of life. The next two chapters will be a further investigation of both the reality and the more comprehensive nature of the institutional individual as basic to an understanding of the precise nature of the man-institutional relationship. However, first the reality of the corporate individual, its status in fact as much more than a "legal fiction," a status already suggested in part, will be discussed in Chapter 2 from the point of view of a reconstructed theory of individuality. Certain common theories of individuality will be critically examined, theories which have led to the erroneous assumption that the only individual is man—the flesh and blood man of nature or the soulful man of spiritual religion—who may ignore or make of the state what he pleases, or the equally faulty theory that the real individual is the state, men being of no consequence.

CHAPTER 2
CORPORATE THEORY OF INDIVIDUALITY

What is an individual? The usual answer is that an individual is a unique existence, an identity, whose individuality is constituted by his absolute differences from others. To the extent he is like others, he is that much less an individual. Another common response to the question is that the individual is his content, either certain features which are held to be more significant than others (e.g., his spiritual nature or his economic strivings) or the totality of contents which may be empirically described and catalogued. Both these views are so widely taken for granted in contemporary discussions of individuality that their logical foundations are rarely made explicit and exposed to critical review. However, is the nature of individuality as uniqueness or content so obvious that analysis is not necessary? Jordan's reply is that the nature of individuality is a more complicated question than ordinarily conceived, and false assumptions about it vitiate much of current social theory. Perhaps, as Jordan argues, this failure in the idea of individuality largely explains the disastrous condition of contemporary society. He maintains that questions of cultural unity and public order—in fact, all issues of modern culture—are ultimately questions as to the nature of individuality, and that the manner in which the public life progresses or fails to progress will depend upon the adequacy of the theory of individuality.[1]

Ironically enough but also understandably enough, that doctrine which exalted the individual has culminated in his almost complete submergence. The fascists, for example, have frankly justified their system as a solution to the political anarchy created by individualism, just as socialists and communists have justified their principles as a solution to the economic anarchy of individualism. Modern liberals, eschewing all of these systems, nevertheless have been extremely critical of the older individualism, and Dewey has shown how the logic of atomism based on a one-sided empiricism led to an equally one-sided rationalism whose social consequences were authoritarianism in every sphere of life. Exaltation of the individual has failed of attainment in fact because the underlying view of individuality was fallacious, and we may expect a continuation of the tragedies which have befallen man as long as we do not arrive at an adequate conception. Jordan does not propose to lose the individual—the prevailing views have already succeeded in all but burying him— but rather to find him.

While Jordan's effort is primarily to construct a positive position rather than to destroy points of view which he feels are erroneous, to a considerable degree he has attempted to expose the falsity of the assumptions upon which certain definitions of individuality have been founded. In doing so, he has at the same time given us some clues as to the nature of the problem and the direction in which the solution must be sought. A presentation of his critique is therefore valuable because it not only provides an insight into the weaknesses of positions he rejects but also contains within it indications, at this point largely implicit, of his own position and so serves to prepare the ground for his positive statement.

Jordan's criticism of prevailing conceptions is not that whatever is individual is *ipso facto* subjective, but rather that the problem is exactly that of determining what is an individual or what is individuality and that current definitions have erred because they are subjective. The problem for Jordan is to attempt to define individuality in objective terms and thus to avoid, on the one hand, the abstract particularity of nominalism, and, on the other, the abstract universality of realism. Both absolutes and their corollaries, individual liberty and social absolutism, are rejected by him because they rest on the same untenable assumption, that the real may be known through isolation and separation. Individualism assumes the separation of facts from each other and the larger whole of which they are a part, and social absolutism assumes the whole to be independent of and exterior to the facts which instance it. Hence the metaphysics of the granular universe and the metaphysics of the block universe are equally abstract and thus subjective.[2]

In analyzing the attempts to define individuality that have been more or less carefully worked out, Jordan finds that they fall into three categories which, while they overlap considerably, may nevertheless be distinguished from each other. He argues that the first two of these are subjective while the third represents an objective statement. These approaches have conceived of individuality in the following terms: (1) distinctness, what it *is not* or what is *not it;* (2) content, what *is* involved in it; (3) intent, what *may be* in it or what is meant by it.[3]

Individuality as Distinctness

Perhaps the first notion of individuality received its elementary impulse from the discernment, in the immediacy of sense perception, of objects distinct in some way from their backgrounds, and while these phenomena are not necessarily clearly demarcated, the feeling or impression of something or some thing standing out is present. While for sense experience the meaningful object may be taken to be either the outlined physical thing-in-itself or the nothing that is the continuum between these objects, in either case the real is that which is distinct from what it is not. There is assumed to be a one-to-one correspondence between the distinguishable in perception and the object as such in existence. On this simple sensory basis the individual is the distinguishable thing-in-itself taken in the absolute sense as separable, but while this may explain the idea of individuality in its earliest and perhaps unself-conscious stage, the principle received a further impetus in the deliberate adoption of the method of reductionism. Based on the false premise that the real is an ultimate simple, the reductionist method proceeds to denude the object of those characteristics which cover its essence and thus to seek its true objective nature. The real fact is then the bare fact, one shorn of all relations and qualities. The effort is that of isolating, in a real sense decontaminating, the object of the relations which infect it and distort or destroy its true existence as a thing apart. The given is broken into its elements, the simplest that the relentlessness of rigorous analysis and the method of differentiation can yield; and the aggregate of these is then taken to comprise the whole or the complex fact. On this basis the organism is reduced to cells which in turn are reduced to their elements, until at length the irreducible simple is found, the real under its aspect of qualityless, relationless finality. However, at this stage the elements are no longer distinguishable, one is like another, and individuality—the real defined as the unique—contradicts itself in complete homogeneity, the elements being distinguishable only by their assignment to a number or a separate place in a numerical series. The numbers representing the elements are different, but the elements themselves are undifferentiated; one is the same as another and counts for as much as another; hence one may be interchanged with another and its character as real has disappeared, giving place to an abstraction.[4] Paradoxically, the attempts to distinguish individuality through reduction into simple elements culminates in sameness and is self-contradictory. To locate man in his physical-chemical being is to find everyone and no one.

The object having been severed from all connections, what is left is irreducible precisely because it is nothing. As independent, unrelated entities, the products of the process of reductionism are absolute zeros; consequently the "positivistic" approach, while insisting upon the pursuit of the facts, actually leaves them behind in its absorption in the analytical process. The fact is lost in the course of the search in which it was to be found, for reductionism and the method of differentiation results in a denial of quality to the real. The methods of reductionism and differentiation deny the possibility of relations among reals, upon which qualities depend. What is left is a real conceived in negative terms, something not this, nor this, nor this, "the fatuous infinite judgment." [5]

The real is not the simple, nor can universality be attained through these simples taken as an aggregate; there are no ultimate simples in the world, no isolable things-in-themselves which are what they are as self-contained units existing independently of relations. Apart from the system of relations, which is constitutive of their being and meaning, they are literally nonentities. The process of reduction culminates in a thing-in-itself which is unknowable precisely because it is no thing, nothing, a pure abstraction. Subjectivity is just this abstraction of an object or person from the whole system of relations which alone constitutes it as real.

The practical significance of the conception of individuality in terms of distinguishability has been exemplified historically.

According to Greek thought, man was unified with nature, but this conception was shaken by the events which disrupted that culture, and early Christianity evolved a doctrine which not only separated man from nature, but one individual from another and from God.[6] Finding the world chaotic, the state crumbling, man looked within himself to discover principle; thought turned introspective and away from the "outer" problems of politics and the state, and salvation was to be found not in the attempt to order life conditions but in putting off the world. No longer was the natural-cultural order the object of study or that to which the individual was bound; instead of attempting to reconstruct the objective conditions of life, man turned to the inner and the subjective. Sunk in the "cave of his individuality," his immediate experience of a shattered world, in which the idealized end was not attained and seemed unattainable, gave birth "to the most pathetic and mistaken wail which his history records: What must *I* do to be saved?"[7] Instead of building the Kingdom, religion discovered the soul and turned its attention to the salvation of man through the saving of men's souls one by one.[8] The soul was identified with immediate subjective feeling, and the self as soul thus became one with these states. Since such states are not amenable to law and are incapable of being generalized, the self or personality becomes private, inner and "metaphysical."[9]

Thus in religion the same reductionist method found its ultimate in the "simple and undecomposable unity" of the soul, the quality-less residue that remained when the contamination of the body and of the world, the concrete detail of culture and fact, was eliminated from man's nature. Committed to the distinguishability of individuals, "negative theology" had at one pole man defined in such terms as fallen, lowly, and meek, who attained status only as God in his infinite power bestowed grace upon this nothing, and at the other, the ineffable, unapproachably huge blankness completely removed from the defilement of contact with the human.[10] Between these two existences, completely separable, stood an infinite gap which required the establishment of inter-mediaries, the endless process of filling the spaces between individuals with other individuals—hence "the plurality of gods or 'beings' extending from the demi-urge to 'a little lower than the angels' " exemplified in the hierarchy of the Catholic church.[11] Similarly, starting from the other pole, it was possible to construct upward a series of individuals as quantitative repetitions, using the mathematical device of increase of quantity. Beginning with the reduction of fact to a simple, the abstract distinctness of the self-contained unity, the progression is to an equally abstract identity, or, to put it somewhat differently, beginning with the particularism of subjective individualism, the process culminates in abstract universalism, the inevitable result of the attempt to construct a unity or whole through the pluralization of what are taken as discrete entities.[12] As we have seen, the distinguishable simple uncovered through reduction flows into its contradiction in undifferentiated homogeneity. The attempt to escape the cul-de-sac of undifferentiated entities leads to the process of pluralization, the indefinite repetition of homogeneous individuals culminating in the abstraction of the numerical infinite. To express this in terms of social theory, each unique individual is exalted. The basis of his value is his possession of an immortal soul. Alternatively, man may be viewed naturalistically without exaltation, a being whose nature patently consists of his physical-chemical-biological constitution. In both cases each individual has a content common to all men, and therefore all men are equal for they are fundamentally the same. Despite the superficial trappings of culture, in their essence—whether Americans, Russians, Pakistani, etc.—they are alike. Since each unit is the same, this leads to the idea variously expressed as the group, the plurality, or the collectivity. The total collectivity can then be designated as mankind, mankind representing the numerical infinite of men, each equal to the other and merely occupying different space-time positions, whose difference is only one of symbolic designation. However, an infinite can never attain to wholeness, and the numerical infinite as a whole of repetition is a contradiction in terms.[13] The concept of a whole, as distinguished from an aggregate, involves a form and thus limits; therefore nothing that is real can be whole and infinite at the same time. It is as a result of distinguishing individuals through the method of reductionism that both individualism and collectivism necessarily resort to coercion in order to make whole what is assumed to be an infinity of discrete individuals. Individualism and collectivism both fail to see life as the ordered whole it is in fact, whose wholeness in fact needs understanding for its sustenance and growth. Wholeness—the ordered integration of parts in a structured form—is natural, and hence cannot be made or broken but only hindered or helped.

A related practical outcome of the conception of the individual as distinguishable is to be found in the social physics which has pervaded much of social theory and has destroyed the possibility of public order by its application of the categories of natural science to society. A good example of this thought is to be found in the theory of Spencer, who conceived of the individual, after the model of mechanics, as a force center exerting himself from the outside on other centers like himself.[14] Society itself is dispersed into these exclusive, self-seeking units whose relations with other individuals are competitive, external, and negative. Public order comes when each individual pursues his exclusive interest against every other individual, and when this struggle reaches a stalemate, the state enters to effect a resolution of the conflict. The state is thus also conceived as a force center, though one superior to the individual, and as such its relations to him are external. The state is external to man, as is man to man. The negative state reaches its highest form and the peak of its attainment when it lies dormant, when it does nothing; hence "that government is best which governs least." The presuppositions of this philosophy issue in the war of each against each and all against all, man versus man and man versus the state. The possibility of public order thus having been precluded, the consequence is said to be just that order.

As long as the fundamental assumption is that the individual is known in distinctness and is therefore an ultimate simple, the resultant conception of society and of human relations is mechanistic, and this is true despite the attempt of some theorists to make society essentially a psychical phenomenon depending for its unity upon mental events, the similarity of the states of mind of its individual members.[15] The issue is the same whether society is taken to be an aggregate of consciousnesses or any other aggregate; conceived as a collectivity of simple individuals, society is never a whole and can never attain wholeness and unity. The constructionist fallacy, a belief that a whole can be built out of simple parts, is operative here. The whole is not made or built out of such units, but is already there as the original fact; man in his institutions, the person in the environment of persons and things, is the unity that is the unit.[16] The conception of the social mind, therefore, as a meeting of individual minds or as a synthesis of them, and of society as dependent for its unity upon the like-mindedness of its members, remains, despite its implicit dependence upon psychological phenomena, a social physics, and human relations so conceived remain external, analogous to physical relations.[17]

The practical disciplines employing the method of differentiation have been based upon the conception of the self-sufficient, exclusive individual of atomism, the competitive self-seeker living in a world peopled by his like, the "man for himself" with a vengeance, whose welfare depends upon freedom from the infection of relations, an integer whose integrity is maintained only in isolation. As discrete, he is the locus of value, the source of ultimate worth and dignity, of authority and will. The individual as absolute will is a law unto himself, and since there are as many laws as there are individuals, disorder is inevitable from the beginning. It is this will as innate to the metaphysical individual that is taken as political reality, and from the assumption of individual absolutes, the problem arises of how to unite or put together what has been posited as ultimately separate. Having assumed discontinuity and disunity as final, social theory has struggled for centuries with the problem of how to construct society out of individuals, to make whole again what it sundered at the start. It has looked for practical principle in the opposition of wills, where it cannot be found, and has finally rested on force, the very negation of principle. The notion of law is reduced to force; the assumed disjunction between man and man is to be overcome by the injunction of law as the power to compel. Thus, based on a negative and centrifugal conception, law itself has been dispersive rather than regulative, conducive to disorder rather than to order.[18] Tragically, the law has legalized the lawless individual, and as long as property and contract, the ultimate practical concepts and working implements of individualism, prevail in their atomistic form, the continuation of hostilities is assured, and men thought to be exploiting nature in behalf of their own exclusive interests will in fact be exploiting each other.[19]

Individuality as Content

"Negative theology" had severed the individual from his qualities as a natural being by elevating him to his "real" being as a soul,

although one of low status and tainted with evil from the beginning; "natural theology," under the impulses of the rationalistic movements of the eighteenth century, while not neglecting
the soul of man, restored him to his place in the realm of nature,
made him a being of stature, and looked within him for evidence
of his selfhood. The probe was extended into the depths of man,
even into his very soul.[20] However, the search was not prompted
wholly by religious motives nor undertaken wholly by religious
interests. Other moral, political, and legal concerns became involved in the quest which, in seeking the nature of the self,
repudiated the realm of the mystical and the supernatural for
something more concrete, something to be found in the experiences of the living and acting man, the individual of practical
affairs engaged in earning his daily bread and in the other activities of his round of life. The facts that would disclose the
nature of human existence were sought and found in man's distinguishable mental states.[21] This procedure developed an extensive cataloguing of particularized states, the individual being
defined in terms of experience. The irreducible particular is the
isolable, immediately felt detail of content which is pluralized
and thus becomes the total fact of man. Each of these details is
regarded as a self-sufficient quality, and the problem of the nature of individuality or the self becomes the relatively simple one
of delineating all of these contents. It is essentially a task of
getting "all the facts" and of inventorying as completely as possible all of the details of content which, through the inductive
process, yield the whole individual as the aggregate of his experiences or the sum of his mental states. In the facts of the inner
life the self is to be found, and the particular unit of mental
states, of wants and needs, the individual as experience or as
biopsychological existence, exhausts the meaning of individuality
within himself. The fullness of individuality is discoverable in
the fullness of the description of these *inner* states; thus the
method of religious mysticism is used, although not intentionally,
by the social science investigator.

   The attempt to define individuality in terms of content results
in an analysis which plumbs the extent of the conception in the
number and variety of states to which it refers.[22] Despite the
fact that the contents described are mental, they refer only to the
external qualities of the person and do not issue in an individual

as a unity. There is no internal bond among these separable contents; the only self that can be found is a series of mental states which indicate no order among themselves; it is a self without unity and hence the very denial of selfhood. Each psychological or biopsychological state is external to every other, and each individual, as differentiated on the basis of unique contents, is external to every other individual. On this basis there is no continuity of one state with another nor of one individual with another. The definition of individuality as content is dispersive and negative, differentiating in such a manner as to culminate finally in isolation and homogeneity. The negation, which can only differentiate rather than individuate, is taken as the real, rather than the real seen in the instance or the case "of specific and describable and interpretable fact, the fact whose factuality is its meaning, the 'fact as a case of a law.' " [23] To know that this chair has curlicues carved into the back does not yet mean that I know it as a chair, as the individual (reality) it is. The individual is not merely different *from* but different *within* its type. Differentiation without characterization is unintelligible.

The content criterion is subject to the criticisms already made of the distinctness criterion of which it is an example. Society is dissolved into individuals, who in turn are dissolved into their mental states, the process of reduction resting ultimately on the absoluteness of the single experience or inner feeling; or, after the modern trend, society is analyzed into groups which are then broken into individuals who in turn are dissolved into their wants and needs. Then the process is reversed and the attempt is made to construct the individual out of wants and needs, the group out of individuals, and society out of groups. In each case the whole is a sum, the result of the inductive process which issues in an abstract universal or an abstract whole. Yet the facts "do not add up" for the reason that the fact of wholeness is never a mere sum. The fact is always a concrete rather than an abstract universal and as such can never be built of facts as particulars. The particulars do not and cannot account for the fact of wholeness, but themselves require a ground which the whole as fact alone can supply. Chair is the law of the parts; boards, nails, glue, and varnish require rather than give principle. Nor does chair exist independently of its parts. Neither the isolate particular nor the abstract universal are real, but rather individuality is a syn-

thesis of particularity and universality, the type-fact,[24] the concrete universal. Once the original fact of wholeness and unity
is destroyed through the very devotion to the facts, no amount
of effort, however exhaustive, rigorous, and diligent, can succeed
in rebuilding it; hence the continued and inevitably endless
fact-hunting of social science discovers nothing but multiplicity
and process, all going nowhere.

Jordan does not, of course, deny the reality of the biopsychological nature of man, but what he does maintain is that the
existence of mental states as psychological facts precludes their
serving as the basis of cultural order, for the reason that subjective facts by their very nature deplete themselves in self-reference.
Objective order cannot be built of subjective facts, nor can the
meaning of individuality be found in these facts, however fully
they are known. The psychological fact is not ultimate and the
cataloguing of states of mind may go on endlessly, since subjective states may be infinite in number, without furnishing a
clue to the nature of individuality. This is an instance of the
content fallacy, that an idea is exhaustible in the existent quality
of its content.

As an example of the failure of the content idea to attain
universality, Jordan cites the conception of the economic man,
the unit of physical needs and wants acting to gratify itself. Here
again Jordan does not deny the reality of these contents, but he
maintains that precisely because the economic man is a psychological fact, he is false as an idea.[25] This conception is false not
only because there is more content to human nature than that
embodied in the notion of economic man, but because content,
no matter how thoroughly known, is not the individual. To be
sure, man does not live by bread alone, but then the spiritual detail of content that constitutes the soul of religion is as abstract
as the material detail that constitutes the economic man, and
subjectivity remains whichever aspect of content is selected as
primary. Neither is it revealed in the attempt to obtain the whole
man by combining the spiritual and material or any other contents.[26] No one content is determinative of the rest, nor is the
individual an aggregate of contents, just as the contents of the
chair are not in themselves determinative of each other or the
whole. The principle of individuality is not to be found in
mental and physical states, however exhaustively described and

analyzed. Depth psychology gets no nearer to human nature than do other psychologies, and neurology no nearer than physiology. It is not a matter of driving deeper and deeper into the mystery of the psyche and the soma and thereby discovering the real nature of man; all we find here is the biopsychological man, the unit of needs and wants. We may catalogue these facts without end and not know man. Man remains a mystery as long as his nature is sought within him in the states of his organism, and the psychological approach only compounds rather than clarifies the mystery.

The concept of the economic man is too small to accommodate human nature, not because of its failure to include other contents, but because *it makes no connection with ends and so excludes the possible or ideal quality of man,* the potentiality of the individual. Content does not determine the meaning of an idea; rather what a thing is is what it intends to be—an expression of the law or universality inherent in its nature.[27] What a thing may be is the index to what it always is, and ideality rather than content then defines the idea.[28] Don Quixote, the madman, knows that the country girl, Aldonza, is not what her rustic appearance makes her out to be. Not fooled by the "enchanters" of sense, he sees her truly because he sees what she may be: the peerless Dulcinea. To restrict the meaning of an individual to his content is to make him a fixed form. Such an individual is an abstraction because his expansive and dynamic tendencies, his possibilities of growth, are overlooked.

The biological arguments of "conditions within the organism" in favor of the economic man are no more successful in sustaining the contents idea of individuality, for the individual is still viewed as being contained wholly within the skin. The environment is excluded, except in a technical sense where it serves as the means or condition to satisfy the economic wants and needs. Looking directly at the fact, the practical man engaged in practical affairs, the theorists of the economic man find only the technical man. Failing to connect man with the institutional order which is the logical ground of the individual, the conception once more issues in the subjective particular, an abstract rather than whole man.[29] As with all subjective phenomena, the economic man cannot serve as a guiding principle for the practical life, and the practical man so conceived is the very failure of that life. A knowledge of the biopsychological nature of man as inclusive of economic man, though useful for some purposes, is of no value for the regulation of human relations or as a ground of social order. This knowledge does not and cannot suggest what these relations ought to be, for content description and analysis per se make no contact with an objective end as the ordering principle of content. Contents require rather than provide ground for action. By employing psychology as its base, economic theory has become no more than the description of the technical means by which physical wants and needs are satisfied through the production and cumulation of property. By thus separating economic thought from its ethical foundations, the science remains subjective because its method cannot find the fact-whole which gives to life its objectivity and universality. For Jordan, then, the castigation of the practical disciplines because of their supposed failure to become true sciences, or because of the impossibility of their becoming such, does not strike at the heart of their troubles; on the contrary, his own criticism of them is that they are too much, rather than too little, sciences; having too literally emulated the physical sciences, they rest on causation rather than on their logical ground in human nature.[30] The valid study of society, as of anything, requires categories appropriate to the object. The paradox of the practical disciplines is that their sincere but indiscriminate application of natural science categories to cultural affairs, as exemplified by the search for inner or outer "causes" of behavior, is at the heart of their failure to become true sciences.

Instead of accepting the institutional order as a fact requiring no explanation in terms of origin and cause, the theorist operating on the basis of the content criterion seeks to find a mental state, a want or need, to correspond to every public phenomenon.[31] Looking to the outer world and finding an institutional system, he proceeds to account for its existence in terms of its growth out of the needs of man. Each objective fact has its counterpart in a subjective state; a social fact is observed and then a state of mind is discovered to correspond to it. But this method takes us back to the heyday of the instinctivists, when every human act had its source in a corresponding instinct, with the result that hundreds upon hundreds of instincts were "discovered" or, more accurately, created. This heyday is over, and the almost infinite number of instincts which Bernard in the 1920's found to have been listed by various writers is no longer taken seriously. Nevertheless, the method still remains implicit in the content criterion of individuality, and the biopsychological person as the unit of wants and needs is still the foundation of current social science. Hence Jordan's criticism, though often stated in terms used at the time of his writing, is just as pertinent today. He is not simply castigating an obsolete method. Instead of "instincts" as the content of man, we now have "needs and wants." Psychology as the queen of sciences takes as its province man in his total contents, and each of the practical disciplines—ethics, politics, law, sociology, economics—selects from among these states those that are suitable to its purpose while excluding the rest, and hence each is still addicted to the content fallacy. Current efforts to find a basis of cultural unity and public order rest in many cases on a similar approach, and are at bottom employing the same method of resorting to the common nature of man as it is found in his needs and wants. The attempt to establish universality on this basis persists, and the hope flourishes that from human nature conceived in this way can be derived a conception of culture and a way out of the present national and international chaos and conflict. A growing minority of social scientists rejects ethical relativism and maintains that subjectivity can be overcome through the scientific proclamation of the universal, objective human nature, defined in terms of the basic biopsychological needs which all men have; and the satisfaction or lack of satisfaction of these needs will serve as the criterion by which social arrangements are to be judged. However, the content criterion of individuality succeeds only in isolating a particular, the abstract fact removed from the system of relations which alone can give it significance. This succcess is its failure, the failure to attain universality despite the fact that certain needs and wants may be common to all men. That they are common or general does not enable the content conception to escape subjectivity, for these phenomena—the needs and wants—still fail to point outward to the order and the public ends with which they connect. They thus lack the meaning which can only be given them by the institutional order. Moreover, even if it be granted that all men experience wants in terms of hunger, sex, cold, insecurity, spiritual, social, and competitive desires, pleasure, etc., or as many or as few as it pleases the social scientist to find, the problems of to what extent, if at all, and with what priority their expression is to be encouraged, and what structure the institutional order is to take on their account, are largely unanswered. In the mere existence of sexual, spiritual, and social "needs," is there suggested a kind of world in which these needs are to be realized? Does the existence of a sexual need prescribe absolute sexual satisfaction for all persons of every age group? Does the existence of a spiritual need mean, on the one hand, that each man should satisfy this need in his own way, or, on the other, that there should be a universal church? And if the latter, what is the proper function of the church in recognizing religious needs? What attitudes about the world should it encourage? And what does man's social need have to say about the kind of society which he should build? Does it necessitate a government, or are the anarchists right in urging love and kindness as sufficient bonds for the satisfaction of man's social nature? When human needs are conceived as the ultimates of human nature, no logically consistent answer can be offered to these questions, although one can admire the imaginative ingenuity with which some social scientists attempt to solve problems which, since they are grounded in a content theory of individuality, are insoluble.

Jordan's criticism is that subjective phenomena—whether called instincts, drives, motives, urges, springs to action, wants, needs, interests, propensities, or whatnot—cannot be universalized, and that human nature so defined is without ground, lost in the mechanism and causation which are at the heart of the content definition. It is the institutional order that is the logical ground of the natural person, giving significance to his native wants and urges. Without the institutional order these wants and urges may be said to be either without direction and pointless or, what is the same thing, to point only to themselves as containing their own meaning. Instincts exhaust themselves in the contradictoriness of self-reference, yielding no clue to their own significance nor to the order of culture. These drives refer to the unity of mind at a low level and merely mean that the biopsychological organism functions as a whole in attaining social ends.[32] Psychological facts cannot account for cultural order; institution is the fact that explains but itself requires no explanation; it gives to instincts whatever significance they have.[33] The urges or needs make their demands but are mere existents unless given direction by public ends, and the latter are not visible in human nature taken as biopsychological. The biopsychological conception of man is indeed primitive and reduces man to the level of the animal, since it neglects the rational element which sets him off as a self-conscious being and gives direction to his life. Man is not led around by his drives, but rather his drives are directed by ends constructed through the intelligence. The drives get their significance not from their mere existence but from their direction as determined by cultural purpose; drives are not universal, therefore, in the sense that they are found in all members of the species, but rather the species as universal has rational and moral ends in which the individual member and his life are incorporated and which become his ends when he is a rational and moral being. The ends of the individual lie not within himself nor in the satisfaction of his needs, but in public aims; and these again, as public, are objective and universal, not an aggregate of individual interests nor the result of a playing off of the interests of individuals or groups against each other.

Psychological feeling—even love in its most altruistic and spiritualized form—also fails to attain universality. It is subjective, not merely because of a lack of reference to objects, but because it attaches indiscriminately to all objects that are presented to it and does so with respect to their specialized qualities rather than to their total meaning.[34] Ideas refer to total significance or the cumulative modes of the universal which, as particular, are the individual, while feeling singles out particulars without reference to their total meaning. Feeling finds a "nigger"; idea finds the man. Because of the failure to recognize the instance "as a case of a law," subjective feelings never attain to the universality which is necessary for objectivity, and this is true even if the feeling is common to a group or a whole people. Feeling is not validated by appearing in many rather than in one or a few, for the shared quality is no evidence of the fitness of the feeling.

The ardent advocate who is impelled by his conscience to promote the brotherhood, praise God, exalt the flag, lynch the Negro, censor the arts, destroy inequality, does not derive justification for his action from the strength of his convictions, but rather from the end he serves. A judgment gets its strength from its objective reference, and it is knowledge of the end, rather than consciousness of feeling, that validates the act. The passions arouse, but the unimpassioned idea of the end is the guide to significant action.[35]

Because psychological feeling is by nature indiscriminate and does not see the end that the object implies as a member of a species, it attaches value frequently where value does not belong; or if it does connect with value correctly, it does so accidentally or through having been properly formed in a sound education, and not from principle inherent in its being. Feeling, merely because the individual or group possesses it as a content, does not endow an object with value; on the contrary, the object as value is the criterion which determines the merit of the feeling and suggests whether the feeling should be discarded or retained. Awareness of feeling and knowledge of the object are not one. Indeed, feeling becomes important when it is obstructive just as much as when it is constructive, for although it is not an object in itself and contains no principle of order, it may project a disturbing reference into the fact-order and thus disrupt the objective arrangements of reality upon which order is based.[36] The analysis of psychological or subjective feeling, while in itself important for clinical and pedagogical purposes, gives us neither the real individual nor any aspect of the world. Furthermore, society rests on something more substantial than states of feeling. Subjective states do not sustain culture, nor are they the tie which binds men together and keeps society from disintegrating. Society is not founded on feeling or on "magical subjective cements" which call for constant exhortation and propaganda to retain their bonding qualities and hold the body politic together.[37] In so far as feeling is objectified at all, it is as the quality of an object, the aesthetic object being the most perfect instance, or as the quality of an order of objects, i.e., an institution. In this sense religious feeling as objective is the corporate order of the church, familial feeling is the home-person organization, etc. Therefore, the stability in the quality of subjective feeling, the effectiveness with which it may be changed, or even the elimination of types of subjective feeling, are dependent upon the stability, change, or elimination of objective feeling.

Value is substantial as it is embodied in institution, where it becomes stable and active in the very structure of society. That structure, not states of mind, sustains and maintains culture. Society endures though states of feelings change; however, this is not to argue that ideas and feelings may be anything, but rather that social order rests on something more solid than states of mind: institutional order. To operate on the biopsychological contents of the natural individual in order to induce the proper states of mind within him is to apply the wrong treatment to the wrong patient. It is the institutional person that needs treatment, or better, understanding.

Subjective phenomena afford no principle either for their own ordering or for the order of culture, and taken by themselves they remain purely inner and inactive unless they are embodied in objects. States of mind are ineffective so long as they remain mere states, but given a corporate body they are sustained in the world. To point this out, however, does not mean that Jordan is proposing the transfer of any idea or feeling directly into institution. Here he is pointing to the corporate character of all life as maintained through body, and with reference to human affairs that body is institution, without which idea is no more than idle fancy. Far from asserting that all that need be done is to translate ideas or states of mind into corresponding institutions, Jordan first questions the worth of the idea itself. The clarity of the idea, the glow it radiates, the persistency of its appearance—neither one nor all of these is testimony to its validity. The presence of an idea in a mind is not for Jordan evidence of its soundness or right to occupy the ground it holds. Anything may come into mind, but its warrant for remaining there depends upon its connections both inside and outside of mind.[38] An idea asserts its right to remain in mind only as it accords with something external in the impersonal world. Failing to meet this standard, it is justifiably evicted in favor of a better qualified tenant. Whether the idea be true or false does not, then, depend upon its having made itself known or felt as content, whether in one mind or many, but upon its ability to give an account of an objective world.[39] That a group, however large, is of a common persuasion, "of one mind," is no assurance of the competence of that mind. The single judger may be right, the "social" judgment wrong, and in either case the soundness of the judgment does not depend upon numbers. Judgment is not validated by a pluralization of minds; states of mind do not become objectified by their appearance in an ever wider number of individuals, and they are not sanctified by agreement.

Similarly, interest, however widely shared, is not an adequate criterion of value. However, the interest theory attempts to establish the universality of value through another method which upon examination, however, proves to be based on the same subjectivistic assumptions. Jordan agrees that the real is universal, and hence he is in accord with the attempt to establish the universality of value, but his criticism here again is that the method used precludes the attainment of that end. The abstraction of interest from objective continuity assures failure, despite the apparently guaranteed success of the definition of value as "any object of any interest," because it leaves the interest itself with no objectification but what it derives from being found as an aspect of every mental state. Then the case of the interest theory is easily won, all too easily, for by assuming value as a constituent of every such state or process, its universality can readily be found as fact. However, universality cannot be established through abstract extension, the "any" of scientific method; Jordan maintains instead that objectification can only be attained through the "whole" of logical method.

To consider value as any object of any interest is to avoid the question that may be directed at any content, namely, what status should it have in man's life? "A psychological disposition for or against something" is no ground for determining the value of the object. Value is not determined by the appearance of the disposition; rather it is the other way around: the worth of the interest is itself determined by the value object. It is the good, the true, the beautiful, as logically discoverable realities in the world, that determine the fitness of the state of mind, the interest, or feeling; such states by themselves are not determinative of, nor constitutional to, objects of either the natural or cultural world. Categories are not imposed by mind on objects, but rather knowledge is attained through categories which are deducible from the object, and the problem is to determine those constitutive of the object and necessary to its intelligibility.[40]

The practical sciences pride themselves on sticking to the facts, on their objectivity in refusing to make value judgments, with the result that they have abdicated in this area and can offer no principles to direct the practical life. The end is not theirs to know, they say, not an object for their study. Individuality as the analysis and knowledge of content is thought to furnish the solid foundation of these disciplines, but if Jordan's criticism is sound, this turns out to be exactly what individuality is not, and the knowledge edifice which the social sciences have built tumbles to the ground. The objectivity of the social sciences on analysis proves to be anything but that, precisely because of the failure to incorporate the ideal in the theoretical conception. Exactly at the point where these sciences are most proud of their achievement they fail most utterly. Since they are dependent upon an adequate definition of individuality, which no account of contents can give, their concentration on mental phenomena, though these are facts, means the disappearance rather than the furtherance of objectivity. Jordan's criticism, therefore, is not to be taken merely as referring to the failure of these sciences to accept a responsibility which should be theirs; it goes further. He asserts that because the social sciences do not incorporate ideality in their definition of individuality and continue to adhere to the content criterion, they do not yield knowledge of their object of study, which, inasmuch as it is the sociocultural reality, must involve a logically valid determination of ends. Ends are in and of their object of study, and any discipline which fails to yield significant knowledge of the object of its study is no science, despite its assertions to the contrary.

The lesson to be gleaned from the idealist Don Quixote is to hold and courageously pursue ends of value, and from the positivist Sancho Panza to take cognizance of the empirical realities in the development and attainment of ends. The error of the positivist is that of interpreting the empirical event as final; the error of the idealist is that of naïvely ignoring existent conditions. Despite Jordan's strenuous criticism of the content idea of individuality, he is not thereby arguing that knowledge of man's current content—biopsychological, economic, spiritual, cultural, or whatever—is without meaning. For example, we should know what the Negro or the businessman is like, what his present personality is as an empirical fact, not in order to define his meaning through this method, but to have greater success through appropriate legislation, education, psychotherapy, etc., in attaining the man. The ideal as the goal to be attained is the law of individual growth, for it is the law of the content to be incorporated in man's public world as well as his subjective life. Knowledge of content sets the legislative problem for any age in achieving the ideal. The social scientist's conception of an individual in terms of what he empirically is ignores the ultimate law of all living things—growth. Since growth has ontological status, the idea of individuality needs illumination through the imaginative but logical perception of what the individual may be. When Don Quixote is diverted from his vigorous pursuit of truth, goodness, and beauty to the byroad of normalcy, of acquiescence to appearances, of acceptance of the realities of empirical sense, Don Antonio Moreno cries out: "Consider, sir, that his cure can never benefit the public half so much as his distemper." In the same sense, as presently constituted, the social sciences are of little value to the public since they expend their major efforts on the description of facts and values which are the current content of experience.

The plea that the social sciences are young and hence to be excused for their incompleteness at this early stage of their development, Jordan finds unconvincing. That they are young no one denies, but their failure is attributable not to their youth but to their method. Given time they will no doubt discover yet more facts, but unfortunately with the same result. The difficulty is not overcome by getting more facts or all the facts; this effort leads nowhere, and the practical disciplines as presently constituted issue in no law because of their insistence upon hunting for more of the facts.[41] The practical life cannot be based on the present premises of these disciplines, for public order is not to be found in states of mind, and hence social theory for this reason cannot be based on descriptive psychology. The social sciences have left the fact behind in the search for the facts. The fact of society, as a unity evidenced in a structure, has been reduced to the facts of mental contents, with culture existing as or validated by states of mind, the final subjectivity, whereas states of mind should be validated through knowledge of cultural reality. It is time, Jordan asserts, for these sciences to leave off the endless pursuit of the facts and to take on the task of evaluation, but that means that the problem is of another nature, that it is a problem of logic.[42] The facts of the practical disciplines are not of the stuff of ideas, and the practical life, if it is to have law as its guide, rests on a logically speculative philosophy rather than on descriptive science.

Individuality as Intent

Jordan's criticism of individualism indicates the direction of his positive theory. The rejection of the "dark regions of identity," where individuals are reduced into homogeneous globules, and of the negative unit of difference, where each individual is a unique entity and hence not knowable, suggests the possibility of, or perhaps better, the necessity of the integration of identity and difference in the constitution of reals. Neither absolute likeness nor absolute difference, relation with indistinguishable relatees nor relationless entities, are real. There is no universe without universal, but neither is there one without diversity. Knowledge presupposes necessary connections, wholeness, a world; individualism, in whichever direction it goes, precludes the possibility of a world and so of knowledge. A universe without a multiverse, as well as a multiverse without a universe, destroys the possibility of thought and world. Since there are no isolable objects in the world—if there were, they would be unintelligible and thought would have no ground—the movement of thought is not backward and inward, severing relations as it goes in order to find an inner essence of the individual, but outward to the whole of relations in which the individual stands and which is constructive of his being. Ultimately, this means going to the cosmos itself as a whole of relations.

The specific does not constitute an individual in terms of particularized, severable, unique characters; its true meaning is the species-indicating or species-forming universal. The case is always a case of a law; the individual is always an individual of a species.[43] To understand a particular individual requires reference beyond him to the continuity of individuals in the species. It is the universal character as individuated in a person or object that constitutes the reality of an individual. These individual forms are real and knowable, as "education" and "book" are knowable through instancing the universal character of education and book. On the one hand it is continuity with the species that transforms raw fact into a real object, and on the other hand it is the existence of the universal in fact and as the law of the fact that testifies to the universal's reality. Raw fact and universals in themselves assumed to be discontinuous from one another are abstractions and hence unintelligible.

Not the unit but unity, not isolation but continuity, is the principle of reality. Real continuity, however, is impossible on the basis of undifferentiated homogeneity or identity without difference; all this can yield is mass man and not an individual. Neither is real continuity to be found in the causal relations of atomism; all that atomism can offer to view are uniques who are in theory their own law and who, when lawlessness inevitably ensues, are arbitrarily aggregated or collectivized. This is exemplified in contemporary "industrial relations" whose "order" is maintained through management, union, or governmental force or fraud. The causal relations of atomism emphasize the specialized trait rather than the individuated character of facts, and so destroys wholeness.

As characteristic of all reals, the principle of continuity retains both difference and identity, object and relation in their union. The abandonment of reals as simples requires the rejection of the correlative analytic and dispersive logic. The corporate theory of individuality has as common to its metaphysics and its "logic of reality as unity" the principle of analogical identity. Viewed from the side of the universal, all reals are identities of differents; education as the universal type is instanced in each school individuated within the type. From the side of the particular, all reals are differents within identity; these specific schools, each in its own way, instance the universal, education. In either case, individual or object and relation are inseparable, and the logic required is one of synthesis and mutuality. All judgment is of differents within identity.

Order or wholeness, or wholeness as order, is necessitated by the demands of thought. With respect to order, Jordan states that there are two choices: either order may be assumed to be given with the facts, or it may be conceived as produced out of the necessities of thought and superimposed on the facts.[44] However, if the earlier discussion of action is sound, order is not created by thought but is there as the ground of thought and action. Disorder could not even be recognized or conceptualized unless order was already fact and idea. Wholeness is an immediately given fact whose comprehension makes it possible to single out the facts; or, said somewhat differently, order is given with the facts rather than constructed out of them or out of thought itself. To say that there are no isolable facts in the world is to say that there is no fact apart from the fact-order which individuates it. Fact and fact-order, particular and universal, part and whole are given together. Neither the sense experience of the particulars of atomistic empiricism nor the conceptual whole-ness or universality of rationalism makes or breaks the con-tinuity; relation is there in the world, and reason does not make it nor experience break it.

To avoid externality and to make relation, as a tie between differents, significant—that is, to avoid cause and its endless repetition of fact moving on to fact—it is necessary to assume an ultimate unity as interrelatedness. "But unity is then continuity. And continuity as fact is the subject matter of science whether natural or social." [45] The social scientist studies the social con-tinuum; the natural scientist, the natural continuum; and within the latter, as an example, the biologist studies the continuity of organisms.

Jordan's discussion of the organism as limited individuality may serve in part to illustrate his general theory. The question of biology—what is the nature of the organism?—leads not to the "element," the cell, but to the fact-order or the species as the continuity of the life of organisms. Within the biological order, the ultimate fact is the species, which as a universal is the law of organisms. When real, the organism is not a unique entity, but in its growth intends the species which is its law. Organisms are not atomistic wholes, but organism is whole, the whole of law "which specifies unities of fact in multilateral continuity." [46] The organism is a unity or synthetic whole of life-structures and functions or activities. As a unity and the medium of the con-tinuity of life, the organism is itself individuated within the more comprehensive unity of the species. The wholeness of the or-ganism is to be found not within itself but within the continuity of organisms in species; otherwise the organism-as-a-whole has merely replaced the cell as element, with the result that the facts of reproduction, regeneration, etc., are unintelligible in the question of the ultimate point of origin of an element. This elementalism would then result in the separation of organism and environment, each being conceived as an independent entity whose relations are external. Then the questions of the influence of each on the other, and which is primary and which secondary, would involve difficulties impossible to eliminate.

The important question concerns the relationship of organism and environment, since the hypothesis taken here will form the basis of the logic of living things. While there are three ways of looking at this relationship: (1) the organism is a function of the environment, (2) the environment is a function of the organism, or (3) both are functions of their own unity taken as a whole, in which the significant factor is their immediate unity,[47] the latter is the most defensible view. The environment of organism is primarily organisms; the environment of life is life; the meaning of the organism is found essentially in its reference to functions, such as those of reproduction and regeneration, which inhere not in itself as an exclusive entity but in the continuity of organisms. "The relation of the organism to its environment is precisely similar to and continuous with that of structure to function within the organism. . . ."[48] The continuity and unity of the life of organisms is real, not the cell or the organism as a unit or element of life. As realities, the cell is a unity principled by its continuity with the organism, the organism is a unity principled by its continuity with the species. Negation of the more comprehensive fact-order issues in a freak, the self-negation of the part. Said another way, the whole is the ground of growth and the end which the individual shadows forth or means, as against the endless process of elements in causal relation.

In this case we find the organism's function to consist in the comprehension of the external facts of species—life in the form of an end appropriated to the fulfillment of its present activities. That is, what the organism means is the corporate whole which it would be were all its activities fully rounded out in the end and the accomplishment of which would universalize the organism as law. And this is identical with the statement of the principle of individuation: a situation of fact ordered with reference to an end which as law effects the continuity through growth of the situation of fact with its species or universal; and its importance from this point of view lies in the fact that it comprehends within itself the constitution of a system of higher individualities.[49]

The conception of the organism-as-a-whole, when viewed not as the element or unit of life but in terms of the unity of the life of organisms, is then not merely a biological principle but a law of logic.[50] Not the unit but unity is the immediately given datum for thought. But since continuity and unity are only different ways of viewing reals, each implying the other, there is the identity of differents characteristic of individuality. The biological sciences fail to be real sciences as long as they resort to the description and classification of organisms, the multiplicity of fact; only when they leave this particularity in order to achieve synthesis and move on to organism or the organism-as-a-whole, which is the law of organisms as the unity of their life, do they give an account of the nature of things and thus fulfill their task. At that point, descriptive science becomes speculative philosophy, an inquiry into the nature of life; the organism universalized as law is the subject matter of the logic of purpose, and the scientific account of the organism-as-a-whole is a matter of speculative logic.

The significance of the conception of the organism-as-a-whole is that the organism as a particular has meaning only in its reference to the wholeness of life. And the wholeness of life, as the stability of the system of lives, gives to the term species whatever concrete meaning it bears. The species is, with respect to its aspect of law, universal, and with reference to its content in a plurality of particular forms, concrete—the concrete universal.[51]

The organism-as-a-whole is a unity of structures and functions. It is a functional order which, as a system of fact, may be described and observed without any reference to metaphysical realities or first or final causes. There is no separation of function and structure; neither is there any need for a one-to-one combination of them. The organism may be referred to as a whole of either functionally related structures or structurally related functions. The successful performance of any single function requires the collaboration of the entire system of structures and so of the organism as a whole. A function *is* the mutuality of a system of structures, determined for and by an end. The end is not a mystical final cause or any magical purposive agency, but simply is the fact that the system of structures, as organized fact or system or organs, tends uniformly to completion in a more comprehensive system of structures. The belief that it is necessary to refer a function to a special structure in a one-to-one causal relation stems from a misunderstanding of the nature of a function, which is thought to require actualization in a substance. A function, however, is already as substantial and as unique as any fact, but like any fact it has a status within a system and can be known, not in any single relation in the system, but as constituted by and through its relations to all the facts in the system. Nor is there any reason ultimately for limiting its relations within the system. A function is a function of the whole rather than of a specific substance, and like all entities implies the whole as ground, in this case the organism-as-a-whole, and so does not require a specific cause. It is an "uncaused" substance, a fact in its own right, but not therefore independent, and it is related to other substances such as structures, as already defined above. Cause, then, is not necessary to a function's substantiality either in the sense of one-to-one cause-and-effect relation or in the sense of first or final causes, either as explanation of its origin or its end.[52]

The division of biologists into those who assert mechanism and physicochemical laws as definitive of the nature of life and those who find life purposive and employ the concept of entelechy may be overcome, Jordan believes, through a recognition of the partial validity of each view and their ultimate synthesis in the "higher realm" of functional order and the principle of corporeity.[53] He states that there seems to be no ground for denying that the life processes in the organism are continuous with the environmental processes in nature conceived as physicochemical and mechanistic. However, the organism cannot be confined to the categories of space-time and incentric or self-centered or internal individuation. Subjectivism or individualization, which characterizes the space-time or geometric form, prohibits growth, "for it lacks the cumulative power of an order individuated outside itself or eccentrically by the principle of purpose, which is always objective."[54] The space-time form does not originate, since the geometric form is already *in* space-time. Real growth cannot then occur in the causal space-time realm, but only mere process or "growth" by accretion, for the relation of one form to another is discontinuous and movement is therefore repetitive and inconclusive. In contrast, the living form, by virtue of its own order or organization, has the power to come through growth into being in space and time. This capacity of the living organism to reproduce and to sustain and maintain itself in a characteristic organization is what is meant by spontaneity. The source of this power of the living form is not in its internal or subjective constitution per se—the metaphysical will of the individual—but in the fact that it is ordered eccentrically, i.e., its content depends upon materials external to and beyond its specified form.

In sustaining itself and reproducing itself . . . the living form becomes an individuality in that it realizes its end within itself while the end is formed from a content without itself. Its content and meaning are the forms possible to it, the forms which it may become by transmutation. The three processes of origination, restitution, and reproduction are the same process, the expression of what is inherent as growth stages in the order of the living form.[55]

However, the organism is a "limited individuality." Its structure is such as to make it impermanent; it is largely instrumental rather than an end of higher forms of life; its capacity to act— that is, to objectify its end outside itself—is limited at best; the self-maintenance of the organismic form becomes the end of its activities, so that its natural tendency is toward subjectivity; finally, the cumulative growth of the organism is limited.

There is a limit to the cumulative growth of the organic form, and this subordinates it to the forms of individuality represented by the state, the church, etc. The last item of our definition of individuality is therefore the limitlessness of its possibilities of ordered growth which by cumulation joins a given form to its universal in the type. This is the point which was so hard for Plato and Aristotle; to see that in an individuality like the State there is a limit neither to the physical size of the State nor to the complexity of order in its constitution.[56]

The natural individual, in his status as organism, is a limited form of individuality.

The individual as organism is a creature of nature in that biological species law governs his physical processes and growth pattern, and his particular individuation of species law is integrally related to the immediate environment of physical materials, vegetation, and animal life. They are the concrete, ordered possibilities of his growth; put another way, he is their higher or specialized organization. Like every living thing, he is continuous with and a special, more complex organization of the environment. This individual-environment integration is a proof of the unity and continuity of life. No organism can exist without its possibilities being in the environment, so that the environment is not mere inert material external to life processes but plays an active part in the process of organismic growth and reproduction. Environmental energies fuse in a new synthesis with the energies of the organism.

Yet there is more to the human individual than his organism. The "natural individual" is not only natural, he is cultural, and just as he is a unity of and continuous with the world of nature, he is a unity of and continuous with the world of culture. The objects of culture are organized within the object systems of the institutions—family, church, school, industry, etc. This cultural environment is also the *active* condition of his growth as man. He is a new and special organization (individuation) of it: one of the Smith boys, Princeton graduate, lawyer, member of the Rotary, Republican, Methodist, etc. The material used to achieve growth depends upon what is available in the nature-culture medium. This relationship is not a causal one in the sense of the environment as external force acting upon pliant and passive man, or man as external force acting upon pliant and passive nature. It is a relationship of unity and continuity with each other, i.e., growth. As scientist, for example, his mind and life activities grow out of the corporate achievements of science, and his contributions in turn become part of a body of knowledge which becomes in turn part of the cumulative growth medium for another scientific mind. Man in his full individuality is the ordered form achieved through the growth activities of his relations to the nature-culture world, and in its place the nature-culture world represents the objective status of his achievement.

The individual as the type of the real is a universal form which is stable, and as ordered eccentrically is *indifferent to content* and therefore incorporates growth as an essential characteristic. Jordan's principle of indifference to content is the reason for his repudiation of the contents theory of individuality. Stated negatively, indifference to content does not mean either that man's biopsychological nature is to be ignored or that man may incorporate any content and still be man. Jordan is not arguing that the content of the organism is of no meaning, or that man may ingest any material and still live and grow. The meaning of corporate theory is the significance it grants to body, but Jordan's argument is that no matter what the given content of an individual is, content as such is not law. The view of the individual as a creature of nature, as having an original content of needs and wants, conceptualizes his organism but not the man.

The "social" view of man as a role player, and as having a cultural content through his playing of roles, is an improvement over the organismic idea. Yet the obvious fact that a man is a soldier or businessman does not mean that such roles and the "cultural" contents they involve have legitimacy. That men possess a cultural content is true, but the value of this insight has been attenuated through attaching meaning to objects and activities simply because they have become content for man; a case in point is the typical justification of the banalities of the mass media—"we are giving the people only what they want." The meaning of being an architect or a teacher does not derive from the existential status of such activities as content of an individual or group, or the "social" and economic value placed upon individuals who have these contents, but is rather a function of the act and what it does in the world. It is the act which, as universal form, provides cultural meaning for or intelligibility of contents, and not the other way around.

When we look to the existent content of man for guidance, the consequence is fixity and stultification. An act as incorporated in an institution is a growing real, and to effect itself in the world an act will use and develop the relevant men and materials. Education, as the formal institution for the development of intelligence in man, from one generation to the next may undergo vast transformation in content and the sequential ordering of its materials. What matters is the realization of the ideal, for the ideal is the spirit which giveth life while the letter of the law killeth. The eccentric order of an individuality about its idea, rather than the incentric order about its content, is the ground of its spontaneity and growth. The effort of the natural individual continually to perfect industry, religion, politics, art, the city, etc., is one with perfection of the self. Man is not merely what his empirical content is, but what it may be; and what life may be is the institutional medium in its growth.

Individualism argues that the individual is an end for the nature-culture environment as means, but overlooks the fact that he is also means for the nature-culture world as end, just as an organ is both means and end for the organism. Nevertheless, the larger whole is always the principle for the part-whole relationship. The individual's activities as cultural are consciously or subconsciously governed by the ends of institutions, such as the family, religion, art, industry, and school. As a cultural being, the individual objectifies his activities in the world, where they become part of the ends of life: he writes a book, composes a song, teaches school children, digs a ditch, builds a bookcase, or administers a college. His life activities issue then within the corporate complex, are conditioned within and principled by the institutions of which he is an organic part. Just as the organ individuated within the organism has the meaning of its function in sustaining the whole, so man as individuated, rather than individualized, within the institutional complex has his meaning in sustaining the whole. The part-whole relationship is his individuality.

The institution is also a living individual, and current insistence that only "flesh-and-blood" individuals are living is sad testimony to the contemporary hardening of organismic and individualistic categories of thought. The school, for instance, as a living, corporate body is empirically manifested in a structured organization of persons and materials whose dynamic (life blood) is the end it intends. As it progresses toward its end, it is capable of growth, origination, restitution, and reproduction. Moreover, education, like the church, industry, or any institution, is capable of indefinite cumulative growth and complexity. The institution is indifferent to its own content and will use any material to effect its meaning in the world. As an organ of the state, its function is an individuated good of the whole; hence its appropriate functioning is an end for the state. It is principled by the state, the institutional complex as a whole, and therefore it is a means for the state as end. The whole good which the state represents is the end for any institution and the necessary condition of the institution's wholesome functioning. The state is a living individual in the same sense as an institution. Its body is the institutional complex; the latter's ordered growth is one with the growth and well-being of the state. The law for the state, its ideal form always to be realized, is justice: the whole good or the wholeness of order achieved through the complementary and harmonious functioning of the ever-growing realities which its institutional organs are. Thus the state is not a "metaphysical" entity externally acting upon its parts, but is bound to and by the realities of life, to and by the integrity with which institutions attain ends and their harmonic relationships to one another in the sustenance and building of the whole good. If parts unprincipled by the whole (American automobile production at the expense of housing and schools) is the meaning of cancerous growth, then the whole uncaring for the parts (Hitler's *Third Reich*) is a crazed monster feeding upon its own life substance. In either case self-destruction is the eventual outcome, unless the tendencies are arrested.

Then the living, cultural forms of individuality are individual-institution-state, the more comprehensive form serving as principle for the less developed one. Since each is a unity continuous within the larger form, there is no inherent opposition within individual-institution-state. Institution as the mediating nexus of the individual-state relationship is both means and end for the natural individual and government, government being defined as the special organ for taking an overview of the state. The key individual, critically needing to be understood, is the institutional one.

To summarize Jordan's argument as developed in this chapter, the individual is not constituted or known as such by discovering analytically the differentia which make it unique; nor by cataloguing and enumerating its contents, no matter how exhaustively; but by discovering its intent, the law of its order and growth, that which constitutes it the individual it now is or is to become. The automobile, for example, is constituted an individual and known through its law of order or wholeness, which binds its varied components together into a unity, as a form of mechanical propulsion over roads for human beings. The principle of any individuality has no necessary connection with certain of its unique features (the dual exhaust) or with the common qualities of its content (four wheels), for these may be pure chance or may represent peculiar accidents of history. Individuality is the concrete realization of a universal meaning, and may compose itself of any content (wood, charcoal, gasoline, or atomic energy as fuel) in order to effect this meaning.

Thus while most social theorists assume the individual to be real, and Jordan agrees, he has in mind another meaning which he holds to be more consistent with an understanding of the realities of the world: that an individual is always a structure or unity of some form which is principled by or continuous with some larger order or whole as its law. This car which through its structure manifests its intent, or intends its principle, is an individual when it realizes its ideal nature, or, to say the same thing, is what it is by virtue of the law of the whole which principles the order it takes. It is true that *the individual is real,* but more profoundly it may now be seen that *the real is always individual* as a fact-type or particular-universal. The realization of the universal as the particular is the criterion of reality as it is of intelligibility.

Man, when real as an individual, an individuation of the type man, is in, of, and for the institutional order, just as the reality of each corporate person depends upon its being an organ of and principled by the whole good. For natural individuals, institutions are the concrete universals of life, the whole which the individual instances as the law of his life in so far as he is man and not beast. As biological law is law for his physical functions, institutions are cultural law for his acts as a human being.

CHAPTER 3
INSTITUTION AS HIGHER INDIVIDUALITY AND CORPORATE PERSONALITY

Institution as Objective Mind

Through action man builds an institutional world that gives to human life new capacities and qualities. But man, in objectifying his ideas, in forming the world, forms himself, since he is continuous with it; thus the *via regia* to the understanding of man is to perceive him in his unity and continuity with the world which he has objectified about him. The principle of the unity and continuity of life is crucial to an understanding of the organism in terms of both its functions and development, as the biological sciences amply demonstrate, but it also has great significance for the conception of mind. It implies, for example, that mind does not consist of separate faculties, but is a unity and always acts as a whole. Were this not the case, it would be impossible to have an organized mind. It is the ability of the mind to center itself as a whole on an object that is the basis of its organization.[1] Psychology lends support to this conception of mind in failing to discover will as a separate faculty; instead, will is found as an ever-present factor in the workings of the whole mind.[2] Furthermore, mental states as well as ideas are continuous with one another. No matter how we examine mind, we find not isolation but continuity, unity, and wholeness.

Already indicated in the foregoing is the continuity of mind with object. Mind implicates objects in a variety of ways. Ideas are *of* objects, having objects as their content and their referent, and are constitutive of them. A table or a civilization is a content of thought and also the *realization* of man's idea of a table or civilization. Furthermore, objects are the test of an idea and determine its truth or falsity, since an idea of the world must be examined in relation to the world. To say that a man is "out of his mind" is to say that his ideas "are out of contact with reality" as independently existing objects, that is, his mind manifests marked discontinuities with important elements of reality. Similarly, we know the quality of a man's mind by examining the quality of his objects, all of which indicates that mind is known only in and through objects. Action implies both idea and object, and these can be unified only in the act, for ideas grow out of objects and their relations, while objects are formed by the ideas which control the process of action.[3]

The concept of "objective mind" is founded in the fact that ideas tend to objectify or to become embodied. Ideas become realized in the objects in which they find a body that stabilizes them as effective components of the world. Thus mind makes itself up of objects and is realized in them. The development of mind is dependent upon and continuous with the development of objects, and mind is controlled through the control of objects.[4]

That mind is bodied—not only in the sense that it employs the body as the instrument of its action, but even more significantly in that it finds for itself an object in which it is completed and lives in the world—indicates that the most profound meaning of corporeity lies in the root of the word: corpus. The corporate theory of individuality is a theory of embodied mind or will. It is through this bodied mind or minded body—or as Jordan has also referred to it, this ensouled body or bodied soul —that men are related to each other, and that the minds of natural individuals are made up of and continuous with each other. Mind is then public or corporate, and culture is objective mind. The development of aesthetic mind in individuals is continuous with a world of beautiful objects, and so with all the other "minds" or "worlds" that constitute the unity of mind. The objects that constitute these worlds also constitute or make up the mind of the individual. A world of common objects is the community of mind that is the basis of the common mind of individuals.

Mind then cannot be separated from object. In fact, the definition of mind is best expressed in terms of object; moreover, Jordan states that object may be defined in terms of mind, or mind in terms of object. This conception of mind eliminates the epistemological problem of the peculiar relation between mind

and its object, and thus relieves the practical disciplines of this
burden.[5]

The starting point, then, is not the division between the inner
and the outer, with the subsequent attempt to effect their union
or to reduce one to the other. Characteristic of the corporate
conception of mind is its assumption of the synthesis or unity of
what is traditionally taken as separate and real only as separate.
The inner-outer problem, the attempt to distinguish between
what is in mind and what is out of mind, or between the mental
and the nonmental or extramental, is dispelled by continuity.
Whatever is is in mind in some sense, although this is not to be
taken to mean that apart from idea nothing exists.[6] At the same
time, mind is the principle of objects, so that objects are in mind,
idea is their intelligibility, and they are also minded. Mind—for
example, as in the idea of education—is ordering principle, and
the order of related fact—the existent educational system—is
mind in public form. Mind is not external to the facts, but is
given with them in their order.

All the effort to distinguish between that which is inside and
that which is outside of mind is, in Jordan's view, wasted. Whatever is is both in mind and in the world; even mind itself is both
in and out of mind. The forms of the mind are also the forms
of the world; space-time as categories of nature are also categories of mind.

As forms of the intuition *and* categories of the understanding space
and time *are* the physical world *in* mind; and time and space are
forms *of* mind *in* nature. Mind and nature, thought and the space-
time world of existence, are of one and the same reality. . . . So long
as there is an alternative, *in* or *out* of mind, existence *or* mind, reality
will be uncertain, truth unsubstantial, and the disjunction the mother
of contradiction.[7]

Even when Jordan argues that mind is the essence of reality,
he does not mean to say that distinctions cannot be made between the mental and nonmental. To seek mind, however, in
terms of the *distinction* between the inner and the outer is fruit-
less. He suggests that there is logically something prior, something necessary, if distinctions are to be made. If there were no
common, there would be no unique; if there were no identity,
there would be no difference. Distinction logically requires a
fundamentum divisionis, implying unity or oneness within which

particulars may be defined. This would apply generally. As related to the problem considered here, this ground of likeness is not imposed upon the real in its separateness from mental entities, but inheres in the nature of things prior to the distinction between mental and nonmental. This ground is institution, which (as a synthesis of nature and culture) is the form everywhere manifested by human life. Experience itself is not "mental" in the individualistic sense of private and inner, but is public and universal. Mind, when it is truly mind and not mere psychological states, is not inner and self-contained but objective, and thus has the degree of reality which makes possible its descriptive and logical consideration.[8] Institution is objective or objectified mind. Social life is rightly characterized as mental, not, however, as belonging to individuals but as objectified by institutions: that is, the mental quality of society is not derivable from separable individuals but from institutions. The mind of the Greeks or the medieval mind is found in Greek and medieval institutions. The unity of mind that characterizes society is not, then, a composite of individual minds, nor is the problem of order a question of unifying such minds. Mind is characteristically institutionalized or corporate. As such, it is the ground of individual minds, of whatever minds there may be.

The separation of mind and object is responsible for the difficulties of mind viewed as individual or as social. In asserting that mind is characteristically institutionalized, Jordan does not mean to say that mind as individual or social is influenced by institutions. Though this is literally true, it is relatively unimportant. Were he to propose such a view of mind, he would be in the same position as those theorists whom he opposes, for he would be assuming a separate, unique, given mind as the basis and explanation of all the problems of social life. Such a magical entity, itself unexplained but the principle of all explanation, is precisely what he wishes to avoid. While he agrees that mind is the essential form of reality, he spurns the mysticism involved in the ontology of mind so conceived, which in its logical and scientific usage becomes sheer magic. The error in such a view lies in the theory of individuality which seeks the essence of mind in the distinction between it, assumed to be a reality in itself, and that something external which influences it. The self-sufficient mind offers no possibility of moral or universal quality.[9]

The corporate view of mind as institutionalized maintains the continuity and unity of mind-object. This view does not take mind as given, i.e., acting upon or reacting to institutions which are also conceived as given and external to mind. While both mind and institution must be presupposed, the important question concerns the meaning of their interaction. Generally, the interpretations are made in atomistic, mechanical terms.

And they are such because they all rest upon the assumption of distinctness between mind and its object, man and his purpose, life and its objective institutionalization, in general between means and end. The problem is precisely one of seeing the unity and continuity of means and end in such relations as that between mind and object, life and objectified purpose. . . . Mind *is* just the synthetic purposiveness of institutionalized life. . . . Mind is the constitutional law of reality embodied in the various forms of purpose as purpose becomes organized, i.e., assumes organs and thus becomes effective. As law, it is the synthesis of just those purposes in stable and permanent objective forms. The study of these characteristic forms in their universal aspects will then give us the genius of the law of life as mind. These forms as known in experience are the mutualized forms of purpose as objectified in the common-ends of politico-moral life—corporate associations.[10]

Thus Jordan does not confine the definition of mind to thinking or to conscious natural persons. In speaking of mind, he refers to the existence of fact only as ordered; he means that fact implicates fact in an order, that orders implicate orders.

. . . a system of fact ordered with reference to an end which is qualitatively specified or universalized in the characters of the facts involved, that is, referred to a type, is a mind.[11]

That is, the educational system is a mind, one form of the public mind of the civilization, since it is the structured order taken by an end. It is a minded order in that the educational idea or purpose serves as the ordering principle of the objects and persons that make up this institution, and by ordering principle Jordan has something concrete in view: that every element of the institution has internal to it, as made manifest in its relations, the idea or end of the whole. In the preparation and conduct of the teacher, in the laboratory, the library, the room for music appreciation, etc., is the educational idea. He states further that

. . . a group of relations ordered eccentrically in respect of objective content and with reference to an end recognized as principle within content so ordered, is a mind, and there are as many varieties of minds or forms of individuality as there are qualitatively specifiable kinds of such groups. It is this order of content which embodies the mind or clothes it with corporeity. It may then be called the corporate mind.[12]

An order always has a content external to its form, and in growing it comprehends even larger portions of its environment; but it is nevertheless not restricted to the specificity of particular qualitative content. It is conditioned *upon* but not *by* content, and may use any and all contents indiscriminately.[13] An order is able to maintain itself as an individual while the quality of its content vastly changes. Therefore, one may speak of an "American educational system," meaning essentially the continuous attempt by Americans to develop their own intellectual competencies, despite the enormous changes that have occurred in the content of the system from the days of the early colonists to the present. The crucial point to be borne always in mind is that an individual should be conceived in terms of its intent rather than its content; content is merely whatever matter falls within reach in the stages of growth.[14] Content is not the law of the individual, and the transcendence of qualitative limitation means that any content is subject to order but does not create order itself. As developed in the preceding chapter, specificity makes content a principle and thus confines, while indifference makes possible the use of any content for self-realization and thus frees. This principle of the indifference of an order to its content explains the unity and continuity of life in its simplest conditions, as in a living body, as well as in the purposive organization of property in an institution.[15] Man's every act confirms the principle, for the whole of civilization represents the appropriation of varying contents to human purpose.

Precisely because individuals are not restricted to the specifics of content, they are able to maintain themselves amid a variety of changes. As indifferent to content, they can realize themselves through the appropriation of any content relevant to growth. Furthermore, the more comprehensive the individuality, the greater is its indifference to content and the freer it is to realize itself. Indifference to content is the principal factor in the freedom of will. Will is free not because it is without content, as in those spiritual conceptions which divorce it from the material world, but because it is freed from the specificity of content, and hence there may be the widest diversity of institutions. Thus individuality or the fact-order as will is able to embody or realize itself in limitless ways. As the form of will, institution is the constitution of *any* fact, e.g., the same object or person may serve a religious, industrial, or educational purpose, and from the same principle which makes possible the indefinite multiplication of institutions can be derived the property of order as effective will or freedom. The necessity for any individuality to have access to content indifferently in order to grow is the basis for Jordan's severe condemnation of the "private" property conception. The withdrawal of property from utilization for public purpose is antithetical to the freedom and growth of will; the requirement of will is that any content be available for the realization of public purpose.[16]

The growth of any individuality, its reaching out for and especially its self-embodiment in materials, is the concrete evidence for the existence of will. The growth of individuality is the key to Jordan's theory of will.

This tendency to self-realization through growth is taken as the type of the real, and its final form for practical purposes is will. It is therefore in a theory of will that any doctrine of individuality must issue.[17]

The Growth of Mind and Will

Jordan's treatment of the development of will or the action life of man is at once historical and "nonhistorical." As historical, it is the story of cultural evolution from low corporate development to the much more fully embodied purposes of the present. While this growth takes place in time, time is not a principle of will development, i.e., time does not in itself cause things to evolve. More fundamentally, the problem is a metaphysical one as to the nature of will and is independent of time in the sense that time is not a constitutional principle. With respect to this problem, there is a synthesis of several components which are present simultaneously, though in varying degree, in any instance of will. It is also this variation in the degree of influence of particular components that differentiates stages in cultural evolution. Jordan distinguished four stages in the development of will or action, with different principles characterizing each.

1. *Nature.* Nature is present as independent fact prior to man's purposing, and influences his life whether he is conscious of it or not. Such external circumstance as the chance position of a mountain range may throw men together whatever their intention, and may to a very great extent dictate the manner of their living, whatever their own desires may be. The same range differently placed may have a much different effect. This is the element of chance or accident which inevitably affects human organization, and since it is ever present, it takes on, somewhat paradoxically, the character of a principle. In any event, it is not merely man's own nature that determines his life-forms, for the character of the nonhuman world affects the character of the human realm. The situation of physical fact, independently of man's nature or purposes, enters into his social situation or institutions. Nature sets conditions, and in the early development of culture these are not merely limitations but determining elements. Here the institutions of man, such as they are, are heavily influenced by forces not of his own making. Where corporate development is very limited, nature dominates the social order. Nature tends to be dominant in all primitive societies, where comparatively few purposes have found adequate embodiment, but it is a factor also in all social organization. However, Jordan is not arguing for geographical or any other kind of determinism, and the fact that nature has such a large voice in "primitive" societies does not mean even there that it has the sole voice. The point that Jordan is making relates to the continuity in the development of will, with natural circumstances playing a larger part in lower stages of growth and playing a successively smaller, though always present, role as society advances toward more corporate development. In the latter stages, or for that matter even to a lesser extent in earlier stages, the institutional system develops momentum of its own and tends to retain its "independence" in the face of environmental changes.[18]

2. *Human nature.* The culture principled by human nature is one whose institutions, in a sense, just grow. They are untended by man as well as unintended, in that they arise largely unconsciously out of his needs rather than from deliberate design. The development is reflexive, inhering in natural human tendencies; corresponding institutions provide for each indispensable. The state is the harmony of these institutions necessitated by human

nature. This is the life according to nature and the basis of Aristotle's characterization of the state as natural. The motives underlying the state are not clearly delineated by individuals or groups, but are simply native impulses objectifying within the limitations set by nature in the broader sense. While this stage of culture is no longer dominated by the external elements of nature, it is nevertheless a low form characterized by the "socialized mind," Sumner's creature of custom and habit addicted to traditional usage and bound by fixity. This is essentially the passive, adjusted, or adapted mind, rather than the active, adjusting, and adapting one. Such a description of the state as natural is not meant to rule out reason completely, but at this level of cultural evolution institutions are the largely unintended outcomes or ends of the activities of the "socialized mind." The intelligence of man confines itself to matters of means. While an artifact, the state is not man's deliberate creation, since it grows unconsciously out of the necessities of human nature. At the same time, it is not artificial but exists there in the nature of things, and to some extent therefore is independent of man's purposing. Perhaps this is part of the meaning Jordan suggests when he warns contemporary man to walk humbly in the presence of the constitution of things and reminds us that institutions do not need our precious godfathering. Here he seems to be affirming the Platonic view that the state needs to be understood or constituted rather than reformed.[19] Jordan is not, however, asserting that man is the mere creature of the state, even while cautioning him to recognize his limitations as creator.

The state principled by human nature is still a low stage of cultural evolution. Man has not become sufficiently conscious of the idea of the state. The state is formed by the principle of his nature as reflexive, rather than by principle constructed by him out of his reflection.[20] It is not yet the state founded on reason or conscious purpose, one in which man by taking thought may transcend the weaknesses of nature in order to design and effect an ideal mode of life.

3. *Reason.* Purpose, which in the state as natural had largely been unconsciously maintained and achieved, now becomes a fully deliberate motive, and the idea of the state becomes directive of men's common efforts. The problem then takes two forms: (1) the outer or institutional order as achieved values

receives the attention of men's thought and issues in the theory of the state and jurisprudence; (2) the internal character of the state or its foundation in human nature leads to an analysis of the latter, resulting in modern epistemology and psychology. The attempts to solve these problems led historically to the establishment of modern national states on the one hand and to the institution of the natural individual on the other. In both cases atomism is operative; the idea of the State disperses into particular nations, while humanity is divided into individual men on the basis of a false conception of individuality. Both views issue in correspondingly inadequate notions of freedom, property, and contract. Yet there is the effort, nevertheless, to see the state as a whole and to organize groups into wholes with definite purposes, along with the construction of constitutions to fit preconceived ideas of human nature, e.g., the French and American constitutions. Even more significant perhaps, in this growth of organizations with a purpose, was the development of secondary or lesser groups with a wide variety of ends, such as chambers of commerce, labor unions, credit associations, etc. Although this tendency developed ludicrous aspects, as in various "reform" or "uplift" organizations or in other groups whose primary interest was to distinguish its members from nonmembers, nevertheless the movement is important because it exhibits the possibility of attaining objective ends through a conscious, common effort to use corporate bodies as instruments of reason.[21]

Rationalism, however, did not recognize the validity in Plato's assertion that the state needs to be understood rather than reformed, with the result that it attempted to construct the constitution of the state out of men's heads and on the basis of certain theoretical views. It was generally thought that, once devised and written, the constitution would stand as originally conceived and as such would provide for the exigencies which might arise in the future. If the life of custom and habit is limited by ignorance of the ends which have developed naturally as the outcomes of the expression of the socialized mind, then in the state as rational, where ends are deliberately envisaged, there is a failure to recognize the self-contained dynamic of institutional development. As a result, reason becomes prescriptive in a way that hampers the growth of new purpose. The excessive exaltation of reason failed to allow for the autonomy of life urges, with the result that the ready-made constitution, probably already outdated at the time of its adoption, did not describe or meet the realities. Life will not stay frozen within the formulations of doctrine and is constantly outrunning, circumventing, or breaking through the confines set by men. Furthermore, if the constitution will not bend, then it must break and be mended, and so there are the amendments. The attempt to impose or force doctrine on life is unsuccessful, and the hardness of the constitution is by its very inflexibility an obstacle to the attainment of newer and higher purposes. Neither does the appeal to judicial interpretation work out satisfactorily, since generally the courts adhere to the letter of the law while the real constitution is to be found in the "spirit of the laws." The problem of judicial interpretation is not that of attempting to determine what the founders meant or to examine what subsequent legislators and judges have made of the original. To be sure, interpretation is necessary, but the usual conception of it is inadequate and results in a looking backward to find principle for contemporary and future events which have developed and are developing their own principle. The foundation of the law is not precedent but the objective intent or trend of institutions—will getting itself expressed by indirection. Neither original intent nor the letter of the law is substantive, but rather the real governing elements are found in the ongoing state of life conditions, and this frequently maintains itself "outside the law."

New purposes come into being quite apart from and even in opposition to conscious designs, and manage to make their way in the world in the face of deliberate intent of men, so that government gets bigger under the very noses of men bitterly opposed to "big government." These purposes have achieved ends which are perhaps higher than any ever attained before, although they have had to evade or surmount obstacles set in their way by the existing social machinery that tends to serve outmoded purposes. The constitution is constantly being enacted, not however by the fiat or decree of legislature or court, but by the institutional system which has a will and a way of its own. Institutions are the law of the land, the constitution and the reconstitution, or perhaps more accurately, in Jordan's terms, simply the constitution considered as dynamic. The durability of the written constitution, which at best can only state the broad outlines of larger ends as an ideal for legislation, is dependent upon its flexibility rather than upon its unyielding quality. Otherwise it tends to live on as a written document while the determinative currents of life go on outside it. Legislatures pass their laws while the real enactments of legislation take place elsewhere. When sound, the laws passed by such bodies are expressive of the living reality of contemporary life. The constitution is found there in the propulsive tendencies of the institutional order, in the dynamics of public mind, rather than in the heads of legislators or in the conflict of wills or interest groups. We need to understand the public mind, but as Jordan sees it this does not involve opinion-polling; the public he refers to is the body politic rather than natural individuals or groups. The general will is not the sum or synthesis of wills of individuals or groups, but is the will of higher individualities. It is institutional in nature, inhering in the life of the life-forms which institutions are.[22]

Real as distinguished from virtual government is found in all these conditions which affect the attainment of human purpose. It exists in the form of utility companies, the supermarket, garage, bank, etc., which have the most intimate connection with the achievement of ends, while the ostensible government is often much more remote in the most important matters of a person's life. Stated another way, "public" government residing in Washington or the state capitol is often relatively insignificant, while "private" government assumes the greatest importance. Moreover, Jordan points out that public government itself has come under the control of the so-called "private" corporation. The neglect of the fact that real government is in the order of institutions accounts for the unsatisfactoriness of most government. There will be no rational order as long as existing institutions—industrial, educational, and other—are themselves irrational, no matter what men may think or devise, since it is their expansive tendencies which constitute real government.[23]

Jordan is not decrying the use of reason but rather warning man against *hubris*. Neither is he suggesting that the way things are is right. He has little praise for existing institutions or for what pass as contemporary states. That men should so far as possible take their destiny in their own hands is highly necessary, and Jordan is arguing for the urgency of foresight and planning; at the same time he points out that life is not completely amenable to man's rational will, not merely because of man's natural limitations but because life as established in institutional forms has a will of its own. The constitution is not given by man out of his head, but inheres in institutions, living and dynamic forms that contain their own growth tendencies. Rationalism erred in believing that reason might superimpose a constitution upon a people and neglected the fact that a people always inevitably possesses a constitution already in the order of its institutions.[24] Despite the weaknesses of rationalism, however, it has led to a rather clear definition of the larger ends of life, to their embodiment in more or less corporate form, and to a universal interest in these ends.

Although Jordan criticizes political rationalism, he does not discard the role of reason in the conduct of life; he also insists on the role of a superpersonal will. Public purpose finds expression despite the fixity of the written constitution. New institutions are being created by the public will more or less independently of individual or group wills, and often without individuals being aware of what is taking place.[25] It is in this will that he finds the basis of such order as now exists in human affairs, and of such higher order as may come into being.

4. *Objective mind or plupurpose.* In the discussion of plupurpose, Jordan seems to be emphasizing two points: (1) that institutions contain their own expansive tendencies which outreach the influences of nature and reason; and (2) that while men plot, institutions are acting, with the result that the ends attained are often neither anticipated nor intended. By "plupurpose," as distinguished from the mere "purpose" of rationalism, Jordan denotes "the complete act of will" as a synthesis which incorporates the ever-present components already discussed but which involves a further element. Man's reason is not the sole determinant of the direction life will take, even though it enters into the control of his destiny. Nor are external nature and human nature themselves ultimate directors, though again they are factors. These elements, either singly or jointly, are not comprehensive or inclusive enough. There is yet another factor which in Jordan's view is dominant, and that is the overriding expansiveness of the cultural order itself. Once established, it contains its own dynamic of development and manages to effect its own growth independently of and often in opposition to the efforts of men, as well as in the face of the changes of nature. Reason cannot impose fixity and authority

over this movement, which continues to evade and elude reason's confines. The compulsion of the fact-order breaks through the fixity of establishment, and legal "fictions" or mythical entities are created as means of getting around the outmoded forms. Men use their ingenuity to circumvent the existing machinery, meanwhile declaring their loyalty to the old regime. The plea is that we should cling to the established institutions, and many believe that we are doing just that when we are in fact busily engaged in evading them. The "fictions" then turn out to be the realities, while the "realities" are themselves myths.[26] The most significant example of this is to be found in the conception of corporate personality, which Jordan maintains is the living reality even though it is commonly viewed as a legal fiction, a person of the law rather than a real person.

The judicial interpretation which goes back to precedent cannot give guidance to the life urgencies that are always present and making their way on their own hook. Because institutions act, it is not precedent but incident that is of major importance here. Envisaging certain ends, men act, but while they do so the cultural order also acts, and other ends as the by-products or incidentals are achieved which are perhaps among the highest ever reached.[27] The unconscious results of conscious attempts at control indicate that men have often wrought better than they knew or intended. As instances of this development, Jordan cites the institution of procedure in law, the system of equity, and governmental agencies, particularly administrative, but even more important, those that grow out of life habits and relations; for example, the development of industry from its inception to its present form.[28] Nobody intended or created the corporation; its dominance in the present state of things was not planned, hardly foreseen. Jordan's examination of the problem of the nature of will as order leads him to the belief that the directive principle in cultural development is essentially indirection, deviousness, possibly even "chance."[29]

Institution as Public Order and Public Will

Order in human affairs cannot be found in the separation or opposition of wills, as contemporary theory maintains. That interest

has become the central practical category is proof of the subjectivity of modern thought. While Jordan does not deny the
existence of interest group conflicts, he nevertheless does not
regard these as political reality, nor does he look to them as the
locus or source of law. Interest, which by definition is private
advantage, and right stand opposed to each other. Interest itself
is not a practical category and does not provide a ground; on
the contrary, it requires one; it is private in its reference, whereas
law and order are public in nature. As an illustration of Jordan's
point, no principle, for example, is to be found in the conflict
of wills in the transportation industry between the busses, truck-
ers, railroads, and airlines. There is no basis whatever for settling
these disputes rationally on the basis of interest. The same would
apply to any of the other group struggles manifest on such a
large scale in contemporary society. Similarly, there is no rational
ground for settling international questions if each nation is regarded as an interest group. Interest groups are not publics. It is
not out of these groups as publics that the universal, the public,
is to be born. The public for Jordan is not to be constructed out
of wills taken as private and individual, but is to be conceived
as already existent, not something to be brought into being.
Cultural unity is fact, original fact. Far from serving as a practical category, the individualistic conception of will, with its
necessary extension in a negative and subjective pluralization
of wills, is the primary cause of the breakdown of practical life,
and only by moving away from this view to an objective, impersonal will, or away from the natural individual to the corporate person or institution as will, can order be found in practical life and higher degrees of order attained. In short, only on
the basis of will construed as universal can human affairs be
grounded in law. Will, then, is not particular, private, individual,
or collective, but public, corporate, institutional. Political reality
lies not in the will of the human individual, but in that of the
superhuman or corporate person, the pluperson.

The organization of a system of objects with which to attain
universal human ends in a mutual activity of persons is an institution. Purpose objectifies—that is, is realized—in objects
which are ends, but which become means to further growth.
These objects are indifferent to their specialized qualities or functions, and so are not particularized in their reference to specifia-

ble minds or persons; they are the generalized objects of mind as such. Similarly, they are dissociated from individualized wills, since a system of organized objects perpetuates itself spontaneously and thus becomes the objective or general will. These objects, therefore, are the means to human purpose without reference to special individuals.

Objects organized as meanings then are the generalized instruments of *human* purpose, mind effectuated as common end or commonwealth in the institutions of life. And as institutions of life or objectified mind these systems of objects are the dynamic order through which life attains its successive stages of integrity—institution is the constitutional law of human life.[30]

The theory of corporeity or of individuality, as has been indicated earlier, issues in a theory of will as corporate. It is a theory of institution as objective mind or will. Jordan finds it difficult to understand why those who assert the reality of particular will cannot accept the reality of corporate will, for the qualities of the one are the qualities of the other. If these qualities were not common to both, then it would be necessary to assert that only particular existence is real, for there would be no identity of individualities. But this would be self-contradictory, for it would negate the logic which yielded the conclusion that only particular existence is real. That logic reduces the universal to the particular by the method of differentiation, continuing the process until no more differences can be found. At the end, therefore, there is identity, not difference as the real, so the outcome is a contradiction. The real is individual; the individuated will, not the individualized will, is the corporate will as a personality.

As distinguished from cause, which is endless process, repetition to infinity, will is expansive and implicative. What differentiates will from cause is that the former is identified with the propulsive tendency of an idea.[31] Ideas do not live unto themselves alone but progressively reach outward, a quality of ideas which the idealist describes as the "reference to an object other than itself." [32] This is the peculiarly characteristic feature of will as function. Ideas implicate and in their fluent and expansive qualities tend to grow into interdependence with other ideas. Ideas once objectified or embodied, enduring in the world in an object-order, as such grow into different stages themselves and also influence other fact-orders. Will tends to objectify itself in some permanent form, and thus develops institutions as structured orders of objects. Once institutions are established, they develop propulsive tendencies of their own. There is, therefore, an institutional will which need not be connected with human consciousness but which in terms of its effectiveness has a driving force of its own or develops its own spontaneity. Embodied in objective form, purpose becomes a stable, enduring, practical phenomenon, as also by virtue of objectification it becomes dynamic with reference to its effectiveness on other fact-orders. Thus the growth of science was the basis of the industrial revolution, which in turn revolutionized agriculture, family living, the status of public health and the practice of medicine, the mobility of individuals, and made possible an expanding public school system and the realization of the idea of universal education. The growth of these orders of fact in turn recoils upon and reinvigorates the others, as the development of various industrial materials provided science with the tools to grow further. The agent then is the order of fact itself as responsible for other orders of fact that follow it, since no natural individual or group of individuals can claim responsibility for these developments in the sense of doing all or any large part of what is involved in the achievement. Even admitting the claims of rare creative genius, such a person never stands alone, but only in connection with scientific, philosophic, literary, or industrial developments occurring about him, without which his "individual genius" would not have been possible.

The Institution as Effective Will

The ordered arrangement of materials and persons directed toward the achievement of an end is effective will; will is in the world as a corporate entity. To define will as merely the private mental state of an individual is to make will of no consequence. For example, the natural individual may will with every fiber of his being but achieve nothing except a mind state and its associated bodily tensions. The natural individual dreams and cannot will—unless fantasy be equated with will—without connecting himself with the order of fact present in his objective circumstance, since to have a will at all he must co-operate with these dynamic fact-orders and the tendencies immanent in their structure. The truck farmer orders his means to the end that certain types of vegetables will grow, but then it is the entire related order of fact which manifests will and not the egocentric immediacy of his own impulse. Will is not mere impulse and is to be identified with no peculiarly psychological fact whatever; it is simply the dynamic tendencies inherent in facts by virtue of the relations in which they stand. Man is only one fact among all the facts, and insofar as he manifests will it is through his rational, logical comprehension of the facts, i.e., thought is man's contribution to will. It is the antithesis of will for man to violate the elementary requirements of nature, e.g., by exploiting the soil without care for its continued fertility, by destroying animals without regard for their replenishment, by polluting the atmosphere, etc. Will as related to action is objective and regulative or orderative of the world, and thus sustains itself. However, the relatively stable order of means, organizing the world toward the achievement of objectives, is the institution or corporate person, the ordered form which the man-nature synthesis has taken, and therefore it is culture, as the system of more comprehensive persons, that is the effective will, the basis in fact upon which will as a biopsychological striving in the natural individual may become real. Said another way, the will of the natural individual is immaterial, that of the corporate person material. The will of the corporate person is objective will, will as concrete in the nature of things, or simply facts as ordered with respect to the attainment of an objective.

Just as the active tendency to be an oak tree is immanent in the structure of the acorn, and as the movement patterns of organisms are determined by their structure, so is the will of the corporate person and its active tendencies immanent in the order which its body of property has taken. The superindividual will is not a mystical will outside of and extraneous to the facts, but is the dynamic tendency to effect itself that is internal to the facts as ordered. The car company, the tire factory, the furniture company, the university, etc., have the effective will to realize themselves in their own ways; they have their own typic products as a result of their peculiar organizational structures and the objects which make them up. This internal constitution is not to be viewed as static but as having dynamic tendencies toward self-expression in certain specific ways, against which the psychic energies of the individual are powerless. Men all over the world subjectively desire peace and friendly relations, but corporate persons pit them against one another in war and hate. The corporate person, as the synthesis of man and objects in an order, has a new quality of will which neither had possessed alone, much as salt has a quality which neither of its constituent elements exhibits by itself. Man as seen whole in an object system has will. Will is the *property* of the corporate person.

The scholar in the library, the scientist in the laboratory, the housewife in the home, the doctor in the clinic or hospital, the worker in the shop—all have will. Yet without the ordered system of objects embodying an objective, no will exists for the attainment of their respective purposes, or their will as mere mental stuff is idle daydream or, if taken seriously, gnawing frustration. Then to say that will is corporate, is bodied forth in property objects, is to say what will truly is whenever it refers to reality.

Not only is it true that property, as incorporate in the social structure, is the instrument of the individual's will, even while he is following his most subjective and 'personal' interests and purposes; but the same corporate property is the instrument and object of all the common motives and activities of men when those motives and activities have conditions proper and favorable to their realization. That is to say, before there can be any act of any person that has a guaranty of reaching its proper end, there must be the system of environmental things set up in institutions as the stage upon which the act is to take place. Further, the same system of things must be his instruments and his materials, the tools he uses and the stuff he works on. And this system of things alone can give reality to his ends. But this means that these things become the embodiment of his will; and, to an extent greater than we often know, the spontaneity and freedom of direction of the will-energies come to be determined by the body of things through which they work. That is to say, that to a greater extent than we are aware our action is dictated to us by the setup of fact in which we find ourselves immersed. What we are to do, how to do it, what is to be the end—all are largely predetermined in the institutional structure, which suggests the action and is thus responsible for the idea or impulse from which the action flows. We become, as agents, that is, institutionalized. What was in a hypothetical primitive condition the mere impulse and effectiveness of our conscious organism becomes, in cultural conditions, the effective agency of our larger life as it is embodied in the corporate unities of the things we use.

The real will, then, the will that is genuinely effective in getting things done, in realizing ends, is the effective power which these cultural agencies acquire from their own spontaneity and the wont and habit of men. But we must think of this wont and habit as themselves objectified and conserved in the forms of material and social objects, objects of real property. As property objects they become the ground of institutions, and as institutions they implement and condition the expression of will in all its forms. It is then these corporate property objects to which we must look not only for the fulfilment of individual aims but also for the maintenance of the interpersonal relations upon which the solidarity of culture depends. These corporate property objects are the substance of every personal or interpersonal relation. They are the effective wills, and they maintain a stable world for us even at the times when our passions and ignorance and stupidity and folly make our own wills as 'personal' the instruments of a chaotic hell. The fact that a social order can survive the frenzy of war is a miracle that no individual will can even comprehend. It is the corporate will that is the basis of our hopes for the continuance of a significant form of interpersonal life.[33]

Yet evil, too, may be incorporated in the structure of things, and as so incorporated the evil will—the antithesis of true will, which is always world-building—achieves demoniacal power. The air force general, as bodied in fleets of planes and bombs with personnel appropriated to this function and resting on a base of munitions plants and associated industries, may "will" the destruction of a world. In his corporate capacity the power under his control is awesome. The same man dissociated from the military body through retirement is only an impotent old man. Analogously, the problem of the criminal "will" is the problem of the institutionalization of crime so that it continues as a driving force in life, frustrating the endless and pathetic efforts made to manipulate the minds of natural individuals. God and the devil—the good will and the evil will—are the order and disorder of corporate life.

Attempts to correct the evil wills of natural individuals express themselves in two forms which, on the superficial level, quarrel violently with each other: (1) exponents of the method of education hold that re-education, psychoanalysis, getting at psychological "causes," and other forms of mental massage are the fundamental methods of coping with crime; (2) exponents of punitive methods argue that severe and instantaneous punishment will scare good will into these basically evil minds, the trouble being that these minds were not frightened into goodness early enough or often enough. Yet in every case, whether the individual is punished with violence or cajoled with kindness, the basic assumption is that the source of the criminal will and the fundamental object of treatment is the natural individual. The "plupersonal" or superindividual nature of will is overlooked, and so long as the property system is a criminal order, so long as it is instrumented to "acts" of negation, the criminal "will" will effect itself despite education, re-education, prayer, psychoanalysis, and other forms of exorcism. Mere mind may will anything, but the effecter is will as instrumented. Therefore, although it is true that "it is the corporate will that is the basis of our hopes for the continuance of a significant form of interpersonal life," as incorporated toward perverse objectives corporate power— for in this case it is no longer *will*—may become the death of all hope for the continuance of a significant interpersonal life.

If will as effective is the will of the corporate person, then will grows with the growth of comprehensiveness of the corporate person. It grows with the growth of objects in the world. The enormous growth of public schools in the last half of the nineteenth and early twentieth century is a growth in the will for education. Federal financial assistance to veterans who wish further education is the growth of will in fact; without it the psychological will would not exist for many veterans, or if it did, would be devoid of content or incapable of fulfillment and so meaningless. The transformation of America from a rural to an urban economy made possible and real the will of women to equality with men in voting, education, and vocational and professional opportunities. The growth of effective sanitation procedures, reservoirs, medical schools, clinics, and hospitals is one and the same with a growth in the will for health. Will, to be real, to be effective, does not need to be psychologically felt. Will is objective, corporate, cultural, present in the facts as ordered, and this implies that change in will is one and the same with change in the order of facts—*real change is cultural and not psychological; psychological changes have their stable basis in the cultural.*

If the corporate person is the stable basis of life in property and the effective will by virtue of its instrumentation toward ends, then it is the actor. Neither the natural individual nor any collectivity of individuals can act, although, to be sure, individual and group energies loomed large in simple societies; but just as early man never produced an object out of his own innards and was compelled to co-operate with natural energies to achieve anything, so modern man is incorporated within his institutions and is compelled to work with institutional energies to realize an object. It is within the body of the corporate person that he acts, or more precisely, *the corporate person acts,* for it is General Motors which builds a car, the shipbuilding industry which builds an ocean liner, the medical school which develops the doctor. Men as individuals or collectivities are impotent to create such objects, since these ends are possible only when there exists a highly organized system of ordered means instrumented toward their attainment. Then to say that "man acts" always means for Jordan that man acts within the corporate person or, more correctly, the corporate person acts through men and a relevant body of property. To procreate, the individual acts through the family; to worship, through the church; to realize an education or to teach, through the school system; to work, through industrial organizations, etc. As Jordan points out,

Practically every act in modern industrial life that comes anywhere near completion is the act of some corporate body, even those acts which are immediately implemented in the individual. What I do either as employer or as employee in an industrial organization is designed and determined by the organization, and my 'freedom,' whether I am doorkeeper or owner, consists in the alternative to do what is assigned me or lose my connection with the organization. What I do is not my act but the act of the corporate body in which I live and move and have such being as it allows me. And something of the same sort is true almost equally in every other connection.[34]

Jordan intends this quite literally. The corporate person is the real person who acts, and is therefore the fundamental object of jurisprudence, ethical theory, and politics, for it is the order of objects of the corporate person and not the order of mental states —the latter are notoriously unstable and incapable of order— which must be controlled if man's practical action is to go aright. Far from the natural person being real and the corporate person a fiction, it is the other way around—". . . the 'individual' of modern ethical theory has no existence and never had existence."[35] To act, to do, to realize, to effect—this is beyond his puny capacity.

That the corporate person is the real person with a superindividual will empowered by its body of cultural objects to effect changes in the world, is a difficult idea for the modern mind to grasp, a difficulty of which Jordan was not unaware. However, he never wavered in his insistence on this point, and as recently as a year before his death he said,

When I say that it is always the corporate person who acts I mean simply that when we think that *we* are acting, in reality we are acting always in and through some aspect of the corporate nature. In that sense we act in the corporate person or, better, the corporate person acts through us. Certainly we see corporate persons acting every day—as churches, as states, as schools, as industries, and so on. I do not see that an 'individual' can act outside of a corporate structure for the very definition of his individuality depends upon his corporate nature, upon the interconnecting institutional relations which make his individuality possible. I read somewhere in a paper recently that an Episcopal church in Washington had bought a dumping lot in order to transform it into a playground for children. No single individual was responsible for this action. It was the corporate person of the church who acted.[36]

While the individual may for purposes of simplicity speak of "my will" and "my act," the will and act, so far as they are more than mere psychological stuff, are properties of the corporate person. That is why, when institutional energies are stacked against the individual, his will is aborted and his idea unrealized; that this is an ordinary fact of experience may be noted by such expressions as "You can't fight City Hall," "You can't beat the system," etc.

The data for the practical sciences, then, are not individuals or groups, but are

the situations of related things which represent not only the will as a creative force, but the will as 'willed' in an objectified purpose. It is the fact that the orders into which facts do get related have two essential aspects; in the one case, will tends to the ordering of things permanently in institutions; or, institutions are the permanent tendencies of fact systems to significant order; and in the other, institutions tend through the very fact of their organization to develop propulsive or driving power which expresses itself in will. And these are for 'social' sciences the ultimate facts. Once get rid of individualism . . . by transforming the individual into the individuality through the recognition of its degree forms, and we have not only the key to the knowledge of the facts of life, but also the tool through which the control of those facts toward ends of worth is to be accomplished.[37]

Institution as Higher Individuality

Life is always the corporate form, has ever been institutional and objective form. Life is embodied order. Not the original distinctness of parts is the real, but the positive unity that makes distinction itself meaningful. Ground rather than cause is the social *fundamentum,* and this ground is institution—institution which, as the objective and plupersonal or superpersonal order, gives significance to all distinctions among the lower forms of individuality that comprise its content. The natural person or human being is the lowest of these personal forms, and as such is principled by the larger order of which he is a part. As a self, he is continuous with a larger Self in which he is realized. This need not imply transcendence into a supernatural realm; it merely indicates the unity of man and institution or person-Person. If the upper case is used here for the institutional person, it is meant to distinguish higher and lower persons with no necessary implication of superordination and subordination in the relationship between the two. As a matter of fact, this is precisely the conception of authority that Jordan is attempting to negate, for it is one which he finds embedded in individualism of every stripe. What are signified are distinctions within the orders of persons on the basis of degree-forms of individuality, for although all persons have a common law, they may be distinguished in terms of the degree of comprehensiveness of life organization. The human or personal is not confined to the natural individual or the human being, but is more inclusive; it becomes a distinction in the order of persons, a unity or whole within the larger system of wholes. The distinction then is not between whole *and* parts but between whole and whole, or, in other words, is one of differences of degree among a system of wholes. Each of the various degree-forms is a whole that assumes corporate form in the unity of lower forms, and at the same time incorporates in still higher forms. All of these forms are held within the same specific type by a principle which is simultaneously the law of the whole system and of the nature of the parts. This principle of individuation is the basis of the distinction of single unities or wholes and the law of their organization into system. It converts distinction from a *constitutive* principle of reals, which it cannot be, to a principle of *discrimination* among reals. As objective, universal principle, individuality eliminates once and for all the problems centering around the supposed contradiction and opposition between the "individual" and the "social." [38]

The corporate form is beyond the distinction of internal and external. By this statement Jordan does not mean that there is no distinction to be made, but rather he indicates the continuity between the two: the law internal to a unity is also the law "external" to it. Another way of putting this is to say that the law of the individual and the species are one. All the members of a system share the same content and are ordered in their relation to it by the same law. The individual or real is a synthesis or unity of particular-universal. The principle of individuation thus abandons the real as isolable, and by individuating rather than individualizing provides simultaneously for distinction and identity, for the real as a different within identity. As concrete identity, the universal is evidenced not in but *as* the particular when it is individuated as a corporate whole.[39] The individuated universal maintains the identity of particular-universal and eliminates its disjunction or opposition in constituting reals.

There are various classes of reals distinguished through qualitative similarity or difference become universal, and consequently they display a *type* of difference. What distinguishes one class from another is the degree of unity or order it evidences as its organic or constitutional law. Within the class, degree-forms may be identified on the basis of adequacy of organization toward individuality. Among these large classes within the real is the class of personalities which includes all the forms having direct contact with the human. In the class of persons, there is the human or personal level, below which there is the subpersonal and above which the superpersonal. The subpersonal consists in the main of machines or instruments principled by causation and used by human beings for individualized or "private" ends. The superpersonal consists of all the institutions of life which, as active and effective agencies, organize men into permanent corporate forms. Institutions maintain the integrity of organization of the real "within the variety of changing quality into which the real differentiates through growth." [40]

The individual person is determined as particular with reference to the system of institutions as universal. There are no individualized entities; rather a thing is individuated through the mutuality of its relationships to its kind, and thus is identified with its species and becomes the particular realized in its universal. Similarly, individuated again through its proximate species with a more inclusive type, it becomes identified with a higher individuality, for real series is cumulative while abstract series is repetitive.[41]

The principle of individuation suggests that there is no difference in principle between the individual and the general or corporate will, but rather a difference in degree.[42] The constitution of the state is individual, identical in principle with the cultural institutions of which it is the synoptic whole and with the human individual.[43] There is then no difference in principle between man, institution, and state. The human as well as the institutional individuals or persons are degree-forms of individuality, differences within identity.

Human relations then embrace more than man-man, man-group, group-group relations. They are interpersonal, to be sure, but the order of persons is larger than ordinarily conceived. The relation of man to man involves a mediatory or mediating person, that is, institution. Institution is the expression of a universal relation with the individuals who are involved as the points of particularization of that relation. While individuals are thus the particulars through whom specific aspects of life are expressed, they are not the locus of principles for the problems of practical life. These must be approached objectively, which means that we must look beyond the individual or individuals to institution.[44]

For example, the case offered in the instance before the courts as A versus B is one in which the interests represented are personal rather than private or individualized, i.e., they are functions of higher persons. When examined, the conflict turns out to involve the relations of institutions to each other. What appears to be a conflict of property interests between A and B is actually a conflict, for example, between the institutions of property and education. These institutions are at the bar. Jordan says that it is always institutions that are on trial for their lives. The conflicts between institutions are objective problems of justice and of law viewed impersonally.[45]

The problem of human relations is one of interinstitutional relations, and only superficially one of interpersonal or intergroup relations. This further emphasizes the necessity of transferring thought away from the individual or the group to the institution or the corporate person, but the question of the personality of corporation is one of fact and does not extend into mysticism or the creation of metaphysical entities. What does require a mystique, according to Jordan, is the conception of the "metaphysical" individual or soul of traditional politics and religion. He thus reverses the argument by maintaining that the "metaphysical" individual is the abstraction and corporate personality the reality. The fact readily seen in the world, if men were not blinded by false concepts, is the tendency to the objectification of mind, which once embodied contains its own dynamic of further development. Such a view of mind and will need have no reference to any transcendent entity in the supernatural sense, nor to any conception of Absolute Reason or Spirit manifesting itself in institution. Institutions are minded—minded order or objective will—and thus exhibit the characteristics of persons. They have a personal organization and content. Like other persons, they require the appropriation of an external content in order to realize themselves through growth, and they have the ability to maintain themselves and to reproduce themselves through the acquisition or incorporation of a wide variety of content. Further, as realized idea, institutional persons continuously reappropriate themselves, as orders of objects, to human functions.[46]

Corporations have . . . a status in human relations that is unique and peculiar to themselves. They are personal agents objectified; that is, they are rationally ordered systems of purposes realized in physical objects and constituted as organic structures. They are then, in the legal and political sense, persons. As such they constitute and embody the public will.[47]

The distinction between natural and artificial persons is then a false one, since it is made in terms of kind rather than degree. What are taken to be natural and artificial persons are in fact identical in principle and are different stages of individuality. No basic distinction is possible among kinds of persons because all persons are such by virtue of the fact that they are constituted on and by the same principle.[48] It has already been pointed out that all will is universal in nature, while the distinction between the wills of natural and corporate persons is one of degree. Jordan states that whatever is true of the natural person is also true in the same sense of the corporate person, although in a different degree.[49] The corporate person, then, has all the legal and juridical qualities, capacities, and liabilities of a natural person. Presumably, it does have a body to be kicked and a soul to be damned, for institution, as we have said, is embodied soul or ensouled body. Rather than a bloodless abstraction, it is a living reality of exactly the same order and principled by exactly the same law as the natural person, with the same ethical, political, and legal status. This is true whether the law recognizes it or not. Law neither creates the corporation nor endows it with personality. Jordan calls the theory of legal fictions the most monstrous fiction of the law.[50]

Summary

The ongoing action life of man—his culture—may now more clearly be understood as the system of corporate persons through whose active presence the individual is incorporated into life. They are the life of man defined, for "the source, the means, the materials, and the end of his act will be found within this corporate medium. It is the ultimate object of every act—every act intends or is designed to create and maintain this medium as the condition and ground of all action." [51] The life of culture as the system of objectives instituted in the structure of the world is the good life, life realized, the life of achievement. The corporate person as the act performed in order to realize objectives made permanent in the nature of things is the organ of the good for which it stands, and the interrelated system of instituted acts is the state; culture and the state are one. The state of culture is then the whole good, not as a separate good additional to its parts but as principle for them, the synthesis of all goods in the Good; thus just as the corporate person is objective end for the individual, the state as the whole good is the ultimate end of every act of the corporate person. Therefore, every act is to be judged according to whether it maintains or destroys the state of culture. Since it is through its relation to the whole that the quality of the act may be known, the state is the objective ground of moral judgment. That Jordan is close to the common sense of people may be noted in the fact that ordinary reflection on what the individual is to do about any relatively important problem typically takes into consideration its bearing on friends, family, community, job, or other factors of the world which the individual's act will affect.

We have seen that in Jordan's corporate theory of society the chief point to be understood is what action involves, so that man's world-building nature may be made intelligible. Through his analysis of action—not man and action—the institution, as the means and end of an act formed in a structure of objects proper to it, emerged as the more comprehensive individuality mediating man-to-world and man-to-man relations. The institution, since it incorporates thinking, is the type of mind which the man-nature synthesis has taken, and as effective will, as the real person who acts in fact, it emerged as the agent of destiny, the key cultural category to be understood. It seems apparent that Jordan's thinking is rooted in the ideas of the ancient Greeks, who argued that the beginning of wisdom was self-knowledge, the self being not the biopsychological innards of the natural individual, as it is in modern thought, but the public order of life, the self "writ large." [52] If man was by nature a political animal, it was the *polis*, the city-state, that was the ultimate object of thought if his nature was to be made intelligible. Aristotle's view that man conceived as "unable to live in society, or who has no need because he is sufficient for himself, must be either a beast or a god" is one with Jordan's. Man as man is a creature in, of, and for culture.

Man has no choice but to be man, to live in accord with what "being a man" means, to engage in activities appropriate to his nature as these are already defined for him in the corporate embodiment of action. Law has authority for man only so far as it is rational, in accord with his nature, and to maintain the types of action is duty and law for the natural individual as a cultured being. "The natural is the rational, and the rational is what the system of ends demands that the merely natural shall become." [53] The moral law must be heeded because it is of the constitution of reality. Jordan says that the triangle, in order to be real as such, must obey the law of triangles, and in the same way man must obey his own appropriate law. If it be argued that man can ignore the law while the triangle cannot, the reply is that he can do so only by ceasing to be a man. A true man like a true triangle conforms to the law of his nature; for man to violate the law is to violate himself, to become something less than man.[54]

It is fundamentally the public will, operative in and expressive of the corporate personality, that is the creator of law and the center of obligation. Man owes it to himself to owe himself to institution; his obligation to himself is an obligation to culture manifested in corporate or institutional form. His will as a member of the human species is identified with culture, the locus of the objectified and objectifying public will. Men are met in culture as embodied value, a value they achieve through their participating existence as elements of the corporate agency. It is the corporate agent as end that binds, and in that bond lies not bondage but freedom and self-realization. While it is true that freedom must refer to a self that wills, this self is not to be thought of as unique.[55] The reference to self and to will is not to an isolate entity but to a form of individuality incorporated in a system of higher individualities or Persons. Language might be employed here which Jordan does not generally use. Self-transcendence is not loss of self but self-realization; "losing" the self is gaining the self. This is to be likened to the idea often expressed in religious terms as selflessness, the abandonment of egocentricity in favor of theocentricity as the finding of the true self, and the like. Jordan is defining the self-Self relation as self-Culture, but this identification with corporate value is not a mystical act. The natural person for man to be is the cultural person.

CHAPTER 4
INTELLIGENCE IN THE
CORPORATE WORLD

Man as Thinker

What role does the flesh-and-blood human being play in civilization? Frequently it seems as if Jordan has lost him altogether in making the corporate person the important figure in his theory of culture. However, Jordan would argue that on the contrary, by attending to the relational medium in which the natural individual achieves his cultural being and in which he makes his contribution, one has located the source of his individuality as human. His individuality is constituted of institutional materials, and hence concern over institutions is one and the same with concern over individuals. Nevertheless, Jordan definitely intends to reduce the individual from his falsely sanctified position as the principle of the institution and the state, for while it is true that in a real sense they are for him and exist as his means, nevertheless he is not their principle. As the larger, more comprehensive organs of the state, in which he is included, they are his principle, and the whole state of things is principle for institutions; but the individual as a part of the corporate person is highly significant and must not be overlooked, since he is the only being within the cultural whole who thinks.

The person as individual and as a concept of pure theory is limited strictly to the function of thinking, since thinking is the only act of which the individual is capable that does not also complicate his activity with that of other individuals.[1]

In other words, the act of thought is the only act of which he is capable *qua* individual, and its issue is not a concrete object but a logical object. The outcome of the individual's thought is a plan, the formulation in the logical imagination of the design of some object or objective.[2] Through speculation new purposes are foreseen, not yet realized in the present constitution of the facts, still "merely ideal." However, as a result of action based upon the designing intelligence, these materials become a house, i.e., thought canalizes the will energies and powers of action of corporate persons. In this sense will may be seen to have a dual but interrelated character, a thought phase representing "will as intelligent prescience" and an action phase representing "will as effective agency." [3] In order for an act effectively to complete itself, the corporate person requires (1) that the organization of men and materials manifest such wisdom that every feature is relevant to the attainment of its end, and (2) that individuals as thinkers be continuously concerned with the guidance of corporate energies on behalf of the corporate good. The obvious difficulty with the "thinking" now going on in corporate agencies is that much of it is more akin to scheming for advantage than to the use of disinterested intelligence in the advancement of public purposes. This leads to the corporate person becoming a Hobbesian *Leviathan* blindly effecting itself.

Diagnosis and Solution of Cultural Failure

The diagnosis of cultural failure or success may now be understood to mean for Jordan the success or failure with which man's institutional life has been built. Recalling that institutions are the synthesis of man's mental energies with the energies of nature, one may see that two basic factors may be involved in institutional failure.

1. The realm of nature may be the source of difficulty, since man when poorly instrumented, as he has been throughout most of his history, is prone to be victimized by it. Chance factors, such as changes in climatic conditions, the destruction through disease of animals which provide the main source of food, etc., may uproot the work life, the family life, the aesthetic and other activities of a people. The space-time realm of nature historically has presented many insuperable difficulties which man with his own pathetic physical energies was unable to overcome. Within this context certain typical efforts which he made to order his world, such as the delimitation of boundaries to protect his food supply, the exclusive possession of property as against other clans or societies, or the development of warriors to raid other societies for food, had a certain degree of sensibleness about them. However, these devices for overcoming natural difficulties tend, when

they become corporate, to effect themselves dynamically and blindly. Once having brought forth armies and munitions plants, a society may be virtually powerless to prevent this effective power from expressing itself.

2. Then the other fundamental source of institutional failure, of the continuance and growth of negative developments within the structure of culture, is the failure of thought to guide institutional energies in accordance with changed life conditions or to think out new possibilities for them. With the problem of the nature realm having receded into the background, owing to man's magnificent if relatively recent triumph over it, the question of institutional order is today chiefly a matter of thought. The problem is not one of an inevitable "cultural lag" as a kind of perpetual treadmill upon which man is stuck, but of having terribly misconceived cultural reality; for while man has been searching the crevices of his mind for new data and attempting to order his mental states into systematic unity, he has also been neglecting the public disorder clearly present in the institutional world about him. While practically all people sincerely wish adequate nutrition and decent living conditions for themselves and others—and this is now objectively possible for all Americans, thanks to agricultural and industrial developments—the "order" in fact taken by economic institutions insures malnutrition and squalid, ugly, pestilent homes for many. Every person may wish, but Persons will. Thus the basic contemporary task is the encouragement of a new thinking that will understand the complexities of the corporate reality now dominant in the affairs of man. Through such understanding institutional energies may be directed toward objects of significance and value. The "right," indeed the obligation, to think inheres in the dynamic nature of the corporate reality.

If the will of the corporate person is in itself blind, man as thinker provides the vision. Should Underwood continue its manufacture of typewriters or develop a new product? Corporate persons may be maladapted to their ends. Is this hospital's interest in profit compatible with its end as an organ of public health? The compelling tendency of the corporate person is to grow, but it does not know in what direction or at what rate. Should the University of Illinois establish a four-year branch in Chicago and at the same time expand rapidly in Champaign-

Urbana, or do one and not the other? Corporate persons tend indiscriminately to aggrandize themselves without regard to the type of material incorporated. Should this hotel expand at the cost of this playground? Should this department store grow by building upon the adjoining park? Corporate persons inevitably affect one another, but what ought their relations to be? What should the relations of Ford Motor Company be to General Motors? General Motors to U. S. Steel? U. S. Steel to schools? Schools to church? Church to family? Etc. The natural individual as thinker, as projector of plans, developer of new purposes, guider of will and action, is essential if the institutional act is to issue in an object that has fitness in the whole scheme of things.

Corporate persons "came into being to give objective reality to ends created and designed by individuals, but to which individuals were powerless to give body and expression." [4] If man's life is to survive and prosper, his fundamental obligation as individual is to know the corporate realities around him, since the ponderous momentum of corporate persons left to themselves is likely to drift into irrational and antagonistic expressions, as witness the ineffable insanity of our industrial "order." Corporate persons *enact* law, that is, they make the facts of life with which men must come to grips, but *thought* creates law; in advance of the facts, it designs what they are to be. "This function of making law belongs by nature to the speculative or knowledge motive." [5] Then political activity, as the governor of the state of things—the intertwined system of institutions—is itself dependent upon thought. Thus corporate life can only be sound when natural individuals as organized in the professions or "theoretical institutions (institutions in which the speculative knowledge function incorporates itself) determine the laws by which politics directs the movements of life in so far as those movements are to have moral quality." [6]

Several Key Acts of Man

Since the corporate world is the human world of action, the person "writ large," but with capacities for effecting acts and realizing ends which no natural individual has by himself, it is the prime cultural reality to be understood. However, the persons in whom the thinking function is incorporated as a professional obligation, the "intellectuals," have failed to comprehend the institutional object of thought, and so it is incumbent upon Jordan to make some preliminary speculations as to the nature, functions, and interrelations of several significant practical institutions. This he does in *The Good Life*, where the family, industry, education, religion, art, and politics are taken up, and the following discussion will be based largely upon the analysis found there.

It is noteworthy, in his analysis and evaluation of the corporate world, that Jordan considers genuine institutions to represent positive, creative outgrowths of nature. What is relatively inchoate in nature achieves form through culture; its random beauty becomes organized art. That is, through institutionalization the crude elements of nature are objectified more perfectly. Through action, elements of existence with a low degree of order are transformed into ends of life, and so institutions, the means and ends of the active life, provide, out of the concrete substance of nature, all the meaning and value that may be vouchsafed to men.

FAMILY

The family centrally connects with the instinct life of man, to which it gives public form. The family is the organization of instinct. Instinct when right takes on the form of family life, and it is in this sense, as institutionalized, that instinct does not operate by some mysterious inner potency but is itself determined in experience by the institution of marriage and family.

Young human beings do not grow up impelled by an irresistible desire or some inner inevitable urge to go seek out the opposite sex and thus provide for the continuity of the race. Long before the 'instinct' of sex has asserted itself the boy and girl have by play institutions mimicked the whole life process of the race, including its idea forms, so that later they enter the marriage relation largely by mere habit, and, it may be, against the influence of sex 'instincts.' [7]

The natural activities of sex, as well as the primitive biological urges so dominant in the first few years of life, are reduced to order in the family.[8] The orderly expression of instincts is a fundamental precondition to leading a cultural life, and hence is a significant contribution to it.

The nature of the instincts ordered by the family lead into two interrelated functions of the family: (1) " . . . the breeding and nursing of children through the first few years of life." [9] The realization of this function becomes an important integrating factor in the life of the parents. (2) The establishment of the physical structure of the home and all the objects requisite to it, so that it may effectively sustain physical-emotional being. The home needs to be a place of comfort in every sense of the term, the locale where eating, sleeping, toilet, play, school, and recreational activities can be carried out. [10]

Essentially the family is a reproductive institution, reproducing the organisms through which the species is assured continuity, but the reproduction of the species which the family insures is not only biological but cultural. It endeavors to produce physically and morally capable individuals, individuals who, through the give and take possible in the protective milieu of the family, learn how to control the objects and persons of the environment in order to effect their purposes. In the process the child becomes disciplined, not self-disciplined in its negative meaning of suppressed subjective impulses, but the learning "of how to adapt the forces and circumstances of his environment to each other in such a way as will offer greater promise of, and opportunity for, action." [11] The child learning to build with blocks or to master the piano is becoming self-disciplined in the most important sense of developing a positive capacity to realize himself constructively in the world. Then the moral obligation of parents is to know the relative worth of objectives accessible to the child. The parents must be competent people, must possess the knowledge and have access to the means with which the child may make his beginning acquaintance with the truth, beauty, and goodness present in the world. Obviously the family is the first institution through which the child makes contact with culture, and the parents are the critical mediators of that contact.

The obligation of parents to know is peculiarly accentuated in contemporary life:

The family is the point where the educational, social, political, legal, industrial, and religious institutional relations and connections of life all meet. Not only do they meet in the family but the family is the point where what there may be of difference of direction, etc., among these institutions and their trends must be brought to some degree of unity. The motives of education and industry, which frequently run at cross-purposes to each other, must somehow be composed if either of them is to reach any important conclusion. And the family is the place where the most immediate conflicts among such institutional tendencies must be resolved.[12]

The family as the harmonizer of the various forces found in life is a miniature state, the realized model of what the state ought to be.

The family has kept before man throughout his career the ideal that all his purposes may be made harmonious and that he could realize all his ends not only without interfering with the purposes and ends of his fellows but while actually furthering and contributing to them. This is man's noblest ideal and his profoundest conviction, and the family has immortalized it in his 'heart.' But it is more than an ideal and a conviction. The family has kept it continuously and constantly demonstrated throughout history that the way and the only way for man to reach his ends is through cooperation with his fellows. And the family has proved that no half-hearted method will work; cooperation, mutuality, brotherhood, is the one ultimate and absolute law, and it may not be ignored in any detail.[13]

INDUSTRY

Industry is man's work energy made more effective through organization. The basic function of industry is the development of objects of value for the maintenance of cultural life; its end is the provision of the objects so central to every cultural activity, without which ultimately every cultural activity would perish. Therefore, both with respect to its control over nature and its direction toward cultural ends, industry is the work life brought to a high level of effectiveness under the direction of intelligence. Industry as ordered with respect to the public ends—family, education, religion, recreation, etc.—is therefore a moral endeavor, since *it is central to any good that there may be as fact.*

If this is true, then it is the *qualities* of the object, *the consideration of its place in the scheme of things,* which motivates the industrial act. When the worker attempts to create an object because of his vision of its ultimate significance, then his work is directed by his intelligence and is free.[14] The law of the object is aesthetic law: it must be such as to fulfill the mental-physical energies of the worker and be the logical completion of everything that entered into its creation, including his personal capacities, and when fully realized it is an exemplar for others of its type. The principle of the industrial act is the object's perfection.

That is to say, the law is that the object produced must be the perfect embodiment of an act, and all the relations of persons to the object, or of persons to persons as mediated by the object, are controlled in the interest of maintaining the adequacy of the object to the act. The object is then the standard principle of all judgments relating to the act and, as such, the basic law of morality. Work thus is dignified and ennobled, since it has become the very principle of morality and the standard by which the adequacy and competence of acts are to be judged in all fields.[15]

Industrial activity, when it is governed by the idea of creating a fine object, demands the utmost intelligence and skill of man, and is integrative of man with his world and with other men. All the mental-physical energies of which the man is capable are brought into play, and since the man fulfills himself in his work, the result is "pride in workmanship." This is work whenever it is *real* work, as distinguished from drudgery. Therefore, the mechanization of work, as in the factory organization of the "process of production," is not work at all but is the reduction of men into robots who are not able nor expected to see any relation of their movements to any end, much less their own end. Such relation as they have to one another is purely mechanical, since their own thought and purposes are nowhere involved in the production process; moreover, the need for their ideas in bringing forth the object is reduced to an absolute minimum.[16]

With respect to the distribution and exchange of the objects brought forth by industry, the principle shall be their *function* in relation to the realization of human ends.[17] The common wealth is to be *utilized* in the furtherance of the Commonwealth.

EDUCATION [18]

Education is the institution which developed out of man's need to control his world and his recognition that intelligence is indispensable to such control. Education is "the organization of intelligence." The distinctive feature of intelligence is that it projects situations in ideal form in advance of action, under the assumption that action will realize these ideal forms in fact.[19] Thus the knowledge process operates in a form "essentially imaginative and projective"; it is speculative and reflective. The assumption which education necessarily makes in developing intelligence is of an integral relationship between mind and the ordered facts of the world, i.e.,

. . . that there is an organic relation between these facts and the inner processes and functions of the individual mind, so that, if you control the relations among objective facts, you not only determine their qualities but you also modify the inner makeup and arrangement of the mind to which the facts are present and thus determine the qualitative form of the mind.[20]

Therefore, education does not proceed primarily through the direct relation of mind to mind, but through the ordering of the environing object system, for this ordering, as determinative of the behavior of the individual, also determines the content and organization of his mind. The development of intelligence is effected *mediately,* through the ordering of persons and things in the environment of learners, this ordering being done under the most favorable conditions possible for learning. The school is a laboratory for learning in which the individual is stimulated to expend his energy in the direction of developing control of the materials of his world and concomitantly his mind.

Since intelligence represents for Jordan the "unity of mind" running through all of its manifestations, the development of intelligence is at one and the same time the development of will, character, and the emotions.[21] That is, the idea of a thing which the individual has determines his feelings about it and whether and how he acts toward it.

The intelligence which Jordan is concerned to have the educational institution develop must be distinguished from the technical or specialized intelligence. Technical intelligence, the knowledge of *how to do* things, is of course necessary, but the characteristic of intelligence as specialized is its narrow isolation of the thing from the whole which environs it and within which it has import. As has been pointed out in the discussion of action, the act that is cultural, or "the moral quality of an act, is just its reference to the whole which the act wills to create, and this element of wholeness is precisely what action lacks in so far as it is specialized." [22] If men know how to do, but not what to do, they are not yet acculturated. Then the intelligence to be developed is the broad, comprehensive intelligence, in which a synoptic view of human affairs may find acceptance. To such a mind many possibilities for action are opened up, since there is no necessity that it follow a narrow groove. The end of education, the type of instrument for moral accomplishment which it is, is the awakening of the mind of the student to the world in which he has his being. As Jordan puts it,

It is the very essence of education that it should open up to us the abundant life, and this life consists primarily in the wisdom by which we see things in their proper relativity of value. Its purpose is then to prepare us for life; but life is not the biological and economic process only. The life for which it should prepare is that which adds to the natural existence the abundance of the cultural, which enables us to see in the good person the good world.[23]

RELIGION

If in the main the family, industry, and education are the respective realizations of the biological, physical, and intellectual energies of man, religion through its institutionalization in the church is the realization of his emotional or feeling capacities. Intellectually, in the cold gray of reason, men design ends to be made real in futurity, but the intellect itself does not impel men to their actualization. Ideas as sheer logical constructs in themselves tend to be "satisfying and quiescent. . . . It is only when an idea glows with the warmth of feeling that it fires us to the pitch of action; and it is only in the heat of action that the good is realized." [24] Ideas provide the design or *form* of the objective, but feeling instructs man here and now as to the experiential *content* of ends.[25] The idea of the brotherhood of man is a static intellective vision until the feelings pronounce it an ideal worthy of man's highest and most persistent efforts.

Furthermore, once an end has been realized, though all the facts needed to satisfy the intellectual side of cognition are never in, the feelings nevertheless insist upon the sacredness of the act and the necessity for its maintenance and advancement. The world being what it is—a world in which one cannot know all the consequences of an act prior to the act's objectification, a world in which chance is real—faith is necessary. Religion, then, as the "organization of faith," through its special means, its ritual, worship, and art, directs the feelings into the celebration of the realized good now present in fact, and heightens the sensibilities of man to the good ever beckoning beyond the realized present. It pronounces the family sacred, but the family must realize itself more completely. The life of man is good, but he must bring it to a greater pitch of significance. In other words, religion is not an outgrowth, as so often assumed, of needs, drives, instincts, inner tendencies toward the magical or mysterious in human nature, or of any psychological causes whatever, but has ontological status; and in this fact the explanation of its persistence and its universality resides. The function of religion is defined for it by the nature of cultural reality, and this reality is the corporate person with its two interrelated aspects: its stable basis in property (the good in the here and now) and its will toward objectification (the good to be realized). Religion celebrates and sanctifies both elements of the good, so that man may have the strength of heart to protect and promote the values of life. It is in this integral relationship with the Good that religion is to be distinguished from superstition.

If the preceding is correct, then religion, as the organizer of affective impulses toward the realization of ends, has a dynamic, prophetic, or even radical function, for the good that must be may contradict many elements now found in human life. In the sense that it relates man to the existent good, religion has a conservative or priestly function. Before man could think with any degree of profundity, religion through its intuitive grasp of life had already defined for him the meaning and value of the realities present to his life and those toward which he ought to aspire. In terms both of its emotive definition of the good already existent and of its prophetic function in projecting ideal values, religion is essentially a *practical* institution, as Marxists and liberals implicitly admit when they condemn it so harshly. It is practical since "religious objects . . . have their existence and meaning within the world of action." [26]

The identification of religion with the emotional capacity of man when he is impelled toward an end is frequently noted in the observation that strong feeling toward *any* end—democracy, communism, football, etc.—is at bottom a religious attitude. However, religion must be critical of the ends it sanctifies. The fact that religion may place its blessing upon conflict, as in a "holy war," suggests that if religion is to be truly practical, if it is to be a moral agency in life, it must receive its direction from intelligence. The danger of faith is that it may be blind.

ART

Art is "the organization of the sensuous and imaginative elements of life" [27] to the end that beauty may be created and appreciated. It is, of course, because art has a grip upon the feelings that religion so naturally uses it in the furtherance of the religious function, for men are likely to dedicate their lives to ideals that are fleshed out in the form of beauty. Yet art itself achieves its own end whenever beauty becomes a reality in the world.

More importantly, art becomes the principle for the whole of life through its peculiar relationship to it. Truth and the good, since they never can be finally known, announce themselves in the forms of beauty.

It is through the aesthetic capacity in this general sense, the capacity for beauty as such, that we are enabled to know the good when it is done and to apprehend the truth when it is achieved. It is beyond any of our intellectual or moral capacities to apprehend the good as the good or the true as the true; they can be known only in the form of beauty. There is ultimately no *reason* we can give that the good is good or that it should be good; or that the true is true or should be true; and there is no moral end that justifies itself to us merely by being a moral end. The good and the true must appeal to me by virtue merely of their sensuous and imaginative perfection in an object, and it is from this latter that we derive both the notions of true and good.[28]

Men feel no obligation to an ugly world, for only through the existence of beauty does the world assert itself as true and good. Proportion and harmony are the law of every act.

The object of beauty demands that no detail necessary to it be omitted, nor any detail alien to it be admitted in the complex of qualities which constitute it a harmonic whole. As the complete fulfillment of the ideas, activities, and materials which have entered into it, the aesthetic object is the perfect act, and since the object of beauty is the perfect realization of man's ideas, beauty is the only end which man achieves completely. In all of his other activities there is imperfection, the inevitable falling short of an ideal state of things, and this inevitability of imperfection is the ground for the continuance of action. However, the aesthetic object is the archetype of "that wholeness and completeness and harmony" [29] which is characteristic of any end, and through its grip on the sensuous and imaginative capacities of life pronounces that *the* end object, the state as *the* end, or the wholeness of the good, is to be the harmonious completeness of all ends.[30] The aesthetic object *is*, and it testifies through its presence that culture may be.

POLITICS

Any fact or relation regarded from the point of view of its immediate qualities and attributes is content for specific institutions. The conduct of the day's work, the procreation of a child, the development of ritual, etc., are respectively specific facts of industry, family, and church, that is, "in its peculiar quality or character, and in its more immediate relations, every fact is a fact of one or more of the major institutions of life." [31] However, politics has no such content peculiar to itself; rather it is concerned with the relations of institutions to each other and to the state, or the state of the whole, which they constitute. The political relation is any relation that is interinstitutional or that has reference to the whole good. Jordan points out:

Doing a day's work is a fact of industry, and all its specific characters and the technique of its processes are to be determined from the viewpoint of industry alone. But when there is a question of the quality of the product, or its price, or the effect of the product upon the worker or his relations to his fellows, or upon the general conditions of order and the peace of the community, the day's work is a political fact. It is such because, in such relations, its very meaning is a reference to the whole and not a specialized reference to the local situation and circumstances within which it occurs. [32]

Political facts are then public, objective, and moral. [33] They are public both in the social sense that they are the concern of all—all men are citizens—and in their character as referring to the whole life. They are objective in that political facts refer to existent facts and relations and to the type of order they are to take in the future. These facts constitute the whole good, but the whole good is itself the system of objective relations, so the moral quality of political facts is precisely their fitness "into the scheme of things as a whole." This public character of the appropriateness of facts to the ordered world of culture makes them the concern of political institutions. Politics has then as its object the state of the state; its aim is the maintenance and development of the "unity of life."

The politic state is one which acts positively to further the whole good, and it sees that the Good is the principle which guides every institutional act and relation. In order for any institutional act to continue properly, it must issue in an ending which is consonant with all institutional acts. Industry must function in such a way that it ends itself in objects of value which at the same time promote education, family, religion, art creation and appreciation; the family and education must produce biologically and culturally competent individuals fit to take their place in the work life; religion and art must infuse the whole life of action with conviction and dedication in order to convince man that action's worth is real now; etc. The many practical problems confronting political thought then concern the proper structural organization of the great life institutions with respect to the appropriate ending of their functions, and the consideration of how interinstitutional relations may best be harmonized.[34]

Political institutions do not negate the state; they act positively in the ordering of the whole action life so that every end may be achieved and the whole maintained. This does not mean that the political act is authoritarian, since law is made *within* the institutional process itself. The law of the act inheres in the structure that the institution itself has taken in the course of the historical process, so that political order is not the institutional life; rather it co-operates with the institutional will already present in the dynamic order which the facts have taken. The political will is nothing more or less than the harmonious synthesis of all wills in the realization of the whole good. Politics must not, indeed cannot, perform the acts of institutional persons, but it can submit policy for the guidance of their respective acts and it is able to do this because it alone possesses the whole view that is its special province.

Since politics is itself a positive process, which endeavors to enhance and harmonize acts themselves positive in nature, the policies it designs are based upon speculative activity. Jordan says that it is "experimentation under logical conditions, and corresponds to practice as the use of intelligence in experimentation under temporal conditions." [35] The speculation of politics is a synthesis of the idealizing capacity with the capacity for observation, which together are implemented in experimentation. The politic solution of life problems, then, has little or nothing to do with "acts" of repression or negation, as in legislative onslaughts upon "evil" conditions; the solution it offers is the logical thinking through of the nature of institutions, their directional tendencies, and how they may best be adapted to their respective ends and to each other; and the policy enacted is viewed as experimental in nature, thus requiring continual study and reflection as the institutional life unfolds.

CHAPTER 5
CORPORATE THEORY OF LEGISLATION

The corporate world must be minded by the legislative intelligence since ideas are indispensable to the ordering of institutional energies. Men must see what new ends are emerging from the corporate process and think through the ends to be realized. They must reflect and experiment to discover the best way to instrument these ends within the corporate body, and they must oversee the mutual fitness with which the various institutions perform their functions, so that institutions do not work at cross purposes, as they so largely do at present—nation against nation, church against school, economic organizations against the family, etc. The legislative quality of mind and character to be developed in natural individuals by the educational system may best be understood by looking at the various phases of the legislative act, since it is the reality of the act that determines the type of intelligence to be developed in men.

Legislation as Speculation

Man has vision but is incompetent to achieve; institutions can achieve but cannot see. It might be said that institution does but has no idea of what it is doing, and consequently in following its own urgencies it may interfere with the functioning of other institutions. Since it is blind, its idea needs formulation and clarification, particularly if the achievement of its end is to be harmonious with the achievement of the ends of other institutions in the whole as End. Institutions have a life of their own and manifest spontaneity which men must respect but which requires the guidance of intelligence. The act of institution or of the social body is not that of intelligence; the act of man is not that of will. The act of intelligence must be completed by the act of will.[1] The act of man is confined to thought since the actualization of an object is only mediated through an institutional corpus. Man's function is to know, and in doing so he fulfills his moral and political obligation. He attains his highest capacity in the creation of ends in idea, and he is limited to that function and can exercise no other.[2] The practical man is the thinker, the man of ideas, the idealizer. Life must be organized and ordered with respect to the Ideas, which are earthbound but still must be extended to their fullest reach. It is precisely in the distinction made between action and movement—and Jordan indicates that perhaps this distinction makes all the real difference in the world in a quite literal sense [3]—that planning is necessary, and this, of course, is beyond the capacity of institution. The responsibility falls upon man to think through the largest or most comprehensive ends, to look constantly ahead to see what may be made out of present possibilities. This calls for the widest use of the speculative imagination in anticipating what is to be realized, the conceptualization of ends before they exist in fact. It is the continuous task of legislation to redefine ends in the creation and maintenance of the state. In this sense legislation's essential function is not the enactment of specific statutes, but the creation in idea of the constitution of the state. As the stuff of constitution is institution, the object of legislative thought consists of institutions and their order or integration in a corporate whole.[4]

Since the state is constantly growing, the law is never fixed or final. Change itself makes final formulation impossible; therefore legislation is always characterized by adventure rather than certainty. This is necessary in the nature of the case, since it is not possible to know in advance the outcome of an action or what the end will be in fact. Thus speculation is an adventure of ideas, and it plans action but does not undertake it. Jordan defines speculation as experimentation under logical conditions, attempting thereby to avoid the dangers of both a priori rationalism and naïve empiricism. Speculation implies the fullest freedom for the imagination, but not in the sense that thought is remote from objects or the hard realities. Thought is of objects, to which it gives outline, structure, and logical substantiality.[5] Further, the ideas or ideals must be tested in practical life, where they will be experimentally verified or proved wrong. If ideologies refer to systems of ideas, then the speculative intelligence must be given free range to construct such schema, but these are not

reduced to law until experimentally verified in social practice.[6]
Ideologies should be viewed as tentative constructs for experimental validation rather than as rigidly fixed dogmas to be used as weapons of "ideological warfare."

Issues arising in practical life require logical formulation, and this is the legislature's task. As a speculative body, it works through the examination and critical comparison of ideas. This is the stage of pure thought, in which temporal experiences are put to the test of ideas. Unfortunately, such testing is seldom done in present legislatures, which proceed generally on the assumption that the principles are already known and need only be applied to immediate circumstance, whereas the crucial legislative task is that of formulating such principles.[7]

In place of the "thou shalt nots" and the general negativism prevalent in contemporary legislation, Jordan proposes a wholly positive view. Legislation is not concerned with enactments against evil nor with proscription. It is not a check against growth to prevent life from going too far. Legislation is not limiting in nature. Neither is government confined to keeping the struggle between private interests from going beyond certain limits. Government is neither a policeman nor simply an umpire or referee. The lack of accomplishment of current legislatures, renowned for their inability to act effectively, attests to the futility of negativism in politics. The checks and balances conception has defeated law rather than safeguarded it, and has assured the futility of the state [8] and its domination by plutocracy and/or tyranny. In America under the Eisenhower administration the drift has been to plutocracy, and in Germany and France to tyranny, and each in its own way is a reaction to the anarchic result of the democratic theory of checks and balances as well as to the contradictory interpretation of government as made up of interest groups for which it must at the same time serve as referee. The only real meaning of the checks and balances conception lies in the idea of assuring that the various life urges will fit together in attaining the whole good, so that the function of each will be preserved and will not interfere with the others. However, even here there is basically a positive conception, the preventive aspect being related to the proper functioning of all individualities. Legislation looks forward to the attainment of ends and is positive throughout, giving full range to the various life purposes.[9] It is permissive and enabling rather than prescriptive of limits or proscriptive of acts.

With reference to democratic political theory, Jordan sees in it important elements of value. His own assumption is that while the ends or objectives of life are not to be found in people as such, in their biopsychological processes, nevertheless the state ultimately is founded upon democratic principles as its major premise, by which he means "that the whole people ultimately carries political responsibility and assumes all the burdens of policy as well as decides the major questions of political method." [10] Because the whole people bears the burden of policy, each person should have knowledge of his relation to the whole.

So important is this knowledge of the whole for all persons functioning in a system that it may be asserted that the highest order of persons within the system should have no function other than to see that the status of the whole was known to every part.[11]

The chief value of democracy is as a political methodology, according to Jordan, a useful way of handling problems of detail that come up within the political process, but this must be qualified by his fear that like any technique it tends to the irrational when it is not based upon a logic of ends. At the same time, to the extent that it is a mere methodology of politics and has no rational view of the ends of culture, it is the source of a great societal weakness. Another crucial democratic principle which Jordan accepts is the thesis of "popular origination of law and of the institutional structures through which law is made effective, as well also the popular referendum control of the entire public process." [12] However, Jordan has different grounds for justifying the popular origination of law than the traditional democratic theorist. For Jordan the people may originate law and suggestions for institutional structure, not because of their inner metaphysical being or some inherent right that they have as such, but because they man the institutional stations at which action is an ongoing process and therefore have a view of things which the "higher ups" must always be prepared to receive and evaluate for the sake of action. Jordan's acceptance of "the popular referendum control of the entire public process" is puzzling, to say the least, and is contradicted by the lack of value he sees in the voting process.

Granted this qualified agreement with at least two basic principles of democratic theory, nevertheless Jordan's corporate view of life necessarily leads him into a severe critique of democracy as a politics. The fatal defect which Jordan finds in democratic thought is its acceptance of the individual will of the natural person, which when pluralized becomes the mystical general will, as the fundamental fact of politics. This means that public reality is a state of mind. On such a basis democracy cannot yield a constitution of the state nor say anything regarding public order. It cannot suggest how life, as instituted in the various public forms, can be integrated into a harmonious whole. Since political theory has as its object the design of the state, since it is concerned with the structure and relations of institutions as constitutive of the state, democracy is not political *theory*. Instead, democracy exhausts itself as political *method* in attempting to find specific instruments for the expression of the people's will in particular cases. Democracy can only tell us how to operate the state once it is established and ordered, but it cannot establish the state. Even its success as method, moreover, is dependent upon the public order, whose institutional ground it does not know. Not knowing its moral basis in the corporate order of the state, method becomes endless, an infinite process going nowhere, whose vacuum of purposelessness becomes filled with subjective considerations of utility.[13] Democratic theory is correct, according to Jordan, in recognizing experimentation as the method of politics, but it is wrong in failing to see that only in dealing with ends does experimentation become a logical process, and that speculation is then experimentation under logical conditions.[14]

Furthermore, democracy makes it unnecessary to come to grips with the difficult administrative task of implementing mind states, even when they are worthy ones, because it assumes that public realities are such states of mind. The education of the public, the establishment of constructive attitudes in people (e.g., desire for morality in government, hostility to crime and union corruption, in short, the achievement of an "informed public"), which at best is but a means, is thought to be the end of the democratic process. Mind states are accepted as real, and governmental "action" is then no more than a statement or exercise of mystic fiat. For democracy the mere passing of laws will be the fulfillment of acts.[15] The recent handling of the television quiz show scandal is a case in point. The proposed passage of a law making certain specific types of dishonesty in the mass media illegal is thought to get at the crux of the matter. But all that is seen is the "little fix" of dishonesty in some people directly involved with certain programs, when it is the "big fix" of the business organization and control of the policies of the mass media, as well as the business organization of the industries who therefore use the mass media in behalf of their interests, which needs alteration. The "smart money" knows that despite individual self-flagellation, despite an increase in self-serving publicity for some politicians, despite public catharsis, nothing real has been altered. If action means the issuing of an idea into a changed condition of fact, then democratic "action" is typically inaction or reaction.

The failure of democratic theory to understand the nature of will, and correspondingly the nature of law and the state, is again evidenced in the conception of representative government.

. . . [Representative government] means that political obligation may at will be assumed or put off, allowed to fall into abeyance or negotiated, interpreted in terms of interest, or bluffed away. Political obligation thus lies on the neck of the political agent not as a burden of moral necessity, but as a detachable collar whose forms and colors may vary with the winds of fashion or the whims of interest.[16]

Jordan argues that the breakdown of representative government lies exactly in its assumption that there can be a vicarious discharge of the political function, in the superstition that one will can take the place of another.[17] In fact, he blames this belief for the tremendous growth of the power of the executive, who has taken advantage of the indefinite status of his position to enlarge his own dominion.

If will inheres in the natural individual and is of his essence, then it is difficult to see how this political unit can be maintained as such once his will is delegated to another, who presumably also has a will of his own; in these circumstances the delegate must give up his own will, so that what he expresses in the legislature is not his but that of somebody else. This raises the question of what the representative represents. Is he simply an automaton who registers the will of his constituents, or is he supposed to do his own thinking? The assumed individualized character of will makes it impossible either for the voter to transfer his will and political obligation to another or for the representative to lose his own will. There can be no substitution of wills in any case. It is dehumanizing for an agent merely to act at the behest of a will other than his own, but it is also contradictory for him to act upon his own will, and as proof of this Jordan points to the widespread corruption of such representatives in democratic government. Jordan asks these two questions in support of his contentions: "How could a unique and 'free' person represent another unique and free person? Or, if this question is not a conclusive answer, how could one such will represent a *plurality* of similar wills?" [18] He concludes that representative government is a contradiction in terms, and its day, like that of the power state in which government is supposed to rest on force or authority, is over. In their place and already here is the concept of the *"administrative autonomy of the corporate person,* which is the basic category of politics, and at the same time the elementary reality of fact to be dealt with in the practice of government." [19] However, Jordan states that representative government is not intrinsic to democracy nor implied in its political purpose.[20]

The faith of democracy in the ballot is tragically misplaced, according to Jordan. The vote is thought to accomplish political miracles, including that of the transfer of will. However, a "mandate from the people" may be right or wrong, rational or irrational, because it has no necessary continuity with the living, growing corporate realities whose acts neither wait nor depend upon the vote. The necessity for a new school building or the reconstruction and extension of the city's sewer system is independent of the electorate's will. The people vote for economy in government and tax reduction, and government grows bigger, more costly, and taxes increase. Fundamentally, the constitution and design of the state are not established by the vote.

On that most important question of all, the nature of ends, democracy is silent, or it assumes that social ends are only individual interests in their plurality. From Jordan's point of view, it is no improvement over this type of individualism to suggest that ends are not aggregates but syntheses, as long as the individual is still taken to be the seat of value and the person to whom obligation is owed. Democracy is a social rather than a cultural theory, and as such it lacks definition of ends. It is concerned with the social question rather than the political question.

Consequently, its attention is centered on the relation of men rather than on institutions and their relation. Whether viewed in terms of the individualism of classical liberalism or the social democracy of modern liberalism, its basic premises nevertheless remain the same as far as their subjective nature is concerned. When Jordan says that the "social question" is a relatively unimportant one for politics, he means that social relations do not constitute the state and that the problem of the relations of men is but an aspect of the more fundamental political question of the relations of institutions. Institutions, as fact-orders within which natural persons are integrated, furnish the state with its constitution. As long as democracy concerns itself primarily with social relations conceived as separate from the property order, it will not be a politics; it will not be capable of finding the state's constitution. Neither will it solve the problem of human relations, whose order is identified with the order of institutions, for this is the object of speculation. The problem of human relations is incorporated in the problem of institutional relations. Once the interinstitutional relations are harmoniously arranged, men will be brought into harmony also.

Democracy does not recognize that value is an object, not an attribute of one or more subjects; the object as end or part of an end is value. The object does not have value but is value; *valet* and does not have worth bestowed upon it.[21]

Jordan seems to be charging democracy with asking the subjective and therefore fatal question of "who shall rule?" If democracy gives a different answer from autocracy, if for the one or few democracy substitutes the many or all or the people as a whole, *popular sovereignty is yet sovereignty and a denial of principle.* The constitution is not to be found in the people any more than it is to be found in an elite or any ruling group, but it lies in institutions and in their interrelations and their order. To be sure, there must be competent personnel, but the law does not inhere in them. The quest for law must go beyond natural persons and the people's will; stated somewhat differently, the public will is not the will of "all of us" but is contained in the momentum of institutions. The law lies in the public will, but public will is corporate or cultural rather than social. An objective politics which would avoid subjectivity—whether of one, few, many, or all—must ask "what is law?" rather than "who shall rule?" Jordan asserts that even were democracy not challenged from without, it would disintegrate from within, for its destruction lies in faulty presuppositions and the failure to design a state. The state is an organized whole constituted in its complex of institutional organs, but democracy does not see the constitution and bases itself upon people. Democracy gives us a faulty metaphysical ground as foundation for the state.

Democracy attempts to establish public will and public order upon a synthesis of interests, but this attempt is bound to fail according to Jordan. There can be no harmony of interests, no unity and continuity, since interests are private by nature and will not submit to order. Interest converts all the meaning of objects to private terms, their significance for the abstract individual. Consequently, interest is identified with feelings and desires, and subjective states are notoriously intractable to order or organization. The legislature as an organ of the public body is not representative of interests or interest groups, nor are these groups the locus of aspects of the public will. There is no such thing as class legislation or legislation on behalf of any interest, that is, when it is true legislation. The object of legislation is culture, not men or their interests.[22] If a group is a functional group, then it is not an interest group; moreover, if it is a functional group, its justification for being, its rights and obligations, all lie in the nature of its end as cultural, and "its" end is in no way private but Personal.

Jordan would not be in agreement with those who argue that geographical representation be replaced by that of interest groups. He stands strongly opposed to the idea that law can be made out of a conflict of interests or wills. As individualistic and private, the latter cannot be brought to harmony, while real law is the tendency toward unity of individuated wills in a higher personality.[23] Contract, not conflict or struggle, is the basic law of life. Speculation harmonizes the ideas which are embodied in various institutions and fits together all their constructive functions, so that their wills are joined to their mutual benefit.

Interest and right are not identical, but are inherently opposed to each other; interest refers to private expropriation, and right refers to appropriation to public function. Culture cannot be made intelligible on the basis of interest, with which it has nothing to do. What, asks Jordan, do such aspects of culture as art, religion, and ultimately politics have to do with interest? The interest state is a contradiction. If culture is to survive and progress, interest must be abandoned and disinterest must take its place. Such culture as we currently have and shall have is detached from interest and allied to disinterestedness. A rational public order depends upon a harmonizing of interests only in the sense that the private is viewed as the raw data of contemporary disorder, to be converted into public and universal ends, and not to be allowed to dominate and pervert such ends to private advantage.[24] An "interest" in cultural ends, such as health, art, and the like, is a purpose and not an interest at all, since it is public in nature. The only relationship that interest has to culture is a negative or destructive one, and when culture comes under the control of interest, as it has under the dominion of business, then culture is doomed; art is debased to "commercial art." Jordan declares that the choice is between interest and culture; in our time, between business and culture.

The present outcome of the belief that the state is a harmony of interests is a state dominated by organized interest and turned into an instrument of private advantage. Far from interest being able to furnish the design of the state or the law of its order, it continuously and everlastingly guarantees that there shall be no law or state. The subjectivity of interest renders it the enemy of law and order, inapplicable as a practical category. Even if it be argued that interest is not subjective but objectifies itself in property, which, to be sure, is the basis of public order, nevertheless property is here viewed as private and hence cannot serve as a principle of law but only as its disruption. Consequently, despite the materialization of interest in property, property itself remains subjective and its current "organization" disorganizes the state. Property objectifies itself as corporate rather than private, and it is the basis of social order only when it performs a public function.[25]

The effort to unify the state through unifying mental states, all men becoming "of one mind," is mistaken. It is not possible for people to be all of one mind; neither is it necessary or even desirable. In any case, public order is not a matter of a consensus of subjective states, but rather of objective life or life as objectified in institutions. The goal of thought is an object, which once realized becomes generally accepted as the precondition of all persons in their practical lives and thus becomes an institution. Such an object is independent of states of mind; it does not require the agreement of individuals in order to be sustained as a reality. Consensus or majority vote constitutes no reals. The acceptance of an object as an end does not depend upon conscious agreement as long as individuals preconceive it as end in their activity, like the complementary efforts of husband and wife in the care of the home. This acceptance is often quite unconscious and grows out of common experience in the common natural-cultural environment. Even when men consciously disagree, as in many university departments, they may still act harmoniously together. In any case, agreement is not important as a practical concept.[26] Institutions and states do not rise or fall on its presence or absence.

The speculative task requires a body of men endowed by nature and culture with the necessary capacities and abilities. Who these men shall be is in the laps of the gods. From what Jordan says, it appears that these elect will not be elected. Presumably, as with many other functions today (e.g., those of the various professions), the question of choice will be solved through a recognition of the nature of the position or office, the "job specification," on the one hand, and the competence of the individual to perform the required act, on the other; likewise, their development will be the task of a rational educational system. These philosophers are not kings, if kingship implies sovereignty. Jordan is attempting to avoid sovereignty as a power conception of politics and law. Nor are such men representative of anything or anyone—the farmer, the businessman, the consumer, or others. If one is to speak in terms of representation at all, then this body represents cultural ends and these alone, and since ends are the antithesis of interest or private advantage, the legislature is not a composition of interests or of representatives of interests. If the philosopher-king conception has any validity, its meaning is that political life shall be rational and culture maintained at as high a level as possible. The principle says nothing, however, as to the nature of the political act in a specific case; neither does it point to a particular class of persons as peculiarly fitted for the legislative function.[27] There is nevertheless an aristocracy of mind involved in public order, but this is not essentially a matter of individual men.

. . . the basis of political order is the simple idea of an aristocracy
of mind established upon a basis of corporate social fact as the
medium in which that mind works. This social fact is in its primary
substance the property system as informed with the principle of the
public will, and it is only in its superficial aspects that it can be described in terms of states of mind and of experiences of men. And the
aristocracy of mind is not primarily a selection of individual men; it
is rather the system of cultural institutions which gives meaning to the
property system and determines the directions in which the constructive will-energy of the property system is to be expended in the
realization of ends. Legislation in the strict sense, then, is the intellectual process incorporate in cultural institutions within this aristocracy as it brings itself to the fullness of ideas. These ideas thus fulfilled are the laws of life, and bind us because they are the product of
life in its highest forms, which are aspects of the perfect state.[28]

Speculation develops the grand design of what may be and
ought to be in the form of an idea, which action must effect.
Through legislation there is a control of action on behalf of objects as the ends which are to be brought into existence. The end
envisaged is both the object in which action issues and the whole
for which it is undertaken, and so becomes the object of desire.
It is in this capacity for translating the speculative ideal into the
sphere of feeling that the ideal, in a sense, takes hold of men
and controls their action or provides the law of their conduct.
Design gives form to the material provided by passion, which
by itself is formless. Raw feeling is indeed lawless, but when
infused with reason it combines idea and substance or material
into the formed object. Design operates to develop not only
formed objects, but also orders of such objects. For Jordan, feeling is substance, and passion is quite literally regarded as passive
material to be formed. Idea provides the form or active design,
feeling the material or passive design. Law as idea becomes
realized in material, and that material is provided by the plasticity
of feeling motivated under the influence of the end. The design
developed in speculation brings reason and desire to ordered
harmony.[29]

The speculative phase of legislation is completed by promulgation, the process by which law becomes effective in the intelligence of men. Legislation has the function of clarifying public
issues as well as of defining public ends in terms which make
them understandable to the citizen and which engage his active
support. The needs of individuals, often vaguely felt, must be

identified with such issues and recognized as elements of public ends. As a corollary to these functions of clarification and definition, there is the additional function of implementing the ideas in and through appropriate organs, which are primarily the administrative and judicial agencies. Speculation, it is true, must be carried on by a specialized body of men qualified for the task, but it is essential that the specialized intelligence also inform the intelligence of the citizenry, which is largely occupied with practical techniques. While the legislature then formulates the design of the state, the "common sense" of the people about fundamental moral ideas may be relied upon to actuate particular applications of policy. Jordan emphasizes that in speaking of intelligent men or bodies of men, the important concept for legislation is not men but intelligence as a practical category, which as such must be stated in universal form. He argues that this is the meaning of democracy's insistence that education be universal, a recognition that large public ends cannot be realized until these ends embody an intelligent society or a society of intelligent persons.[30]

Jordan is concerned about the cultism of specialization and says that the legislator of the future will be the man who is competent in *any* field. His activity as a legislator will consist in performing those functions which are the proper expression of that capacity. This modifies the Platonic principle that each man should know his work and stick to his last by requiring that the individual be competent practically. Only the incompetent have no political function.[31] However, Jordan stresses the need for particularly qualified men for the legislative task and suggests that political order depends upon society maintaining such a group of free and independent thinkers. It is a particular responsibility of the educational system to see to the development of such competent individuals. The hope of democracy in universal education, according to Jordan, has not been borne out by the results as far as the development of an intelligent citizenry is concerned. Yet education remains the best hope. What is needed is education that escapes from narrow technical pursuits and from the dominance of private forces and individualized interests in order to return to its public function.[32]

There are generally two ways by which the law is promulgated, the first of which is the *subjective* method of education, whose mode is persuasive in its appeal to the experiences of men. The agencies through which the appeal is made include not only the formal educational institution, but also such agencies as the church, government itself, the radio, press, etc., all of those which in fact are able to promote respect for law. Such agencies have generally operated on the false assumption that cultural effects can be produced by changes in the mental states of persons. Moreover, where they have come under the control of private interests, the subjective, individualized emphasis upon need and want satisfaction has been emphasized. Under such conditions education does not succeed in preparing individuals for active participation in the public life, and therefore fails of its purpose.[33] Nevertheless, it appears that education as promulgation of law should develop the intelligence and enlist the desire of men in support of ideas or ends, but should also be aware of the ever-present danger of falling into subjectivity, the appeal of ends being so closely related to feeling. The *objective* method of promulgation is directed not to the experiences of men as such but to institutions, in which the ideas are objectified through the method of administration. The ideas are incorporated in public instruments and thus become operative in public life. The threat of subjectivity here lies in the danger that public instruments will be perverted to private interest.[34] Administration must be much more broadly conceived than it usually is, so that it will include not merely those agencies associated with government but *all those which perform public functions even though they be regarded as private agencies. The need is to convert these functions to public instruments.* Such agencies in private hands prevent the full implementation of law and in fact stand directly in its way, yet these are appropriate instruments of promulgation. All institutions—industrial, recreational, etc.—as public bodies promulgate the law by bringing it directly to bear upon the individual's thought and action. Administration is public throughout.[35]

Legislation as Administration

The experimentation which in the speculative phase of legislation takes place under logical conditions as a trial of ideas becomes empirical in the administrative stage under conditions of time and cause. This is not to imply that administration is a mechanical process involving no thought, but to indicate its distinctive function as that of actualizing in the world those ideas developed in speculation. The ideas are to be enacted, not just thought. Reason must meet experience, the rational will become effective will, ends find their means. In the administrative process of experimentation in the laboratory of society, all these are joined, and the image or vision becomes a reality in objects. The administrator works under the guidance of the large idealized ends of speculation, and it is particularly his province to take new social experiences in their uniqueness and to fit them within these broad categories. The ideals are hypotheses, not fixed in rigid form, under which the new experiences, in fact any experience, may fall. The administrator, like any other scientific experimenter, has an open mind, not one that is devoid of idea but one which constantly keeps principle in mind and implements facts accordingly. It is, in fact, the characteristic outlook of the experimenter to maintain a flexibility within his concepts, to which the form and character of the facts will give the form needed to fit the larger system of categories as a principle.[36] The administrator can proceed effectively only if he understands the ideas and the world of fact, and can mediate between them. While never losing sight of the whole or of general policy, he must be able to administer a great amount of detail. Therefore, he cannot be the narrowly conceived practical man who is the idol of the present, the man who gets things done in behalf of interest. Disinterested himself, he must prevent interests from interfering with public life. His responsibility is that of realizing ideas or ends, not interests.

The ideas of speculation then are plans of action to be undertaken. They are not mandates from on high, but hypotheses to be tried out in the course of their implementation. In application the ideas developed in speculation may need to be changed as they encounter the hard facts. The administrator is not merely the passive receiver, unquestioningly accepting ideas, but the tester of their efficacy. He is under the obligation to try the idea, but he need not, in fact must not, affirm the unworkable. One of the functions of administration is to react upon the processes of speculation in such ways as may cause a change of policy.[37]

All the phases of legislation are autonomous in the sense of an organizational unity continuous with its end, administration no less than any other. Administration is obligated to an end which is not imposed by speculation but which is essential to its own autonomy. The negation of this obligation would at the same time be self-negation.[38] That speculation transmits ideas for administration to embody, then, does not in any way interfere with the latter's freedom.

The fear of vast multiplication of administrative machinery and administrative law is largely a needless one, according to Jordan, once the nature and function of this aspect of legislation is understood. Administrative law is the essence of state-building, through its conversion of ideas into living actualities in objects. Since it is innately a positive force, it needs to be promoted rather than feared, and if it is to carry out its job, then sufficient apparatus is necessary. The fear of bigness in itself and the destruction of the large corporation are irrational. There is no danger in numbers or amounts, as long as the machinery is needful and appropriate. The failure to provide the necessary tools for growth will mean that social purpose will remain an abstract ideal because it will lack implementation. Administrative agencies will require co-ordination, but this does not call for restrictive external control.

There is no need to fear that administrative agencies will get out of hand and become tyrannical if they are appropriated to their proper functions. That is what control through business or interest fails to do, and hence the danger in such agencies. Part of the task of speculation is the recognition of the conditions under which administrative autonomy may be assured through the development of spontaneity or self-control. Administrative bodies achieve this when they become corporate persons.[39] Such control as exists "from without" is that exercised by the influence of ideals. The obligation of administration to these ends is at the same time the ground of its own freedom. Self-negation is the consequence when the public end of the agency is not upheld by its personnel, e.g., the recent failure of regulatory commissions to function.

One of the chief obstacles to administration is the fact that its instruments are often not adapted to its functions, as, for example, when property is identified with interest rather than with end. If administration is to achieve the ends for which it is designed, speculation must convert property to a public function, in which case it will then be an appropriate instrument of administration. Maladministration may occur for a number of reasons, including that of incompetent personnel, but Jordan feels that the major difficulty standing in the way of good administration is the property system in its individualized form. As they now exist, propertied interests often control administrative agencies and prevent them from developing their own spontaneity. Public agencies must be divorced from private interest, and the speculative body, in developing ends and designing instruments for their realization by administration, assures the proper control of the latter.[40]

Far from fearing the machinery of administration or administrative law, Jordan suggests that the administrative system may itself be considered as end. In the first instance the perfect society as a system of means appropriated to their ends would need to have all of its processes mechanized as a stage of rationalization. All the processes themselves would be necessary, since all those which were unnecessary would have been eliminated in the progressive appropriation of the growth function. Consequently, every purpose would have its embodiment in an appropriate organ, the organ itself having autonomy as a machine well fitted to its function. Means as machines are necessary to the attainment of ends, and if ends be thought of as peculiarly the realm of autonomy, then mechanism is necessary to autonomy. Thus a relation of dependence becomes a relation of identity or unity, and this is an example of purpose realized.[41]

It is . . . through the mechanisms of growth as effective order [that] an active identity is established between means and end, and a complete appropriation effected between administrative mechanism and the system of ends which as values is represented as social or public life. Adequate or rational administration is thus itself an end, and, in a significant sense, *the* end as practical.[42]

Administrative bodies as autonomous are not externally controlled, either by speculative or judicial agencies or by their own executives. They simply do not need to be run by anybody, perhaps least of all by executives, who in Jordan's view are without function. The executive is not a figure of authority or power, since these belong not to him but to the law. He is not the law, but a symbol of the law and its greatness. He does not order the administrative functions into unity, since this occurs automatically when there is appropriation to proper function by the speculative body. The executive might stand as a symbol or representative of the public will, representing to that will, which is engaged largely in technical processes, the moral significance of these processes in their unity. Men are already governing when they perform their technical tasks competently; the executive can then symbolize through the majesty of his office the assurance that their competence is contributing to the whole good. However, Jordan says that the intelligent citizen recognizes that there is no special function for the executive and so permits him none. Jordan believes that actual tendencies are toward the complete elimination of the executive as not only useless but as a positive danger, a usurper of rights which are not his. Either he tends to become a nonentity, or else he becomes a dictator or an instrument of the most powerful private interests.[43]

Administrative agencies do not need any bosses from within or without. They run themselves when rightly principled and organized, often despite their "heads." [44] Jordan cites the case of the postal service, which manages to function well despite the fact that it is headed generally by an incompetent "politician." One of the great causes of maladministration is to be found in the exaltation of the executive, not only in officially recognized public agencies but also in those great bodies, the "private" corporations, which are in fact public and a very important aspect of public administration, far more important perhaps than government itself. Yet dictatorship is not a principle and supplies no law, and the executive as dictator needs to be eliminated as an excrescence on the body politic. Autocracy must be discarded.

In his reaction against the role of the executive there is little doubt that Jordan is scoring the abuses of executive power which seem omnipresent in the officialdom of industrial, educational, and public agencies of various types. Nevertheless, it may be more accurate to interpret his meaning in the following terms: that if we must choose between the executive who views himself as the individual source of law and authority, will and action, on the model of a despot, and the executive as an impotent figurehead, the representative for simpler minds of the doings of a great corporate body, such as the monarchy in England,

then the latter is much to be preferred. However, both conceptions are false to Jordan's general theory of administration as an
integral part of the legislative act. The very fact that Jordan
gives to administration a distinguishable place within the process,
and stresses the great growth and positive import of administrative agencies of all types, suggests that the executive has a responsible function, requiring an ability that may be distinguished
from the speculative and judicial functions.

The executive executes policy. He is not the speculator, and so
he does not create policy in idea; nor as administrator is he involved in the direct doing of things (the teaching and research
of educational agencies or the work with objects produced by
industrial corporations). His position is analogous to that of the
general contractor in the building of a home. The ideal of the
house is ordered by the architect as speculator, who creates a
plan in conformity to the objective end of family life, but the
architect is responsive to suggestions (popular origination) from
the particular family for whom the home is constructed. The
architect as a result of his greater knowledge accepts, modifies,
or rejects the specific suggestions from the family in terms of the
proper articulation of the home. The general contractor is in
charge of the practical achievement of the objective, and in order
to realize the speculative ideal, the plans of the house, he must
have the qualities necessary to perfom a number of functions.

First, he must be able to grasp intellectually the ideal, so that
the spirit of the enterprise is always before him. Without complete understanding, the ability to achieve is hindered.

Second, he must know how to relate and integrate objects and
men so that the goal may be achieved in the real world. This
requires that he be sensitive to the direct doings of the sub-
contractors and accessible to them, the men on the front line of
action, as well as of the family itself, since conditions may arise
which were unanticipated when the plans were drawn up. In
terms of personality, this requires that he be capable of decisive
action. He must be competent to make on-the-job revisions in
terms of the new conditions after discussion with the subcon-
tractors and/or family, but consistent with the spirit of the
original policy, and to take the problem back to the architect
for final disposition if necessary. In other words, the executive
function is a mediating link between the policy-making body

and the working body. He translates the plans to the working staff and determines which of their ideas about conditions need to be transmitted back to the speculative body. Many of these ideas he can dispose of, but others may require important policy changes or modifications of plan.

Third, as has been implied above, the executive views each implementation of policy experimentally, since life is such that unanticipated realities may stubbornly contradict what seem to be our best ideas. Principle may need to be modified, or facts approached in another way, so that idea and reality may come to living terms with each other.

If on the one hand the executive as mediator understands the policy formulation, on the other hand he sets up within the administrative process the means by which to evaluate the outcome, in order to correct such errors as may have been made and prevent future ones from occurring. The mere technical completion of the house according to plan does not finish the business of administration, since continued checking with the family (consumer, citizen, etc.) is needful to determine how successful the speculative conception and its administration have been and where either may have fallen short. Then a fourth characteristic of the executive is his alertness to and respect for careful evaluations of agency process, function, and accomplishment. While the judiciary in the formal sense, as we shall see, makes the final judgment of the speculative and administrative parts of the legislative act, administration needs its own built-in evaluative devices, such as grievance committees and "consumer research" departments of industry, but principled by the public good. Administration objectifies idea, and the act is best controlled in idea prior to its objectification. Even the majesty of the office of the judiciary cannot, through learned pronouncements, change a *fait accompli;* therefore, the value of intrainstitutional judicial review is in preventing errors in administration from materializing.

Finally, the executive must be sensitive to the relationships of his corporate agency with the activities of others, since the various organs of life are not to grow at the expense of others but are to be fitted appropriately together. This house may need to be heated or to dispose of its waste differently than originally planned, owing to peculiar local conditions which would lead to an increase in an already overloaded gas or sanitary system. The executive is aware of the relationship of his activity to the whole in which it stands, and he attempts to fit the act to the whole as the ultimate law of his act. Ideally, then, the executive is no mere technician interested in personal aggrandizement, but a culturally oriented person with technical competence in the effective integration of men and materials, and with skills in facilitating communication along all levels of the act.

Thus if autocracy will not do, neither will the democratic conceptions of administration, which Jordan also denounces as subjective. Here Jordan finds, among other things, a neglect of *expertise*. Furthermore, despite the stated experimental character of democracy, its subjective presuppositions make interest a practical category and thus make experimentation impossible. One of Jordan's major criticisms of democracy is its failure to be an experimental politics. Lacking principle, democratic administration can only be hazard or adventure rather than experimentation.[45] In effect, Jordan is saying that experimentation is not possible, either under logical conditions or under factual conditions, within democratic conceptions, so that the speculative and administrative functions of the legislative process cannot be carried out. Since policy is not interpretable in terms of interest, insisting on the attempt to do so makes experimentation impossible and is responsible for the fact that "democracy has not been tried." The failures of democracy at the levels of policy and practice stem from its insistence that reality is a state of mind. What is "represented" in all phases of the legislative process is culture, the ends of life overtly manifested in corporate bodies, rather than interest, the reference backward of "ideas" to self-advantage.

The new administration is already evident in practice. A good example is the commission type of government used in a number of cities.[46]

. . . It represents a combination of the democratic principle that the whole people ultimately carries political responsibility and all the burdens of policy as well as decides the major questions of political method, with the aristocratic principle that the performance of a function should be put into the hands of the individual who can perform it best from the technical point of view and in consistency with principles of policy as laid down. It is clearly a recognition that the ultimate administrative responsibility rests upon the person who assumes to be competent to attain a view of the whole situation where action is required and who occupies a position giving the best vantage point for that view. It is also assumed that a man may possess the competency of an expert in the superintendence of vast complexity of detail and at the same time appreciate the significance of general policy and the mutual bearing of policy and factual situations upon each other. It is also an attempt to find a middle course between the narrowness of the specialist and the incompetence of the masses, and to show that democratic equality is not incompatible with aristocratic competence.[47]

However, the idea of equality rightly exalted in democratic theory needs to be redefined. Political equality has been vitiated by economic inequality, and rights have become abstract because the concrete means to their realization have been denied. It is once more a case of the need to allocate property to public function, so that there may be the economic equality of opportunity to function which will assure individuals a ready access to necessary means or "goods" in accordance with their capacity. The new administration would undertake to develop that capacity to its fullest through education, so that the most complete access to the good might be possible.[48]

How would the disinterested, public-spirited, and technically competent administrator be produced? Jordan's answer here is the same in principle as for the development of legislators and judges. First, he is optimistic about the emergence of such persons because, even though there is little effort being made in this direction at the present time and in spite of many inimical factors, such administrators are being produced, perhaps largely through the trial and error of experience. Even business executives now worry about their public responsibilities and exhort each other to more public-spirited behavior. Too often, of course, this takes the form of establishing a "public relations" smoke screen, but at least the awareness of new dimensions in administrative responsibility is there. Nevertheless, if the educational system were to deliberately educate for this purpose and acquaint students with corporate theory and the problems and challenges of institutional life, Jordan believes that much greater success would be attained. In addition, since corporate positions are functional, job specifications, including the search for relevant traits of personality, and appropriate merit tests could be worked out by the legislature, administrative and educational agencies, similar to the civil service and professional personnel agencies. A man may now attain the highest administrative positions through subservience to powerful interests, demagoguery, wealth, or simply by being an inoffensive nonentity, but these must be eliminated as criteria of administrative selection. Criteria exist in any case, and what is proposed are more adequate ones. Finally and most importantly, property must be transferred to public status, so that the administrator will automatically identify himself as a public agent, just as he presently identifies himself as the agent of interest. Would any industrial corporation as presently organized in terms of private interest tolerate a public-spirited administrator in a position of real power? How the orderly transference of property to public function may be effected is for Jordan the great problem of political speculation and experimental action.

Legislation as Adjudication

A most significant description of the nature of the legislative process is to be found in Jordan's statement that it is analogous to the procedure by which science takes the immediate, raw data of experience and converts them to knowledge or science.[49] In this process he finds analogies to the three phases of legislation. The first, corresponding to speculation, is the stage of imaginative perception, which grasps the situation of fact in the large and with all its potentialities of organization. This is the phase of pure hypothesis, the tentative formulation of an idea which suggests an action to be undertaken. Secondly, analogous to administration is the doing stage, in which the facts are dealt with under the influence of idea; their relations are tested, not only in terms of their permanence but also in terms of the possibilities of new relations, even though these may involve actually changing the facts. In the third and final stage, similar to that of adjudication, there is a review or assessment of the process and its results to see whether they have been successful, and if they have not, to determine where the trouble lies, whether in the hypothesis or in the active trial. In this way the judiciary is an inevitable part of the legislative process.

The judicial process, which is reflective in nature, appraises the outcome of speculative and administrative experimentation, and in doing so is always testing the constitutionality of the law that has been made in these phases. In a sense, it might be said that the judiciary, or the judicial mind, attempts to see to what extent there has been a meeting of the speculative and administrative minds. It is ultimately the province of the judiciary to declare whether the meeting of idea and fact has been fruitful, and if not, where the fault lies—whether in idea, in application, or in both. The judiciary must therefore judge the quality of ends as well as the efficacy of means. Adjudication does not stand outside the legislative process passing judgment on it, but is itself a part of that process. "Judge-made" law is not usurpation, but precisely a rightful phase of the legislative process. The judicial pronouncement would be usurpation if it were a personal decree of the judge as a natural person, but the law is impersonal; it has nothing to do with personal feelings, convictions, and the like.[50] The law calls upon the judge to put aside such considerations. Even apart from such matters, the judiciary would be abdicating responsibility and thus failing the law were it not to make its distinctive contribution to legislation. To be sure, the autonomy of each of the phases of legislation must be preserved, but this in itself requires that the autonomy of the judicial process as legislative also be recognized. Jordan maintains that the autonomy which is sought perhaps in the separation-of-powers conception is actually secured only when the triune is seen as the unity it is, with each of the phases of the legislative movement distinguished within that unity. Administrative law and judge-made law, viewed impersonally, are necessary aspects of the total act; when they operate positively as particular functions, each is within its rights, not a violator of rights. The error of the traditional view, which has led to the current difficulty with administrative agencies, is that it regards legislation as the sole prerogative of the legislature and fails to see the parts that the executive (administrative) and judicial branches have to play. In Jordan's theory the importance of the legislature is recognized, but as only one of the legislative phases.

The judicial act brings principle and maxim together in a law which simultaneously sustains the practical life in its two phases: as corporate in political institutions and as moral freedom in the individual. It completes the legislative process by which Man through his intelligence takes his destiny into his own hands.[51]

While the language used here in describing the phases of legislation has termed each of them acts, the speculative and judicial "acts" are those of thought, the first coming before the fact and the latter after it. Thought which is speculative at the outset is reflective at the end.[52]

The judicial act consists of more than merely affixing the seal of approval to the work of the legislature and administration. Adjudication is creative, rendering experience whole in the corporate judgment. It harmonizes all the objects and objectives of life into a consistent whole. Even the unintegrated aspects of experience can be conceived only through the instrument of thought operating as a corporate judgment. Through that judgment life is given whatever unity and order it may have, and the details of life are brought into consistency and harmony so far as it is possible to do so. The fragmentary character of experience is subjected to the authority of order under a law that operates in the name of the wholeness of life. Experience can be made intelligible only through the corporate judgment. Otherwise, experiences are mere scattered facts which cannot even become data without the ordering they receive from the corporate judgment. Experience is simply raw fact incapable of "speaking for itself." Raw experience is life fragmented, without the meaning which it can acquire only when the pieces are put together and each lesser unity is made consistent with and appropriate to the whole as unity.[53] The judiciary takes the various elements and synthesizes them, and in that process, which is the legislative act operating as corporate judgment, order is "born." The judicial act is the principle of ultimate unity in the world and of order in experience.[54] It is the mind enacting into wholeness all of the details of experience.

And when we . . . view the practical act it becomes more evident that its characteristic form is the judicial act, not only because as a judgment it represents the corporeity of the legal order out of which it issues and from which it gets its authority; but we are also reminded that as a judgment it incorporates precisely the reality which, after the act, we know *as* the legal order. That is, it is the act of spontaneity through which the world of fact gives form and order to itself, and lays down the line along which our hypothetical and speculative accounts of reality should follow.[55]

The judiciary is concerned at every point with the whole of life, and its judgment constitutes or wills the unity of the public life or the social order. Its act gives to the law it declares the forms of constitutionality.[56] Knowing is itself constitutional to and constitutive of reality, creative of embodied order. In knowing, man becomes a constitutional factor in social order. In the judicial act institutions are fitted together and all the life forms come to unity. It sees life whole and is able to relate the parts to each other and to the whole. The synoptic judgment which characterizes the judicial function appropriates each institution to every other and gives each institution its characteristic function within and in relation to the functions of other institutions. As an example of this, Jordan cites the case of industry, in which the judiciary balances the claims of the function of labor against those of the material of capital within that institution, and also defines the relations which the institution as a whole may have with other institutions, such as education.[57] Judicial decisions are constitutional decisions. The judiciary declares the law of the order of the whole. The relations to which it refers are not specific but universal. Law that is not universal is simply not law. The law which would refer only to a specific case is "class legislation" and thus a contradiction in terms.[58] It is the antithesis of justice. "Legislation is always, as Plato and Aristotle say, the act of the body politic in its universal form—the *enactment* of principle. . . . The act of polity . . . undertakes to reduce to universality all of the problems arising within the life-whole, and to effect in a final synthesis this whole as a unity." [59] Doing justice in a particular case is a matter of experimentally determining right relations, and this same experimental determination with reference to the system of such relations taken as a whole is politics proceeding to define the constitution of the "just state." [60]

The synthetic character of the judicial act may seem to bring it into close kinship with sociology, but while the latter does attempt to relate those aspects of the practical life with which judicial decision is inevitably concerned, it has no principle for effecting such a synthesis.[61] The judiciary cannot look to sociology for aid in its task. As a philosophical discipline, the law must rely on its own thinking.[62]

An act passed by the legislature is not yet law, nor is it so even though the administration has attempted to effect it in fact. The law is not final until adjudicated. The law passed by the legislature only states what is lawful; it is enabling and permissive in nature, whereas the judicial act synthesizes speculative policy with administrative maxim and thus declares the law as mandatory. When rightly established, the judiciary has a more rational organization than the legislature and possesses a degree of mindedness which makes it an integrated person; its judgment therefore gives to law a more perfect status than that provided by the legislature. Its more rational organization derives from the expertness or technical competence of its members. Consequently, the judicial decision has authority over the acts of the legislature.[63]

That "it is written" cannot be the final word is evident from Jordan's description of the judicial function. The judiciary is not limited to "the law and the evidence" but is a creative body; its judgment is constitutional to reality. The judge must be a thinker and must find the law, not through the resort, eternally retrogressive, to precedent or to *stare decisis*, but by thinking through to principle. The judicial process is evaluative; the law is moral. The judge must look to life rather than away from it if he is to find the law and declare it. Both the speculative and reflective intelligence are bound to the developments taking place within the creativity of the administrative process, and it is in that process that the law lies. It is there that the active reconstitution of society is occurring, and the judiciary will be unqualified to render a judgment unless it recognizes this fact.

In a sense, every case before the judiciary is a fresh one and has unique qualities. It is the task of administration to apply to new experiences the ideas set out in speculation, and the judicial function carries the law to its completion in assessing the new case. However, the case is not to be regarded, after the analytical method, as an unrelated entity. It is always a case of a law and must be referred to the larger sphere of policy or ends for its principle. One of the dangers involved in the judicial function lies in the tendency to regard a particular case as a thing in itself, from which constitutional principle may be derived. All too frequently the case is referred to precedent, its like as previously encountered. The constitution is not simply an induction from similar cases, but is itself the principle on the basis of which the cases must be decided. Hence the case must be referred to the whole as principle; the whole must not be derived from the case. The guiding maxim is located in public policy.[64]

Another difficulty with respect to the judicial function stems from a mistaken notion of the nature of the instruments for embodying social policy. Here it is assumed that the administrative instruments of property are private in nature, a view which is largely responsible for social disorder.[65] If the law is being made in the administrative process, then the judge must recognize that that process is in fact taking place in domains which are regarded as private but which are in fact public, and he must know that private corporations are agencies of public administration. True, the judiciary has increasingly confirmed the public status of property heretofore regarded as private, but it is necessary that this conception be progressively extended to incorporate all property within the public order. For the owner who is at present the final legislative agent and who in fact impedes the law, the judiciary must substitute a qualified agent of the new state, for which a new parliamentary agent and administrative body have largely been found. The naming of such an agent is the fundamental problem of constitutional law which the judiciary must solve,[66] but so far its positivistic approach to the law has led it astray from the consideration of its most serious problems.

The Role of the Citizen

The role of the citizen, deduced from Jordan's corporate theory, is no different in principle from the role of those more directly concerned with legislation. His function is the maintenance and support of the institutional complex to which he is related in an individuated way, and this means that he accepts his responsibilities to concern himself actively with education, government, industry, family, community, church, recreational agencies, art, etc. In his ordinary doings as a constructive member of several corporate bodies, he is part of the legislative act, sustaining or bringing into being the various elements of the state. The business of the citizen, whether he consciously formulates it in these terms or not, is always state business because it exists within and influences the corporate bodies which themselves comprise the state. Therefore, the citizen's basic responsibility is to perform his several corporate functions as parent, worker, church member, community member, etc., as intelligently as possible. All the personal virtues of a "mature," "good," "decent," "moral," "responsible" neighbor and citizen will accrue to him as a result. This does not mean, however, that the citizen slavishly accepts whatever is as right. His sensibilities and ideas must help him to distinguish which choices in life sustain and perfect or contradict and destroy the institutional order. Said another way, the citizen as citizen identifies the good of the public life with his own personal good and acts accordingly. The ancient Greeks believed that the man who has only "private" business in reality has no business as a man.

Democratic theory rightly holds that the people as a whole are to contribute to the political process, but the meaning of this principle must be extended beyond their relationships to formal organs of government and the vote; it must apply to the whole institutional life in which they live. As greater or lesser participants in the activities of industry, the school system, the church, recreational organizations, etc., and as consumers of services and products, they must take part in the evaluation of all corporate action. In opposition to the metaphysical assumption of democratic theory, and of empiricists and logical positivists strictly opposed to metaphysical assumptions, the value of natural individuals and their views is not innate but is a consequence of their relation to action. It is because people are integrally related to action, and not because they possess metaphysical value prior to action, whether or not they act, that they should be heard. Citizens who have no special training, but who are thinking about what they are doing, may be capable of occasional brilliant insights; therefore, lines of communication must always be open within the various corporate bodies to allow the policy proposals of the *demos* to be received and evaluated within the legislative process. Nevertheless, whether policy proposals have a democratic or aristocratic origin, the disposition of the proposal is a function of the intelligence of the legislative bodies. Where an ordinary citizen is consistently responsible for intelligent policy proposals, then he should be advanced to a position where he may perform a function consistent with his ability, and the technical means for "advancement from the ranks" must be worked out for each corporate body. The point is that intelligence, however and wherever it may appear, should be fitted to its proper office. It is assumed that every citizen's abilities will be developed as fully as possible and that everyone will be capable of performing some function(s) contributory to the whole good, but the democratic thesis that every citizen is inherently capable of the most complicated acts of speculation, administration, and adjudication is expressly denied and held to be an important ingredient in the ever-present weakness of democratic states.

Legislation as Aesthetic Creativity

All citizens in their thoughtful relation to the objects and objectives of life are contributors and, as doers, actively take part in bringing into being the structures of fact with which the legislator must deal; but the legislator oversees the whole. Legislation itself in all its phases, though it proceeds often in a mode of scientific experimentation, is in reality a high art. Harmony is an aesthetic concept; the art of legislation is the harmonization of society's disparate elements into an ordered whole. The legislator's objective is no less than the perfection of the state, the creation of a mutual fitness among the acts of life which compose the whole of action. Since every act, if it is to reach completion, depends ultimately upon the condition of the state, and since true legislation refines, cultivates, and improves that condition, the legislative act is the most responsible of creative acts. It orders the colors of life, their shadings and blendings and harmonious forms; but the canvas is not fixed, and therein lies the perpetual challenge of the art of legislation.

CHAPTER 6
THE OBJECTIVE VIRTUES
OF CULTURE

From the point of view of realizing in fact the ordered world of culture, the political act is of utmost significance. Its objectification is *justice*, the fulfillment and mutual complementariness of the significant acts of institutional persons, and it is in this world as objectified that the fundamental virtues are located. The subjective virtues of the natural individual, the highest of which is the capacity to think, are by themselves incomplete in the sense that whatever may be realized as fact is dependent upon institutional actors. It is in the institutional world that Jordan locates the "objective virtues," and this conception provides the solution to the troublesome question so often debated by Socrates and left darkly answered, namely, the relation of knowledge to virtue. Is virtue knowledge, and if virtue has a relation to knowledge, can it be taught? If the good, as we have already concluded, is determined by the quality of relations to the whole in which a thing stands, then virtue does not refer to some separate and distinct sphere of action. Virtue is not a special activity of man, for its reference is to the relational qualities of any and every act. Virtue has its being and completion in the institutional structure of life as something objective; it is a fact of man's moral-cultural world of action.

The commonly celebrated subjective virtues refer essentially to the traits of natural individuals, and as such the virtues are always partial, incomplete, not appropriately ended. My feelings of *sympathy* lead me to love the sinner, but no act comes out of my forgiving and so he has no need to alter his ways and may in fact be encouraged to continue them. Or my *generosity* may impel me to lend him money which unfortunately enables him to commit more heinous crimes. The subjective virtue of *friendship* results in my pouring my life into a friend, yet he may become part of an army intending to kill me. As a responsible family man and a person with *integrity*, I pay the pharmacy and the doctor for their services to my sick child, but they both use part of my payment to contribute to organizations whose primary function is to maintain artificial restrictions on the availability of pharmaceutical and medical services. I may have every conceivable subjective virtue, even that of intelligence, and everything I do may still issue in immoral consequences. Thoreau knew that it was a moral obligation for every citizen to pay his taxes; his rebellion was against the abuse of his contribution when it was used for purposes of war. He found it better to retreat to the simplicities of nature than to become part of a monstrous crime which he was helpless to prevent or alter in any significant way.

Virtue, then, cannot be taught, since the virtue of the individual's acts exists through its corporate embodiment in the world, and this suggests that no subjective capacity, including knowledge, can achieve virtue in an immoral world. Not to pay the pharmacist, the doctor, or the tax bill has its immoral consequences as well. Then virtue has to do fundamentally with right relations in the whole of life and not exclusively with the mind and character of natural individuals. The desire for integrity still present in an advertising functionary is praiseworthy and pathetic. Institutions must be virtuous. For my life to be virtuous, the institutional ends which I help to realize in the life process must be right, since virtue is not achieved immediately in any experience which the individual may have, but mediately through the objectified world of action. Hence the Socratic paradox: if virtue is knowledge, why can it not be taught, and why do not good fathers necessarily have good sons? is resolved, for virtue in its most genuine form inheres in the order culture has taken; hence the role of knowledge is not primarily that of exhorting virtuous feelings in people, but of guiding and building up the objective order. Not merely the complete act, but the completely virtuous act, is a property of institutional order—the good son is such by virtue of his institutional parenthood.

The objective virtues, the moral qualities Jordan finds as fact in culture, are wisdom, temperance, courage, and justice.

Wisdom

Knowledge becomes wisdom only when it is implemented in institutional structures. Knowledge not capable of objectification in public instruments of culture can never be wisdom; thus the knowledge of chemistry which contributes to preparations for war can never be wisdom,[1] since no knowledge is wise which destroys the social structure. Furthermore, knowledge as merely mental, as primarily existent in minds and books alone, is not yet wisdom. Political knowledge, for example,

. . . becomes political *wisdom* when it is made practically effective in and through the forms of political and civil organization, since in this form it gives body to habits and customs, and so becomes an actual part of the acts and purposes of men. So long as such knowledge is mere science, classified and organized knowledge, it is a product of the abstract intellect and is yet to be given meaning in terms of experience by actual application. The application is effected by giving it means of expression in political machinery. . . . As such it is there as a fixed and permanent good, organized into the texture of institutions, available to any who care to make use of it; and we recognize it as the 'wisdom of our fathers' because it comes to us as a heritage.[2]

Knowledge, as an individual attribute, is to be distinguished from wisdom, since the latter refers to the objective order which life has taken and which has been tested in the experience of the race. The intelligence which has laid out the transportation system is now wisdom, for it is an objective factor in bringing the act of any cultural agent competent to use it to a successful conclusion. Its very presence is the ground for the suggestion of acts otherwise not thinkable. The possibilities of actualizing intelligence in the individual and realizing it in the world are grounded upon knowledge already made effective—wisdom.

Temperance

Temperance is the organization of life tendencies in the objective world in such a way that the instincts and impulses characteristic of life may receive effective expression. According to Jordan, the commonly held notion that there is an internal psychic will which through its own force and power is able to repress and "control" the expression of life urges is mistaken, since this view "implies a mysterious power which can operate upon the vital facts of impulse and instinct directly, or through a means which the controlling power develops for each occasion." [3] The mystery is how the individual, who is reduced to a ghostlike housing in which mental functions directly operate upon one another, is able to control himself by his self, and no source of such power has ever been found in him. The failure even of the abstract intelligence of the individual to control his active life is chronic and leads to disillusionment and the establishment of specialized agencies of repression, but it is the purely subjective interpretation of temperance that is at fault. Simply to name the controlling entity "will" or "intelligence" is not yet an explanation of its presence and development in the individual.[4]

The source of control has already been suggested in the discussion of institutional will and action, for the individual's volitional tendencies occur and achieve structure through the features of the culture within which the individual has his being.

A man is ensconced in a matrix of institutions which are of extraordinary complexity, and his 'will' is his and is free in the fact that it is the will uniquely conferred upon him by his relations to his natural and cultural circumstances. The mechanism of control in human relations, both individual and general, is this system of institutions. Through it such changes are made in human life and human nature as can be made, and the problem of temperance or the control of life is a problem of understanding the methods of operation and *modus vivendi* of these institutions, and the 'social' and 'political' control that is possible is effected through the same institutions. We can illustrate this doctrine of objective will and objective control by use of the sex 'instinct' and the family.

Left to itself as the procreative urge of the individual, the sex 'instinct' would express itself without reference to its object, its end, or any consequence. This we see is what happens in the case of the animals. The individual man often, however, does not control his sex instinct, and it is probable that few men would 'control their lusts' if their only means of control were their capacity to think. Relieve the man of the influence of the home, the club, the church, the professional or industrial connection, and his reason will be a poor support under temptation. Without this institutional support a mere idea, no matter how attractive or how demonstrably true, will sooner or later disappear; and with a competent institution behind it a mere superstition persists indefinitely.[5]

The temperate character of the individual is maintained through the harmonious way in which he takes his place in the institutional complex. Through the normal exercise of his various "needs," as structured within the proficient activity of the institutions of life, it rarely occurs to him that he has "basic needs" for sex, food, shelter, clothing, affection, security, etc.; but where institutions do not function appropriately, intemperance becomes the rule.

A community living in extreme poverty or extreme wealth will rot in sexual corruption. And a community in which excessive strictness is enjoined by social custom or religious or 'moral' tradition, and conformity expected through self-control, will find occasional individuals requiring readaptation which can never be effected under the conditions. A cultured existence is not possible where there is a violent conflict between nature and culture, and such conflicts can be avoided only through institutional control, by which we mean the adaptation of the institutions of life to the adequate and appropriate exercise of all functions natural or cultural.[6]

Here Jordan is criticizing the institutionalization of intemperance in corporate structures. It is the objective existence of poverty, discriminatory race relations, sovereign nation-states, business domination over industry, government, and the mass media, etc., which leads to the subjective intemperance of class conflict, rape and lynching, the bitterness of strikes and unemployment, the frenzy of war, and the passion for luxurious living.

What must be allowed the individual is the opportunity for the full and free expression of every normal capacity. This will leave no room or necessity for intemperate modes of behavior. *Self-control,* far from being the negation of the self, *is action directed at realizing the individual's varied capacities.* When institutions co-operate in this endeavor, the result is the objective virtue of temperance, and the intelligence which effects it is instrumented in political institutions.[7]

Courage

Courage, subjectively conceived as the capacity of the individual to hold fast in the midst of danger, presupposes a condition in which the individual faces the world alone.[8] However, such an individual is not yet man; man confronts the world in his corporate being. In fact, it is through the development of corporate human nature that the occasions for fear are prevented from arising in the first place. Beasts of prey do not stalk the city streets. Thus if a brave man may be taken to be the man who in the active conduct of his life never feels fear, then courage has been institutionalized in the world created by action. It is in this sense that planning ahead for adequate social security measures, medical services, and housing for the aged is helpful in reducing the fear so many have of growing older. Similarly, the fears of workingmen induced by the dislocations accompanying the growth of automation may be considerably reduced through intelligent planning.

The "courage" commonly thought to be an individual virtue may simply refer to the rashness or folly with which the individual places himself in situations of danger. That is why Jordan completely concurs with Plato's definition of courage—a "knowledge of things that are to be feared and of things that are not to be feared," [9] meaning thereby that when man has knowledge of things, he need have no fear that his act will not be significant, but when he has no knowledge and must act nevertheless, his awkwardness, impulsiveness, even cowardice is typically a reflection of his ignorance. Then the best that may be said of courage as an individual virtue is that it represents the development of intelligence in the individual who has been habituated in the course of his early life to act on the basis of knowledge. However, the development of such an individual is predicated upon the existence of competent institutions whose influence has enabled him to acquire a character organized so as to act upon reflection.[10]

Courage is an objective virtue because it is an attribute of the ordered world; out of his relations to it flow the active impulses of the individual. Courage represents his determined obligation to sustain the whole good with all his being.[11]

Justice

Virtue completely developed in a wise and temperate and courageous public life and established in appropriate institutions is culture. Culture organized and unified within the political state and given effective power by and in law is justice.[12]

Justice is simply the principle of wholeness or completion of things, i.e., the perfect realization of all human ends in harmonious accord with one another is perfect justice. Justice is not a special act or pronouncement encountered in a court of law, but the qualitative synthesis of all acts. That is, the act which may be adjudged a just act is one which fits into the scheme of things in such a way as to sustain the whole of action. Justice, then, is a type of relational complex to be maintained and developed so that the whole of life activities may go on; it is not something "got" or "had" by the individual.[13] Realizing one's interest, in which a particular is the point of reference for the act, and realizing justice, in which the whole is the point of reference for the act, are polar opposites for Jordan.[14]

In the state of justice peace and order are real, for in this state the individual has both the subjective capacity and objective opportunity to perform significant acts. That is, he is harmoniously integrated in the active life; he lives in a world which collaborates with his purposes; his acts may be realized.[15] In it he has "positive freedom" because the institutional world provides him with the "access to whatever is necessary to enable the person to perform significant acts." [16] Justice is the institution of the good in the constitution of the world. It is morality embodied. Justice and culture—the harmonious order of the corporate world—are one.

CHAPTER 7
TOTALITARIANISM, DEMOCRACY, AND CORPORATISM

In our Introduction the problem of the meaning and significance of corporatism was raised, partially in terms of the relation of corporatism to totalitarianism and democracy, but ultimately in terms of its relation to the nature of cultural reality itself. It was shown that ideologies as hostile to each other as totalitarianism and democracy were identified with corporate theory. The exposition of Jordan's philosophy of culture in Chapters 1 to 6 indicates his overt rejection of both these ideologies, most fundamentally because of their misconception of the nature of society. A further clarification of Jordan's corporatism, particularly with reference to totalitarianism, may be helpful, however, before we proceed to the discussion of the significance of his theory of culture for educational theory and practice.

Is Jordan's Corporatism Totalitarian?

Corporatism has most often been identified with totalitarianism and the totalitarian state, whether fascist or some other variation, and Jordan's theory as a type of corporatism has also been called totalitarian. At times this criticism has been associated with the allegation that he is an Hegelian. Jordan has responded to this charge by saying that he has never been a serious student of Hegel, but that if the criticism is meant to imply a serious concern with and respect for ideas, then he pleads guilty.[1] Between empiricism and its facts on the one hand and rationalism and its ideas on the other, Jordan finds little to choose, for only by holding to both can an adequate theory be formulated. His conception of culture as objective mind forbids the exclusion of either. Ideas are real but are not the only realities, nor are the realities of life mere ideas. The structure of society is a hard fact, in the absence of which ideas would be mere mental phenomena.

It does not appeal strongly to me to argue that respect for ideas and for the Idea, which is good title to 'Idealism,' is necessarily involved in such distinctions. Many things are real besides ideas, even if nothing is true or real in the absence of ideas.[2]

Jordan frequently uses the phrase "with respect to the Ideas" to indicate an ordering of life in accordance with that ideality which is reality, but this never means for him an abstract archetype but a living fact. While undoubtedly Jordan's theory, as a reformulation of idealism, has affinities with that philosophy, it differs at several important points from what is generally taken to be that position. Jordan, for example, does not observe a cosmic dialectic at work leading to some foreordained end; neither does he see a continuous unfolding of Absolute Spirit or Reason. His distress as he contemplates what passes for the state in contemporary society and his bitter criticism of existing public affairs are evidence of his rejection of the view that what is is right. Jordan is very critical of present "states," since they are largely "power states," supreme sovereigns, war-makers and destroyers of law and social order, rather than agencies of culture, and hence hardly states at all.

According to Jordan, all genuine philosophy since Anaxagoras has assumed that the real is ideal. Unfortunately, under the influence of empiricism this assumption was transformed into "the real is idea," and more recently into "the real is a state of mind."[3] Jordan accepts the view that reality is ideal and that "the state is the reality of the moral idea," but this does not commit him to the belief that anything going by the name of the state today is in reality that. No such implication necessarily follows, and it is in fact what he wishes to avoid. His criticism of existing so-called states is that they are not true states or that they are such only to the limited degree to which they are one with culture. Rather than exaltation of the *status quo*, what is needed is profound criticism, and even when the worst features are changed into constructive elements, it will be necessary to experiment continuously and everlastingly. Hence, the *status quo* is not the ultimate definition of the good life, since the institutional world is never a finished piece of thought and work. Life constantly falls short of the ideal, even as the sole reason for men's efforts lies in attempting to realize it. The everlasting disjunction between the existent and the ideal creates the need for action. The

meaning of an idea is determined by its "intent" or by its portent.[4] The real state is the ideal state, the state of culture, but this
means that it is one which is to be realized continuously rather
than one which already exists or will come into being and never
require alteration.[5] The open society requires continuous effort
at improvement, and the task is never done.

When Jordan affirms the Platonic idea that the institutions of
life need to be understood rather than reformed,[6] he does not
thereby propose a fixed or closed society, any more than he
does when he cautions men to become aware that they stand
in the presence of the constitution of things when they stand, as
they always do, amid their institutions. It is to no fixed ideas that
the state conforms; life refuses to stay within the bounds of men's
doctrines and is forever running beyond them. Jordan, perhaps
characteristically, speaks in two ways on this point. He sometimes argues that institutions need to be understood rather than
changed, by which he means to suggest that man needs to know
their nature and not violate it. At other times, he states the urgent
need to modify existing institutions, so that they will be appropriated to their purposes.[7] One can, then, either say, for example, that we do not need to change education but to understand
it, or that what passes for education today is not truly that and
consequently the institution needs to be altered. In both
cases Jordan means the same thing; in neither instance is he
proposing a fixed society, but rather one that is continuously
reconstituted, although always possessing a constitution in its
institutions.

At some points Jordan's criticism of Hegel has been explicit.
He says that while Hegel saw, as Kant did not, that the formal
character of universality is identity rather than quantity, he did
not "see that identity must be concrete, that is, must instance
the universal, not in, but *as* the particular individuated as a corporate whole. Only this concept of the corporeity of the real
can save us from abstraction and subjectivity here. . . ."[8] Hence
Jordan's acceptance of the concrete universal does not imply an
acceptance of Hegel's view nor of the political inference often
drawn from it, i.e., that the state as the universal dominates the
individual as the particular. His rejection of nominalism is at the
same time a rejection of realism and on the same grounds: the

fallacious conception of reals, whether conceived as particulars or as universals, as things in themselves. If atomism is subject to the fallacy of misplaced concreteness in the form of the particular, as Whitehead has described it, then organicism is subject to the fallacy of misplaced universality. The doctrine of the concrete universal, as Jordan defines it, incorporates both in a synthesis, and the real is then a union of particular-universal,[9] a concept which carries with it the most significant implications for social theory.

The political philosophy which Jordan favors must be distinguished from that of Hegel. Haynes warns against identifying Jordan with such neo-Hegelian political theory as that represented by Bosanquet.[10] Schneider also cautions against dismissing Jordan as an objective idealist.

The language which Jordan employs is reminiscent of Hegel and objective idealism, but it would be a serious mistake to label his philosophy as idealistic or to see in it merely a restatement of Hegel. Jordan's objectivism fits into no conventional pattern and must be studied in terms of its application and judged strictly on its own merits. It may well become a classic in the classical tradition, but now it is a fresh, original system of rational criticism.[11]

While classification or categorization may be helpful, it may also impede the appraisal of Jordan if the evaluation is made to depend on his likeness to or difference from Hegel or idealism generally, and the suggestion is, therefore, that his theory be considered on the basis of its own qualities. We may then still ask whether it is totalitarian.

One characteristic generally associated with totalitarianism is the closed society.[12] If this be true, then Jordan's theory is distinctly not totalitarian, for it envisages a continuous effort to realize the ideal. The theory of individuality issues in a concept of the will as supplying the everlasting dynamic of society, and Jordan's theory of legislation, which he has subtitled the "dynamics of public mind," is a theory of a permanent function, not one which is ever ended once and for all. His view is of an ever-evolving society, although no linear development is assured and no end is foreordained. The task of legislation is to maintain the state continuously in its progress toward the fuller objectification of mind, the higher attainment of culture. The state is both stable and dynamic, ever so. Furthermore, Jordan's conception of the tragedy of life prevents him from assuming that perfection is ever attained, for the act always fails of complete realization and a break yet remains between existence and value.

The experimental politics of Jordan is associated with a growing, open society rather than with a fixed, closed society. The element of chance, which he believes to be an ever-present and important factor in the dynamics of society, also precludes fixity. If an experimental politics is antithetical to a totalitarian society, not only in its rejection of fixity but also in the abandonment of absolutes in favor of tentatives and hypotheses, Jordan is the essence of antitotalitarianism. Fisch holds that Jordan, more than any of the canonical six (Peirce, James, Royce, Santayana, Dewey, Whitehead) who are the classic American philosophers, has developed a philosophy suited to an experimental politics.[13] Jordan's experimentalism is a refutation of absolutism in whatever form, whether that of the absolute state or of the absolute individual or people.

His rejection of absolutism is also a rejection of any type of dictatorship or external authority, the characteristic of totalitarian societies. The fact that he maintains that reason shall prevail and that the most highly intelligent shall fill the offices of legislation does not imply dictatorship or external authority either. He is critical of the idea of philosopher-kings if it embodies a principle of *personal* authority or control. Objectivity requires that the various *acts and their wills* be done and that those capable should fill the offices associated with these acts.

A traditional criticism of such a politics as Jordan's is that it is metaphysical and gives abstractions reality, more particularly, that it endows the state with personality; and it is argued that any theory which makes a corporate person of institutions or of the state inescapably involves totalitarianism. Fascism is cited as a prime example. It is said that inevitably flesh-and-blood persons are sacrificed to artificial persons, real persons to fictive ones. Jordan's argument, on the other hand, is that principle or law is not to be found in natural persons, and that any attempt to ground law therein is subjective and results in the subjection of the individual. Quite contrary to the traditional criticism, he asserts that only by installing the corporate or institutional person as the basic concept of political theory will tyranny be avoided and freedom won. This is the Copernican Revolution in politics. While he distinguishes between the natural and institutional person, he rejects the notion that the latter is in any sense artificial. The human realm incorporates more than natural individuals: that is to say, there are more persons than the natural one. Institution is a person organized on the same principles as the natural person; it is real rather than a fiction, and no one endowed it with personality, least of all the law. The corporate person is not a fleshless and bloodless abstraction without soul that subjugates flesh-and-blood persons who have souls; it is itself embodied soul or ensouled body, has indeed a body to be kicked and a soul to be damned, whereas the effort to locate rights and duties in natural persons is doomed to failure and does not serve to explain the character of contemporary society and its growth. What the law condescends to recognize in the form of the corporate person is a reality in its own right, one which makes the law and cultural reality itself intelligible. It might be said that the law has been forced against its "will" to accept the concept of corporate personality if it were to function with any degree of adequacy whatever. The facts with which the law had and has to deal could not be understood upon any other basis. Hence, while the charges that totalitarianism is inherent in corporate personality persist, the concept of corporate personality continues to flourish and to be extended in the law, even in democratic societies.

There is no mystique propounded in the conception of corporate personality; Jordan's criticism, on the contrary, suggests that what is mystical is the concept of the "metaphysical" individual or group. Haynes states that:

The 'personality' of the corporate body does not involve any mysterious concept of a spiritual entity hovering above each center of human activity, a being whose 'rights' will take precedence over those of mere mortals. The 'personality' of corporate bodies . . . is a reference to the fact that the systems of persons, property, and relations which are established in modern life must be an object of ethical analysis, as well as the men themselves.[14]

What creates mystery is the attempt to understand ethics in terms of natural persons. Corporate personality dissolves the mystery. Furthermore, far from freeing action from the control of moral law, corporate personality brings action directly within the domain of ethics. The confinement of action to natural persons, on the other hand, not only makes it impossible to understand the civil growth that has culminated in modern society, but also precludes an insight into further cultural development. Only when institutions are seen as our active agencies can sense be made of the moral world which they constitute and reconstitute. When Jordan says that the corporate person is the central concept of ethics, politics, and law, he is getting to the heart of the matter, which cannot be done by looking to individuals or groups. That the concept of corporate personality has such wide and continuing use in politics and law suggests the value of the idea, particularly if it is divorced from the conception of an entity sitting above and dictating to life. The purpose of Jordan's institutionalism is precisely to avoid external authority and to find law within the ongoing circumstances of life. It may seem strange that the only way to preserve and enhance the stature of man is to look beyond him for human principle, while to stay with him is to subject him to regimentation; yet that is the nature of the case. This is part of the significance of Jordan's insistence that the problem of politics is the need to impersonalize or publicize control. Hence only by going to another person, the institutional or corporate person, can freedom be won and man reach his full individuality. Corporate personality or institution is the assurance of freedom and individuality, not their denial. The social order is the corporate order, the order of institutions, and these are the realities, the actors with whom ethics, politics, and law must be concerned. Instead of being totalitarian and enslaving, they are antithetical to absolutism and are the essence of freedom, if freedom is considered in objective terms. It is these institutions that furnish man with the opportunity to become himself; their growth is at the same time his growth. The problem, then, is not whether man or institution shall dominate, or which shall rule over the other, but how to distinguish the functions of each in the order of the whole; neither can the question be put in terms of a choice between making man end and institution means, or institution end and man means. Jordan would deny both the choice of the atomist and that of the organicist here, and assert that both man and institution are ends and means. Art and the artist, education and the teacher, for example, are ends and means. The art object, which the artist creates and which is incorporated in the institution of art and ultimately in the whole of institutions, is the end for which he is a means; but in the creation of that object he also creates himself. He draws not only upon the world of art, using it as a means to the end of becoming an artist, but upon the institutional whole in becoming whole himself, a person. Once the unity and continuity of persons natural and corporate is recognized, the false choice between institution or man is eliminated. Institution is a higher individuality than the natural person, since it is a more comprehensive form of life, but it is not ruler and the natural person is not subject. Even in the case of the organism, the existence of higher and lower forms does not impose authoritarianism or external law. No order is possible in nature or culture on such a basis. The law does not descend from on high, as an imposition of the higher forms on the lower ones.[15] Law is immanent in individuality, in the constitution and individuation of the forms. Individuality is a system or whole whose principle is identity and all of whose members are distinguishable as differents within identity. The same principle pervades all the forms, which are thus manifestations of degree-difference. There is an identity relation between all the personal forms of individuality: man-institution-state. Each of them is a person and a differentiated form of individuality. Consequently, man cannot be understood as an entity apart from the state, nor can the relation between them be put in terms of man versus the state. The state is what man means; it is himself writ large.

Jordan is not proposing, then, that man be subjugated by institutions; quite the contrary, his condemnation of contemporary society is in large part based on the fact that man has been so subordinated. In fact, he wondered why it was that the very theory which exalted man succeeded only in degrading him in practice, and from this he was led to examine the common theory of individuality and to conclude that it was false. The necessary antithesis between man and institution is a myth. Jordan's effort is to elevate man to his true stature, something the former theory did not and could not achieve in practice because the theory itself was fallacious. When he cautions man to walk humbly in the presence of the constitution of things and asserts that every people has a constitution in its institutions, he means to avoid the excesses of political rationalism, which would write the constitution out of the head and would ignore the constitution in the environing facts, and at the same time to counsel man to maintain a true humility that neither underestimates nor overestimates himself. It is a suggestion that man find his place in the structure of things, rather than continue to regard himself as lord over them. At the same time, "things" cannot be left to themselves, and it is at this point that man plays his distinctive and most important part, for he alone is the creature of intelligence without whom institutions would go their blind ways and interfere with, perhaps ultimately annihilate, each other. The will is both effective agency and intelligent prescience. Without the effectiveness of institutions, man is but an idle dreamer doomed forever to live in his fantasies; without the intelligence of man, institutions lack the guidance they require to effect their ends as incorporated with the ends of other institutions in the End.

That contemporary institutions are inappropriate to their ends is not an indication that the men who use them are evil, but rather that the institutions themselves suffer from defective structure, with the result that they have come to use men. It is institutions that have gotten out of hand, and in a sense they must again be taken in hand, provided that Jordan's qualifications about the autonomy of institution be retained. These institutions are subject to principle rather than to personal control. Institutions cannot think, but if the ends provided by thought are to be realized, they must fall within the forms which institutions prescribe. If the state is not to become the Leviathan "which shapes the ends of man in accordance with the destiny incorporated in its own nature, the problem of control in human affairs must be worked over from the ground up." [16] This is no diminution of the stature of man, but an assertion of his rightful place in accordance with Jordan's proposed Copernican Revolution, which he argues is here already as fact. Man is not a principle, however important his intelligence is for culture. It was a false estimate of man which sent political theory astray. Modern philosophy made man a principle, the source of will and the basic political fact.

The assumption that the elementary fact of politics is the inner will of the individual human being, or that it is that will pluralized and compounded in a mystical general will, is the major premise of modern political theory. It is false; and its falseness has worked corruption into the vitals of every modern state and is now bringing them all to a common dissolution. [17]

This mistaken notion of the fundamental political fact stems from the idea that reality is a state of mind; it is therefore blind to the existence of the institutions which form the structure of public life. Institution is the elemental fact, and its will, the corporate will, is the concept through which to understand politics. The individual is a very important part of politics, but his importance lies in his place and function within the institutions of which he is a part, not as a principle of politics. The principle lies in the whole, which as law provides the basis upon which all persons and things find their places. While it may be said that all things are for man, nevertheless in the construction of the whole as the good life, man is to be disposed (but not disposed of) like any other object in the system, in accordance with his proper place and function. This fitness of persons and things to each other in the whole eliminates any need for authoritarianism or hierarchical "ordering," or for relations of superordination and subordination, which in reality have nothing to do with ordination or order at all.

The elevation of natural persons to a status which is not theirs has released politics from the control of ethics, for the state has been viewed as the "society of persons," with persons here holding a place separate from other objects. This is the collectivity that marks social as distinct from political theory, the unity of such persons being thought to be their common mind states or beliefs, subjective likemindedness, the subjectivism of modern politics. Classical political theory, on the other hand, maintained that the state was a society of institutional persons, and that politics was "the orderly arrangement and organization of the things and objects of nature in an objective whole, and the constituent content of this whole was the order and law which applied indifferently to the persons and things involved." [18]

Jordan affirms the anti-atomistic reaction which asserted the metaphysical status of institution, even while he decries that form of institutionalism which merely substituted the sovereignty of the institution or of the state for that of the individual. Only by keeping institution attached to its human substance can it be prevented from becoming a tyrant. His quarrel, then, is not with metaphysics or the metaphysical grounding of institution, but with that form of metaphysics which erroneously abstracted institution from the life process and gave it a dominant place in that process, which set up institution as an entity over and above life, dictating to it. Jordan, while agreeing with the institutionalists in their criticism of the shortcomings of individualism, has no intention of establishing the theoretical grounds for the subjugation involved in some institutional theories. It is necessary, therefore, to distinguish Jordan's institutionalism from other types. The choice is not between individualism (or socialism) and institutionalism, but between institutionalisms. There is no inherent tyranny in institutionalism as such, but a false form of that theory is indeed tyrannical. Jordan's agreement with those institutionalists who assert a metaphysical status for institution is qualified by his criticism that their theory is a form of social absolutism. While a metaphysical status for institution is a true one, the implication of Jordan's position is that this conception ties institution to, rather than loosens it from, its human substance, and that this bond is necessary for human individuality and freedom. "According" a metaphysical status to institution is necessary because of its objective reality and in order to prevent its being conceived in subjective terms. Far from setting institution above man or apart from the facts of life, such a conception is the only way to avoid the dehumanization of institution and the concomitant subordination of man. Jordan would readily grant that as institutions are now organized they do dominate man, but then the difficulty is not inherent in the nature of institutions. Quite the contrary, when institutions are rightly understood and organized, they are the very essence of man, the embodiment of human purposes. Consequently, when institutions attain their fullest height, man rises to his highest stature.

Jordan has given ample evidence that present institutions as empirical fact are in conflict with human ends, but it is false to think that they are inevitably so. His assertion that the relation of man and institution is one of identity need not blind one to the existing social reality; quite the reverse. When, as at present, institutions are at cross purposes with man, there is a fundamental flaw in the organization of human affairs. The positivistic side of Jordan urges clear recognition of the empirical state of affairs, but not that form of naïve empiricism which takes the way of things as they are to be political or cultural necessity. Because they are not, change is inevitable. Thought is necessary to understand the evidence of the senses, to know what the facts are and what they imply. It is the kind of positivism found in the social sciences, including legal science, that vitiates them, but Jordan affirms the positivistic motive divested of its naïveté. What man, institution, state, and their relations are must be thought out, and this the crude type of empiricism fails to do; hence it is subject to a fatal incapacity, the inability to find an objective ground of value.

For Jordan metaphysics is not subjectivity, the common opinion, but objectivity; as objective it concerns itself with the world of fact and not merely with the world of thought. Jordan is highly critical of positivistic jurisprudence, which looks to "the law and the evidence" and gives the judge merely the responsibility for finding the law and applying it mechanically to the case at hand. The difficulty with positivism is that it really does not know the facts that are involved in a case of law. While such positivism is crude and gives a false meaning to law, "yet the insistence on the necessity to face the facts in the interpretation of law, and the recognition that only from the point of view of fact can law have meaning, indicate a profound insight. The law has its very essence in the facts of human experience and is grounded in human relations." [19] Hence, while then the positivist is correct in his concern for the facts, what these facts and their relations are is not a simple matter to determine and is a question for the legal philosopher to decide. The heart of the meaning of law is found in the relation of law and fact, and the determination of that relation is a profound philosophical problem. That Jordan's solution of the problem is identical with his theory of individuality is indicated in his suggestion that the principle for deciding what the facts and relations are is "that which states the relation of the individual moral person to the corporate moral person and shows at the same time that the relation is constitutional to the corporate person and identifies with the relation between corporate persons as the foundational principle of the state. Such an interpretation is made necessary by the fact that morality is the content and the intent of the law and will therefore determine its form." [20] The ultimate fact with which the law deals, then, is the relation of the moral person as an individual to the moral person as corporate and universal. Authority and obligation are rooted in this statement; in fact, all of the essential concepts of ethics and law find their ground here, and in this relation is to be found the basic principle of all practical philosophy.

The concept of authority is the viewpoint which interprets the relation which the law expresses, interprets the law, that is, from the point of view of its bearing or incidence upon the corporate moral person; that is, the viewpoint that sees the law as universal. Its interpretation is therefore a categorical imperative, since it states the fact of the law as it *is* and therefore as it must and shall be. What the law is, however, is not merely what it is by statutory enactment; its positive basis is metaphysical.[21]

Here Jordan combines positivism with metaphysics. His criticism as well as affirmation of positivistic jurisprudence is allied with his commentary on the positivism of social science generally. The political scientist who looks at the facts of political reality too often takes them to be the circumstances of conflicting interest and the struggle for power. He is perceiving the facts much as does the legal positivist who looks to the statutes and the case at hand, but this kind of positivism mistakes the nature of the facts and their relations, and we might parallel Jordan's closing sentence in the quotation above by saying that the positive basis of politics and the state is metaphysical. Jordan's ethics, politics, and law thus rest on this kind of "metaphysical positivism."

While Jordan's is an institutional theory and has connections with idealism, to call it "institutional idealism" will confuse rather than clarify his position. He has been called and has called himself that contradiction in terms, a "metaphysical positivist." Perhaps this is characteristic of a philosophy which is synthetic and joins seemingly contradictory elements. Jordan is critical of both metaphysics and positivism if they imply such a concept as the "metaphysical" individual or a naïve empiricism that takes "the way of things as they err" [22] as cultural reality. This is at the same time a criticism of rationalism and empiricism in their separatism. Jordan's theory at once joins the rational and empirical, and the experimentalism he advocates takes place under logical and temporal conditions.

Is Jordan's Corporatism Democratic?

Jordan's extensive criticism of democracy as politics would seem to make the answer to this question evident. While there will be no attempt here to review thoroughly those of his objections to democracy which have already been discussed or to add others which have not been treated, some of the arguments will again be cited briefly.[23] Put most bluntly, Jordan doubts whether democracy is a politics at all, since it has nothing to say regarding the constitution of the state. As a politics, it concerns itself with governmental machinery, and exhausts itself with problems of the rights, liberties, duties, and interests of individuals. Democracy disregards institutional problems, and when they become unavoidable, it backs into them apologetically. It is a social theory and consequently it may be said either to have nothing to say about culture, or, what is the same thing, to regard cultural reality as a state of mind, the false principle of liberalism. Whether democracy be identified with the individualism of classical liberalism or with the groupism or "socialism" of modern liberalism, this false principle remains. Although modern liberalism often refers to society as corporate, it is nevertheless a social or collective theory rather than a corporate or cultural one. The group is no more adequate as a political concept than is the individual of traditional theory. Modern society is neither an aggregate nor a synthesis of individuals or groups. Because of its faulty premises, modern liberalism is unable to depict, and therefore unable to control intelligently, the constitution of modern society.

Conclusion

The modern tendency to call all political theory either democratic or totalitarian may not exhaust the possibilities. Jordan's criticism indicates that whatever the differences between democratic and totalitarian theory, they are essentially alike. Both are subjective; both misconceive the constitution of the state. Corporatism may be the answer to the need described by Dewey to retain the virtues of rationalism and empiricism in political theory while avoiding the authoritarianism which is the logical outcome of the one-sidedness of each,[24] and to overcome the weaknesses of monadism and monism, of isolate entities, on the one hand, and of a relational view which eliminates pluralism on the other.[25] As Dewey has made clear, philosophy is not to be identified with the *via media,* compromise, or eclecticism, but with synthesis, the formulation which is more profound and inclusive than the views which it replaces.[26] In our interpretation, corporatism is an attempt to develop such a synthesis.

Far from affirming totalitarianism, Jordan is trying to avoid absolutism in all of its forms, whether that of the absolute individual of empiricism or that of the Absolute Individual, the state, of rationalism. The recognition of the reality of the corporate person and the corporate will is necessary if we are to make sense of modern society and of such order as it has or such higher order as it may attain. Haynes believes, as do the present writers, that this conception avoids the difficulties of traditional political views.

A strong tendency toward political pluralism . . . is manifest as a result of Jordan's transfer of will life from the individual person to the corporate institution, taken together with his insistence that government does not become an overpowering or absolute individual. Jordan's position is to be distinguished from the main trend of political pluralism, when the latter is intemperately taken not as a recognition of an ever-present aspect of political life but as an ultimate and wholesome 'loose-endedness' considered as necessary to liberty. He does recognize the necessity for the maintenance of a studied and legal relation between the various institutions which are themselves seats of legality at least with regard to their own functions. His point is, however, that the harmonizing of these many life centers is not accomplished through any *fixed* legal norm. He sets himself the task of giving a rather full statement of the principles and organization of the non-authoritarian government, thus offering an alternative to both political pluralism and political monism as usually conceived.[27]

Political holism, which characterizes corporate theory, is generally thought to mean totalitarianism, so that freedom is taken to require "something less than" the total conception, yet Jordan argues that tyranny results from a less-than-total view. While he does not put the issue in precisely these terms, the inference may be drawn that to be less than total is to be totalitarian, but to be total in the mode of organicism is also totalitarian; hence the problem is to find that form of holism which is not totalitarian, and this we believe he does in his concept of the corporate person and his admonition that both the individual and the government must respect its integrity. Life is whole and must be seen as such.[28] "It is the function of the state to create and maintain the order and balance of the total system of life, to give to life, that is, its moral significance." [29] Life must be organized, and this is the task of the political intelligence. Above all, the appropriate functioning of the corporate organs of life provides the objective basis for freedom. In this sense a real government does not enthrall the capacities of men; it liberates them.

Part Two   CORPORATE EDUCATION

CHAPTER 8
THE AUTHORITY OF EDUCATION

Introduction

As a means of bringing Jordan's social theory to bear on education and the problem of educational authority, some of his corporate conceptions will be reviewed briefly. When Jordan modifies the generalization "society is now corporate" with the qualification that society is always corporate in greater or lesser degree, he nevertheless agrees that modern society is markedly distinguished from preceding society. In his treatment of cultural evolution he indicates four distinctive stages of development, corresponding to the predominance of one or another of the components of will: nature, human nature, reason, and plupurpose.[1] While all of these components are present in any instance of will, the supremacy of a particular component at a particular stage of development characterizes the constitution at that time. The history of society is marked by changed constitutions, each the product of various will factors that have emerged and gained prominence. To say, then, that society is always corporate is not to say that it is always indistinguishably the same or that the present era does not exhibit unique qualities. To characterize present society as corporate is to say that it has a vastly changed constitution, the plupersonal aspect of will being now dominant. Jordan's recognition of the soundness of Maine's assertion that ancient society was based upon status and modern society is based upon contract indicates his agreement with those who argue that modern society has a unique constitution, even though he does not feel that the transition is adequately described as "from status to contract" but requires the addition of "and on to corporeity," thus combining both in a synthesis.[2]

At the same time, status, which refers to property and the stability it gives to interpersonal relations, and contract, which refers to the actional impulses of the property-person organization, are constitutional to society and provide the law of persons and things in their relations; and this is the fundamental or constitutional law. Jordan rejects the subjective concept of property as exclusive possession of goods, and of contract as the meeting of subjective wills. No constitution is possible on the basis of such a view of property and contract. Institution is the stuff of constitution. The constitution, then, is the living institutional order in both its stable or propertied aspect and its dynamic or contractual aspect. The constitution is ever-building, and what it continuously builds and rebuilds is the state, the dynamic unity of institutions. Property and contract supply the universal principles for ethics, politics, and law,[3] as of all the social sciences.

The order of persons and things is objective fact, and the unity of society derives from the unity of its institutions or corporate persons rather than from the likemindedness of natural persons. The maintenance of that unity does not require propaganda or exhortation, which make up the education of a subjective social theory. Education is not an attempt to induce or to change psychological states in the hope that social and political order will be the outcome. An education for cultural unity is one which recognizes that cultural order is objective, not subjective, and which finds that *the order of men rests upon the objects of their common lives.* Men are met in culture, and property is the most immediate thing which they have in common. It is the corporate or public character of property which joins men to each other in a common world, through which they attain their personal, common ends. Neither their property nor their ends are private but public.[4] Property and contract are corporate and provide the order of culture. If education is to help construct the order of culture, it will inquire into that order rather than into mental states. The import of Jordan's corporate theory here is that an education which will be harmonious with the spirit and body of the constitution is one that abandons the individual and the social conception, neither of which comprehends the state, and adopts the corporate philosophy, which renders intelligible the reality of man's life in, of, and for the institutional order.

By implication there are several prominent conceptions of educational authority which Jordan's theory rejects. The spiritual conception of authority in the person of an other-worldly God is repudiated by Jordan, for authority must stem from the concreteness of facts in this world. The law is in those facts as ordered, and is not imposed upon them by some agency located outside the facts. The same objection may be lodged against the "corporate"—or better, organicist—state of the fascist theorists, since the state, like the idea of a supernatural God, is conceived by them as a willful entity external to and independent of life, an agency which may act in any way that it pleases. The one issues in a spiritual, the other in a military dictatorship, for only a regimented world and educational system, as distinguished from a society that is internally ordered, is possible with this conception of authority. The classical liberal's notion that the individual is the authority for education is also denied by Jordan, since the entity so conceived is not a human being and the ultimate outcome of the idolatry of the absolute individual is educational as well as social chaos. Another conception of authority which Jordan implicitly and explicitly rejects is the social or group point of view, viz., the idea that society conceived in terms of a mystical common will is the ultimate source of political and educational authority. Since, in our times, this idea is the most pervasive one in ethical, legal, political, sociological, and educational literature, we shall discuss it in somewhat extended form, both because of its importance and as a contrast to Jordan's conception of educational authority.

Corporate versus Modern Liberal Educational Theory

The purpose of this exploration is not to develop fully the social interpretation of authority, for this would require too extensive an analysis. Our goal of exposition and contrast may be accomplished more succinctly through consideration of a prominent educational philosophy, that of social reconstructionism.[5] Like its political expression in modern liberalism, which was a sharp reaction against the atomic individualism of classical liberalism, it is grounded upon a "group metaphysic." The universal characteristics which identify this position are clearly brought out in the writings of William O. Stanley, who will serve as the focus of this analysis. To do full justice to this position would require a much more extensive and intensive treatment than is possible here; nevertheless, the consideration of certain aspects may serve our purposes without misrepresenting social reconstructionism.

Social reconstructionism affirms the reality of a corporate society and the need for an educational philosophy in accord with that reality.[6] It asserts the inadequacy of merely changing subjective states of mind or even ideas without effecting change in the social order. Institutional reconstruction as well as personal reconstruction is needed, and if the theory is called social reconstructionism, it nevertheless incorporates both individual and institutional change. Derived from Dewey's famous definition of education as the continuous reconstruction of experience, this philosophy maintains that both the aim and the process of education are such reconstruction.[7]

While the account which social reconstructionism gives of contemporary society cannot be fully developed here, certain attributes bearing on the problem of authority will be described. Present-day society is marked by great change and is said to be in a period of transition, for the old ways of life have been challenged but not yet fully replaced by the new ways. The unity and common mind which marked the United States in the past are for the most part lacking today. Where before the public and the public will could usually be readily identified, now the public no longer exists with respect to many fundamental spheres; instead, there are a variety of interest groups or publics. The old community is gone; in its place have come a host of interest groups, and these are now the referents to which the individual attaches great importance. He is identified with such groups, rather than with the neighborhood or the local community. His well-being is thought to rest there. He speaks and makes his will known through these groups, rather than directly as an individual. Stanley characterizes the present state as a multigroup society, and speaks of the problems of education in relation to the problems of a society so constituted.

Perhaps the profound difference between the views of Jordan and Stanley may be illustrated by discussing the very first sentence of Stanley's *Education and Social Integration:* "The work of the school, as any experienced educator can testify, is constantly conducted in the midst of a conflicting network of social, economic, and political pressures exerted, directly or indirectly, by the more important interest groups in American society." [8] Thus far both theorists would agree to this description of the actual state of affairs, but their disagreement begins at the point where implications are drawn from it. For Stanley this reality is as it must and ought to be. Not that he favors what every interest group attempts to do in society generally or in education particularly; but for him these groups constitute publics, and since the public is sovereign in the creation of social and educational policy, such groups must necessarily have a voice in forming that policy. He denies the validity of the claims of such groups to represent the whole, although he would agree that each actually does claim, and probably sincerely, to identify its interest with the interest of the whole. Stanley warns against mistaking the voice of the most articulate or powerful groups in the local or national community as the voice of the people, while at the same time he holds that the voice of the people is now heard through such groups. On many matters the people are not now speaking with one voice, he says, but if we hope to reach the state in which they will be, then we must recognize the multiplicity of interests represented by these various groups. He insists that a gross misunderstanding of the nature of contemporary society is involved in the belief that such groups are mere self-seekers. They are now "part and parcel of the very core of American society." While there is reason to say that in some instances these groups have advocated their own interests as against the public welfare, they nevertheless cannot be wholly characterized as selfish and opposed to the public good. Such a view is far too narrow and misses their real significance for society.

Each of these groups represents a portion of the public, the more important of them a large and significant portion; consequently, their interests are in some measure a part of the public interest. Moreover, these groups typically conceive their purposes, not in terms of purely private advantage, but in terms of *their* conceptions of the commonweal; they usually regard their respective programs, not as obstacles to the common good, but as an essential condition of its realization. Each of these groups has developed consciously or unconsciously, some social philosophy; each of them must be understood as making, in some particulars at least, proposals to the American public with respect to the goals of American life and the means by which they are to be achieved. Nor can these proposals be dismissed with impunity as sheer rationalizations. The members of pressure groups are also members of society; as such they, no more than other men, can free themselves in their own minds from the common obligation to respect the public weal. Moreover, in order to advance the interests which they represent, pressure groups must frequently secure the cooperation of other groups. Hence, they are compelled both by the moral principles of their mem-

bers and the practical necessities of the situation to relate their particular interests to the general welfare. The tendency of men, where
vital interests are at stake, to erect their particular into a universal
may be readily admitted. But that is a principle which is limited to
no single groups, and it is pertinent to ask where, in a modern industrial society, the impartial public is to be located. . . . The public
interest, in the modern world, is an achievement rather than an original
datum; acceptable standards of public welfare must include in some
measure, as they must also transcend, the particular interests of the
functional groups necessarily involved in the social structure. . . .
While these groups . . . are pressure groups, that label does not
fully define their meaning; indeed, their primary significance cannot
be comprehended at all in such terms. Rather they must be understood as representative of important group interests in American society, and as the bearers of pregnant propositions concerning the meaning of the public welfare and the definition of the ends of public
policy.[9]

Furthermore, interest groups are not unattached entities but
have their roots deep in the social structure itself, growing directly
out of the relations men bear to the fundamental institutions of our
time. The most conspicuous and perhaps the most significant examples
of this category of associations are to be found in the occupational
and professional organizations (such as the Chamber of Commerce,
the Farmers' Union, the American Federation of Labor, the Bar Association, and the National Educational Association) based upon the
functional relationships of different groups to the economic processes
of society; but even a casual inspection will indicate that every major
social institution is surrounded by a cluster of organized associations
representing the particular interests of different groups.[10]

Perhaps, then, the key factor in an understanding of contemporary society is the interest groups and their minds and wills as
representative of the individuals composing such groups. Stanley
does not mean that such groups, as they are now organized, are
fully democratic, or that the ideas of their individual members
are fully expressed. These groups in many respects fall short of
that ideal, but this in no way alters their importance as constituent elements of what will be, when unified, the public and
the public will. Out of the conflict of wills, it is hoped, and
through public communication, free deliberation, and mutual
persuasion, a common will will arise in those areas where it does
not now exist. Two points are very important here for Stanley's
analysis. One is that the public and the public will are unities,
i.e., they exist only when there is a high degree of agreement; the
public is not an originally given reality, but must be constructed

out of smaller publics. The second is that the public and the public will need to be referred to particular concerns; it is false to think that they exist in reference to every matter, just as it would be false to say that they do not exist at all. Hence one needs to examine a particular sphere of endeavor in order to determine whether or not the public and the public will exist with respect to that sphere, instead of talking about the public in general.

These interest groups have explicitly or implicitly also developed educational philosophies and programs, either by indirection and because a social philosophy is also an educational philosophy, or by direct expression of such a philosophy and program. There is plenty of evidence to indicate that all of these groups have in one way or another attempted to influence the aims of the school and its program. Educators have often responded hostilely to these attempts, regarding them as an interference with the task of education. Stanley agrees that undeniably some of these groups have interfered with education, and he cites, in particular, groups which attempt to hamper intellectual freedom or which deny financial support to the schools. Such groups have sometimes succeeded in dictating the content and method of education. The educator, on the other hand, does have a moral responsibility to protect the interests of learners and is duty bound to do so by the obligation of his office.

Obviously, it is the duty of the educational profession to resist demands that threaten either the financial support or the intellectual integrity of the public school. Freedom to learn necessarily implies freedom of study and inquiry, and freedom to learn is an essential precondition of any genuine education. And while it is not always true that there is a perfect correlation between expenditure and educational achievement, yet it is patent that a good educational system is impossible without adequate financial support.[11]

But again, it would be false to view interest groups in their relation to education solely as obstructors; nor is the task of educators primarily to shield the school from interest groups. To act in such a way would be to deny the American public its right to decide social policy. These groups, as has been said, constitute publics whose philosophies and programs are representative of portions of the public. They cannot, therefore, either be ignored or rejected as inherently inimical to education. The educational profession is right in resisting any effort to turn the school into a propaganda agency for a selfish interest group, but wrong to maintain that the ends these groups seek are unimportant for education or to hold that legitimate representatives of these groups should have no voice in determining educational objectives. If the public is to participate in the determination of educational policy, then interest groups as parts of the public must take part in these decisions.

It is possible to argue that a considerable degree of educational autonomy is possible and desirable in a democracy. But it must be an autonomy within a broad framework of purposes approved by the public; and the grant of autonomy itself, as well as the uses which are made of it, must rest on the consent of the public.[12]

Such a view does not, however, mean that educators are confined to being mere unthinking agents, to be commanded as the public sees fit. Stanley says that the educational profession has two choices: either it can passively accept the policies imposed upon it by society, or it can exercise leadership in trying to guide and shape the public will with respect to policy.[13] Educational statesmanship requires that the latter option be chosen.

Although both Stanley and Jordan recognize the pervasive influence of interest groups in modern society, they differ sharply in their analysis of the significance of these groups. Stanley's interpretation means that the locus of will is still the natural person, not as an isolate individual but as incorporated with his fellows in groups, social or public will being then determined as the synthesis of the various group wills. Rights also are social rather than individual. In short, neither the individual nor his will are absolute but are social in nature, and society is seen as the union of groups, the public will as the synthesis of group wills. Conceived as syntheses, they thus transcend the individual and his mind and will, while at the same time incorporating them in the final outcome. Thus new entities evolve out of individuals and their minds and wills, new entities in the form of the group and its mind and will. This conception rejects the idea of the group mind as external to or above that of the members of the group, the "metaphysical" mind or group. Abandoning the atomistic individual as a central concept, this view replaces it with that of the group.

Jordan's criticism, with which we would agree, is that the group offers no better concept than the individual, since it is only the individual pluralized. To this the social reconstructionist would object on the grounds that it is not mere addition or multiplication that he is asserting as the character of the group, but a qualitative difference; he posits a new entity that is something more than a collectivity. He insists on the changed character of the group conceived as a synthesis rather than a sum. Our inference from Jordan's position, however, is that even this qualification does not diminish the subjective character of the group concept. Synthesis or sum, the group itself is left without ground, for it remains a social rather than a cultural concept.

Pluralizing a subjective relation does not make it objective, cannot give it truth. This is the fallacy of all 'social' theories. These theories merely multiply the fallacies of individualism. A group of persons means no more than an individual so far as their subjective experiences are concerned, or until the relations of the individual are thought as mediated through the things of the world, so that the group is constituted a corporate body. And then we are dealing with public relations and not experiences. But cultural 'interests,' as public, are not social but political, and morality becomes the science of the public life.[14]

Jordan's view is that the group cannot provide a ground, but requires one. It is in the same position in this respect as the individual. The only real ground is institution conceived as objectified mind or culture. The group's justification and *raison d'être* derives neither from itself nor from society, but from a cultural objective, and consequently the latter is the only source of right. One cannot start with the group and derive rights from it, even when society at large is taken to be the group involved; but rather culture is the starting point, and the rights and obligations of the group are derived from it. The corporate person, not the individual or the group, is the indispensable concept. The community is ultimate, as the social reconstructionist maintains; but then it is the state, i.e., the unity of corporate persons and not the synthesis of groups. In this distinction lies a fundamental difference between the corporate and the social theories. In the social view, public and publics refer to groups, while in the corporate view they refer to institutions. In the former conception the public is constituted from the synthesis or agreement of groups or publics, themselves constituted from the synthesis or agreement of their individual members, and the body politic thus consists of groups; but corporate theory holds that the public is the synthesis of institutions, which thus are the body politic, the public body. Jordan's theory maintains that the public—the unity and continuity of institutions—is an original fact which is only fragmented by the positivistic search for the facts. Contrary to Stanley's view, which is representative of Dewey's and the social interpretation, the public is an original datum, not something to be constructed out of smaller publics; yet this original datum must not be construed as unchanging. If Jordan's view of the state as both dynamic and stable is taken into account, so that the task of politics is continuously to fit institutions together and harmonize their acts, then we may say that this original datum must be seen not as fixed but as growing, and hence the state as the public body must be interpreted as a dynamic unity. The whole is the Fact, the ground of all the facts, in the absence of which the facts disappear. Elementalism must be abandoned if there are to be "elements," unities within unity. This Fact in its various forms is the ground of groups and at the same time the basis of their public character. Institutions conceived as acts or offices imply actors or officers; the act is primary, person and world are derivative. This again is in contrast to Stanley's conception, which instead derives institution or act from the group.

No principle of social order can be found in interest groups, which must go outside themselves to find their own principle. However, this does not mean that they go to other interest groups or public opinion. There would be no transcendence in such a transfer, but only more of the same. The reference would still be subjective, even though it gets "outside" the self. For the reference to become objective it must implicate culture. To be sure, as Stanley says, these interest groups are rooted in the structure of society, but it is that structure which gives them meaning, not the other way around. Labor and management as interest groups diverge; they converge in the common object of industry, which is at once their common end. Their disputes can be weighed only by reference to the object of industry; this objective is their aim and their justification as an entity, which makes of them a corporate body. Labor and management do not possess interests but rather cultural ends, in which their rights and duties inhere. Interest is self-referent, and pluralization or socialization does not objectify it. Interest, whether individual or group, is private advantage; it stands against the public good, the form of culture or the corporate person.

The appearance of an interest is not the ground of a right, even though it be subjected to social appraisal. Interest and right are not the same, but are opposed to each other; nor are interests moralized simply by being publicized, if publicization means their intersubjective appraisal. Intersubjectivity is not objectivity, even though the conditions and method for appraisal are carefully described. The question is not which methods of intersubjectivity are to be used, with the assumption that if the proper method is chosen the result will be objectivity. Jordan's view is that all such methods remain subjective, and consequently he would be opposed to the use of consensus as the ultimate criterion, however well defined the method by which it is to be achieved. Value is real independently of agreement, and consensus, if it appears at all, is an epiphenomenon rather than the criterion of truth or reality. It is not because the people agree that the good is real, but rather they ought to agree because the good is real.

Although in the following quotation Jordan is speaking of beauty, the position expressed applies to the realm of value as a whole.

Objectivity is not grounded in mere number or abstract plurality in spite of the presence of number and plurality in the universality which is its ground. The 'social' is itself therefore a mere abstraction, and there is no way of arguing logically from the mere togetherness of phenomena whose essence is subjective, in the sense that it implies mere status in mind or consciousness, to the corporate entity which is constituted of the union of beauty objects with other types of objects in the persisting structure of things; and until theory has implemented it with and through other states of mind, and the physical instruments which states of mind always imply, it will continue to lack that status and station. And a real status in the world can never be found for my state of mind by merely discovering that other people have a like state; the *consensus hominum* and universality do not mean anything like that. It is to be very seriously questioned whether there is an important fact or idea that can be validated by a mere reference to the social; and if we will allow the pragmatists a little more time the question will be settled, for every possibility will have been tried.[15]

Jordan would agree that universality and objectivity must be sought; his criticism of other theories is essentially that they fail in the search. The social approach to the problem fails because it professes a false view of what constitutes objectivity and universality. The agreement or disagreement of men tells us nothing about the reality of the object about which they are agreed or disagreed. The object does not become real when disagreement turns into agreement, nor unreal when agreement becomes disagreement. Jordan would apply this view to both the objects of nature and those of culture. When scientists fall out, no change occurs in the natural world. The tree is no less a tree, a natural fact, whether scientists agree or disagree about its qualities; similarly with objects of value. *Valet*, the object is value and does not have its worth bestowed upon it by the people or by anybody. The reality of value, of culture, is independent of agreement or disagreement. To hold otherwise is to make cultural reality only a state of mind, and of course this is what Jordan believes the social conception does.

While Stanley accords interest groups a central place, if not the central place, in public affairs and calls them "social realities of the greatest importance," [16] Jordan says either that they have no place in such affairs, since they are the essence of the private motive and hence are unreal politically, or else that they must be conceived as cultural groups, so far as they can be shown to be such. However, if groups are cultural entities, their position is still not that of rulers of institutions; rather their position is defined by their functional relation to the ends which these institutions seek. In any consideration of public order, interest must be eliminated. Jordan's argument is that legislation for the public ends of the state has nothing to do with interest groups or the selection of voices to be heard in that sense. In fact, quite the contrary; disinterestedness is requisite to legislation.[17] There is no rational basis possible for the adjudication of interests, and no law is to be found in them; as subjective phenomena they do not submit to order. What legislation "represents" is culture in its growth, in its further reaches. Education cannot be made intelligible by an attempt to bring together the claims of the American Legion, the AFL–CIO, the National Association of Manufacturers, etc. These bodies exist neither in their own right nor by grant of the people, but are constituted as legitimate agencies, are legalized, only through their instrumentation of culture. It is by knowing what education is that whatever claims these groups may have can be measured, rather than the other

way around. On the basis of Jordan's statements we have inferred
that education is of, by, and for culture, and hence has nothing
to do with interest. Education is based upon cultural rather than
social foundations.

What Jordan describes as the social conception or theory, in
contrast to the corporate or cultural theory, is then applicable to
the philosophy of social reconstructionism in education. His
critique indicates that despite the frequent characterization of
modern society as corporate by the social reconstructionists, their
interpretation of that society is subjective and does not grasp
contemporary reality. This is true even though their position is
avowedly anti-atomistic and gives great emphasis to the need
for institutional reconstruction; it falls short of being an institutional theory and hence, like atomism, assumes, despite its
contentions to the contrary, that cultural reality is a state of
mind. True, it does reject the view that a whole is a sum, whether
applied to a particular group in society or to society considered
as a group, but its view of the nature of this whole, that is, of
publics and the public, is in contrast to Jordan's corporatism.
The latter asserts that corporate persons or institutions constitute
publics and that the public, which ultimately is the state, is the
whole of institutions. Said another way, social reconstructionism
holds that society is ultimate and that the state is at best but a
means to it as end. In Jordan's terms the state as the cultural
whole is the end, but it would do injustice to his position to consider the individual as only a means to the state as end. To consider the individual only a means is to neglect important aspects
of the relation between individual and state. Individual and state
are both means and ends; and both atomism, individual or social,
and organicism err in believing that the relation must be one or
the other: either the individual is the end for which the state
is but a means, or the state is the end for which the individual
is but a means. There is no antithesis between individual and institution or between the individual and the state as the unity of
institutions, no opposition between the individual and culture.
Neither is there any need to appoint a sovereign or to impose a
dominance-submission relation upon individual and state. Sovereignty is still retained in the social view, even though it abandons the sovereignty of the isolate individual as a will absolute.
To make the whole of natural persons sovereign, or to move

from individual to popular sovereignty, leaves the principle of social organization unchanged.

The social view yet asks as the fundamental question of public life, "Who shall rule?" As has been indicated, the question is a false one, necessarily subjective, and thus carries with it the subjection rather than the exaltation of the individual. Whatever the answer, this is the inevitable result. If the totalitarians answer in terms of a dictator or the rule of an elite, and if democrats answer in terms of the majority or the people as a whole, no change in the principle of authority has been made. If social reconstructionism adheres to consensus, no change in principle is involved either. Even though the whole be conceived as a synthesis rather than a sum, society is defined as the whole of natural persons, whereas corporatism identifies society with the whole of institutional persons. For corporatism, society and state are identified with each other, and freedom rather than tyranny is the consequence of this unity. Culture rather than human relations is ultimate; the cultural conception rather than the social furnishes the principle of human order. Although the social view explicitly abandons the independent individual of atomism as a principle of authority, and although it rejects the mere pluralization of individuals in the group as supplying principle, its insistence that a group and group will and mind are something more than an aggregate of individuals and individual wills and minds still does not succeed in giving will and mind an objective status. Cultural reality is not an independent entity in this view, but comes into existence and passes out of existence according to the presence or absence of agreement between groups. Such a view makes the group itself, conceived as a synthesis, the basic political unit or fact. To believe that the individual is an inadequate source of authority, and to substitute for him the group, still leaves politics with no life of its own and subject to personal authority or domination. It is culture and its objects that are the ground of both the individual and the group as corporate bodies, not the other way around. The group does not endow culture with reality; culture endows the group with reality. Hence the social reconstructionist position, which attempts to find political reality in interest groups, has not found that reality because it has failed to distinguish between interest and right or between interest and culture. Interest is not real, or is real only as it becomes culture, in which case it is no longer interest. The political task is to convert interest into culture, not to accept it as politically real. The concepts of interest and interest group must be abandoned if the constitution of modern society as corporate is to be understood.

What the reconstructionist then takes to be the essence of political reality turns out to be unreality and denies culture its autonomous status in the world. Perhaps this is what Jordan means when he confirms those institutionalists who assert a metaphysical status for institution, while at the same time he criticizes the form of institutionalism which has resulted in social absolutism. For the reconstructionist no institution has a metaphysical status, neither education nor any other, and any institution must be conceived as owing its existence merely to its role as a social agency. Hence rights and duties are social, derivative from society rather than inherent in the nature of institution. Social reconstructionism, like corporatism, is critical of atomism and the kind of institutionalism that is organicist in nature, but while it affirms the necessity of an institutional approach to social problems and the need for a reform of institutions, it does not rest its case on cultural grounds and makes institutions mere means in the hands of the people whom they are to serve. Jordan agrees that institutions are for men, but still maintains that man is not a principle of public order. As stated before, the cultural end is the principle of order, and man is but an object, unique to be sure, but to be disposed like all other objects according to his proper place in the whole. Again, the distinction between the social and the corporate concepts is important here, for while the social reconstructionist holds that institutions are social agencies, the corporatist maintains that institutions are cultural agencies with rights and duties inherent in their own nature and function, or, stated somewhat differently, derivative from culture. It may be said that every institution has a status in its own right as a form of culture or of the good, and that all it need do is to be itself or be true to itself, in which case it cannot be false to culture conceived as a whole. Education may be viewed as rightful because it is a particular form of the good with its authority *ex officio*. The other way of stating essentially the same point is to say that education's authority is derived from culture in the sense of the whole of institutions, the state of which it is a constitutive factor. The latter probably best expresses the cor-

porate view, but the autonomy of institutions must be understood to lie in their nature as ingredients to the whole good.
Consequently, if it be said that the human community is the
ultimate source of authority and the ground of rights and duties,
both the social reconstructionist and the corporatist could agree,
but their interpretation of the community would differ; for the
former the community is the "society of persons" conceived as
natural, while for the latter it is the "society of persons" conceived as institutional or cultural. When the social reconstructionist grounds the authority of education in the public as the
whole of natural persons, he differs widely from the corporatist
who finds authority in the office of education in its own right,
in the nature of the educative act and its object in the Act and
its Object.

Jordan takes the objective side of the question: Is it good because the people love it, or do they love it because it is good?
Whether one substitutes God, or an earthly one, few, many, or
all, for the people does not matter; one answer remains subjective, the other objective. The people love it (or ought to) because it is good. Culture is real and has a metaphysical status.
It is derivative from no one, and like the truths of natural science,
speaks in its own name and on its own authority.

Thus cultural reality is not a state of mind. The reality of the
value of education does not lie in the people and their percep-
tions. Either education is a cultural reality in its own right and
must be understood as such, or it derives that reality from some
source outside itself, the people or some other. If the latter alternative is chosen, it is difficult to see how there can be institutional
and professional autonomy, for the external authority may do
with education and educators as it "wills." In this case education or any act may be whatever the people say that it is. The educational profession is then necessarily reduced to the status of
an "agent" or "public servant," devoid of mind and will.

Stanley indicates, however, that his conception of the public,
the society of persons, as ultimate does not impair educational
autonomy, but that educators can choose to be active leaders
rather than passive followers in forming the public will. To argue
thus, however, is to assert that education is a cultural reality on
its own, which is precisely Jordan's view. Perhaps this is the
significance also of Dewey's insistence that aims are internal to

an act and that education has no aims outside itself.[18] When Dewey and the social reconstructionists generally define education as the continuous reconstruction of experience, are they affirming the reality of education as such, independently of whether the people perceive its reality or not? Are they saying, "To this the people should agree, and whether they do or not, this is the reality of education," or are they saying, "This is what we believe education to be, but whether it is this or not will be known only when there is universal agreement, consensus"? There is considerable ground for identifying social reconstructionism with the consensus position. In addition to the statements of Stanley already cited, there is, for example, the position taken by the authors of *The Improvement of Practical Intelligence,* who maintain that in both the realm of fact and the realm of value consensus is the ultimate criterion.[19] Although, as Stanley says in interpreting this position, a number of tests of the adequacy of practical judgment are described, such as inclusiveness, relevance, continuity, self-objectification, etc.,

. . . there is no doubt that, for the architects of the methodology of practical judgment, these criteria, while highly valuable and suggestive, are not final. The crucial and conclusive test is the re-establishment of an uncoerced community of persuasion, or, to put it in the current phrase, the achievement of a substantial measure of consensus.[20]

He goes on to state that further qualifications, even of this last statement, must be made:

The supreme test is not simply consensus, but a consensus that emerges from the crucible of deliberation and inquiry; and inquiry, whether conceived in Dewey's terms or in those delineated in *The Improvement of Practical Intelligence,* always includes the test of action.[21]

Although these qualifications undoubtedly apply to the position taken in this volume, nevertheless even the judgment of the results of action returns to consensus. Hence the qualifications, particularly that of action, which presumably intend to overcome the subjectivity that otherwise is involved, do not succeed in escaping the criticism that the consensus position rests upon the idea that cultural reality is a state of mind. Reference to the world, which the position insists upon, does not give that world an independent reality as long as judgment is validated by agreement, and this is true even though the method by which agreement is sought is carefully described. In short, the qualification

of method which would exclude the validity of agreements obtained by such devices as coercion, for example, still fails to
eliminate subjectivity. Furthermore, the authority of the method
itself must logically also rest on consensus. Hence a methodological principle of authority is no differently founded. According to
Stanley, in those areas where consensus exists, where the public
is an entity and the public will is expressed, the school has its
mandate. In other areas where this consensus is lacking, he suggests that educators rely upon a methodological principle of
authority, which, to be sure, must ultimately gain the acceptance of the public.[22] If, however, our analysis is sound, this
principle does not escape subjectivity either. Apart from its involvement in infinite regression, the consensus conception means
that cultural reality is a state of mind, and the question then is
only which state of mind is education or art or religion, or any
value.

The social reconstructionists generally believe that the central
task of education in the contemporary situation is to aid in the
restoration of consensus or the community of persuasion. On the
basis of Jordan's position, one criticism applies to both phases of
the social reconstructionist position, so far as they rest on consensus. The first, directed at the conception of cultural reality,
maintains that cultural unity does not reside in a state of mind
or in the subjective likemindedness of the people. The second,
directed at the conception of practical judgment or judgment as
a whole—and very closely related to the problem of cultural
reality or reality as a whole—is that verification cannot be attained by achieving consensus.

It is clear that the social reconstructionist, like the corporatist,
wants to avoid the conception of authority as external. External
authority is authoritarian authority. Perhaps this position is most
forcefully expressed by Dewey. He has insisted that education,
for example, is not subject to such authority and that its ends
are not subordinate to external ends, but are self-contained.
There is nothing outside itself for which education is a means.
Education has no ends outside itself; the aim of education is
education.[23] There is another side of Dewey, perhaps not characteristic, which also seems to give education a status in its own
right. He has said that the great problem of educational philosophy is to determine the nature of Education, and he does not

hesitate to use upper case, which is uncharacteristic of him. The problem is not one of choosing between traditional and progressive education, but of determining what is the nature of education without any adjectives whatsoever, what it is when it is truly education.[24] An inference might be drawn from this statement that education has a nature of its own, independently of the will of the people, to which the people should agree. This is, of course, vastly different from the position which holds that what education is is what the people determine it to be, even though the mode is prescribed by which agreement must be formed. If the people may make of education whatever they will, if institutions are whatever the people declare them to be and ends whatever they prescribe, then it is a very real question whether the social reconstructionists do succeed in avoiding external authority and whether ends are within rather than outside the act. Are the people any less a form of external authority than the individual dictator? Jordan maintains that the autonomy of institution, as contained in the conception of corporate will, is the fundamental fact of politics, and that only by transcending the natural person or the society of natural persons can freedom and order be achieved in human affairs. The theory of individuality issues in a theory of will. Another way of stating this might be to say that the autonomy of individuals is innate in their own nature. What every individual wills is self-realization, but this already implicates the species or the whole as end, in which the individual is fulfilled. What the society of natural persons wills is culture in all its forms and in its unity or wholeness.

According to Jordan's view, then, the primary problem of academic freedom, like that of the freedom of any institution, is one of understanding the nature of the educational institution and the conditions required for the attainment of its object. Practically, it means that the instruments necessary for that attainment, persons and things and their relations, must be provided, and this is the responsibility of politics. Social policy needs to be cultural policy, the will of the people one with culture.

Instead of finding law in the natural person, singly or collectively, corporatism maintains that law is the basis of the order of persons and things indifferently. Law in this sense is no respecter of persons, and persons will respect the law only when it manifests this kind of indifference, when it is "impersonal." If, as Jordan maintains, the great problem of politics is to impersonalize control, then social reconstructionism fails to solve the great problem. Our conclusion is that the social reconstructionist theory of the locus of political authority is subjective, and because it is so, serious consequences follow, not only for society as a whole but for the educational institution and profession. The autonomy of education and the teaching profession is eliminated, although the social reconstructionists argue that it is not. This is not because the social reconstructionist has any intention of subjecting education and the teaching profession to external rule—his aim is directly opposed to that—but because his theory can only issue in disastrous practical consequences. To look to the group or even the total unity of people, the "public," is to admit implicitly that education as an enterprise has nothing to say on its own, that there is no necessary logic inherent in it. There can then be no thinking by educators, for there is nothing objective, no object to think about. When the authority for education is the social whole—whether local, national, or international—educators can only submit to the dominion of the antiquated habits and customs of the community, or to the "power elite's" manipulation, through its direct and indirect control, of the states of mind of the public. Jordan's corporate view, on the contrary, holds that the primary problem of education, as of any profession, is the logical one of defining its proper goals and of designating clearly the structure of materials and persons it requires to achieve these goals; then what is to be done about the mind states of the public, whether to accept or re-educate them, follows from this understanding. If a group believes in irrational medical practices, is the group's psychology to be considered ultimate, or are the principles of the science of medicine the ultimates in terms of which the group's state of mind is evaluated and an educational program developed? The social position can only tell us where people now stand in their views of life, and provides no objective grounds for where they ought to stand, except at the cost of theoretical inconsistency. Indeed, the plausibility of the social point of view is largely the result of failure to recognize the self-contradiction in its tenets.

When he views himself as a hardheaded realist or when he despairs of attaining a consensual utopia with respect to any significant issue, the modern liberal, as a result of his group metaphysic, conceives the social order as a conflicting mass of "power" groups or social "forces." These he then defends as prerequisites of freedom, and the big problem of social order and educational authority becomes one of maintaining a system of "countervailing" powers, in which none shall become big enough to overwhelm the others. For the irreconcilable struggle of atomic individuals he substitutes the irreconcilable struggle of atomic groups. The interest group, assumed to be a power or a force, can achieve no constructive synthesis, since it drives toward its own interest regardless of the effect upon other groups and the institutional whole. *Powers* or *forces* know how to destroy but are not to be identified with *will*, which is world-building. The group makes use of cunning and deception in order to marshal its power on behalf of interest, but corporate persons require intelligence in order to define and redefine ends and the structure which ends must take in the light of the complexities of interinstitutional relations and the whole of which they are functional parts. Then Jordan would find that the attempt of the modern liberal to maintain freedom by preserving "private" areas of action for voluntary groups fails of its end. Relying on empirical evidence of disorder rather than on logical understanding of what a state is, the liberal misconceives the social structure as a collection of force centers. However, the state's being and growth is a functional harmony of wills, whose synthesis is Will, the dynamic objectification of the State of Culture.

Jordan affirms the autonomy of institutions and their professors, but cautions that autonomy must not be construed as private and separated from, or opposed to, politics and its concern with the public welfare. No group has a right in itself, but must be evaluated in relation to its act or the objective which it purports to realize. Power, whether that of a monolithic medical organization or union of teachers, and right are not synonymous. When right, the group affirms a corporate purpose. The right of the group to exist and act is derived from the object of culture which it seeks. There is no enmity between the state and such groups, for there is no inherent opposition between the state and culture. Furthermore, the state retains a positive responsibility to support, and not only in financial terms, all cultural acts. Society is corporate; its every act is a profession of the good, its every object is the basis upon which groups justify their right to existence and growth. Through their acts such groups maintain and extend the state as the cultural whole; far from being free from the state, they require the whole for their own sustenance. Individual and group purposes must be universalized, that is, incorporated in public and political ends. Their privacy demoralizes rather than frees, and only full publicization or politicalization can give them moral status. All acts are public or corporate, and their effect on the whole is the measure of their moral worth. While the problem of freedom in modern society may need to be seen from a new angle, as Whitehead asserts, the autonomous professions (and here Jordan includes all workers as professors of the good) are not safeguards against the inroads of the state, but are maintained by, and in turn maintain, the state as the state of culture. Jordan would disagree strongly with Whitehead's statement that freedom is now dependent upon voluntary associations or groups that have special ends separate from the state or from political objectives.[25] Jordan would agree that institutions and their professors are autonomous, but he would say that autonomy depends upon publicization, and he would say further that only in this way can the state be kept firmly attached to its human substance instead of becoming a supreme sovereign ruling over life. The state has no content of its own; in that statement lies a crucial part of Jordan's theory. Its content is precisely these institutional acts. There is no contradiction or opposition between the state and self-governing institutions; rather they form a continuity and unity.

Jordan distinguishes, in his views of the morality of public and private authorities, between those which *now* exist under those auspices and the *underlying principles inherent in such agencies.* He does not mean that at present all education under public sponsorship is good and all private education evil. Public legislatures, for example, currently motivated by interests, may impose an external authority which interferes with the freedom of the school and actually defeats public purpose. When it acts in such a manner, the public body is public in name only. On the other hand, there are undoubtedly private schools today which exhibit more freedom and are generally superior. Such private schools are then more truly associated with the public motive than schools operating under public or governmental authority. All, therefore, that goes by the name "public" now is not thereby moral, nor is the "private" thereby immoral, but Jordan argues that a distinction must be made between the names and the realities. If so-called public agencies at present do not express public ends, and if private instrumentalities do, they are violating their true natures. Private authority can be moral only when interest is abandoned and replaced by public purpose. On the other hand, governmental agencies may be utterly tyrannical and destructive of education, but only by giving up their public character. Jordan's fundamental thesis is that when private and public agencies are both true to their natures, the former is dominated by private motives and the latter by the public good. Existing so-called private schools may be more public than so-called public schools, but then the former are not really private and the latter not really public; their names belie their character. Jordan believes that the public school has to a certain extent become the servant of private interests, the very antithesis of its public purpose, and requires to be made public in reality. Nevertheless, the reality with which public education is identified is moral, the whole good, while "the possibility of the identity of the private with the public motive . . . has proved a doubtful maxim when applied in practice." [26] When private schools have been superior to public schools, it has been accidental, because the private motive cannot be lawful or rationally controlled, whereas the public motive can be so guided and its outcomes foreseen. Freedom of inquiry is essential to education, but can be realized only when identified with the public end. "Freedom is never effective until it is real and true, until it has become rationalized and made effective in institutional form." [27] The more fully public the act, the more free.

According to the corporate view that the legislative process is inherent in the growth tendencies of corporate life, and that the control of these growth tendencies is through the legislative act of speculation, the essence of true politics and real authority is experimental. Only when government is dominated by some form of interest, when public purpose has been taken over by private, is "authority" characterized by fixity and the perpetuation of the *status quo*. It is interest which rightly, in terms of its own self-perpetuation, fears change. Public authority, grounded in the nature of reality, cognizes and experimentally controls change for the good of the whole. An experimental politics is grounded upon necessities present in life; its corollaries are experimental institutions, of which education is one, and all of which the state itself is continuously to maintain. In this view there is no antithesis between public authority as the principle for a single public system of education on the one hand, and freedom and experimentation on the other, but rather an affirmation that the two are complementary to each other.

Jordan and Dewey agree that the institutionalists are right and the individualists wrong but that the institutionalists erred in subordinating the individual to the institution. They failed, therefore, to avoid the tyranny of individualism and merely substituted a tyranny of their own. While Jordan would agree that institutional idealism evolved into social absolutism, which did indeed enslave the individual, he would hold that the socialization advocated by modern liberalism, while presumably anti-individualistic, does not provide a solution to the authority problem in politics or education. To make "the social" the basic concept in place of "the individual" is not to escape individualism. Publicization as conceived by the modern liberal is socialization, whereas Jordan's publicization is basically different. The distinction here is between "the individual" and "the social" on the one hand, and "the cultural" on the other. Modern liberalism is social rather than political or cultural theory. For this reason the abandonment of individualistic democracy by the modern liberal and its replacement by social democracy is still inadequate and remains ultimately individualistic, despite its avowed rejection of atomism. Democracy exhausts itself with the social question, and when Jordan says that it has nothing to say regarding the constitution of the state, he means that it has nothing to say regarding culture or the institutions that comprise the constitution. Democracy does not relate itself to the corporate world as such; hence Jordan finds no difference but only more of the same in the transference from individual to social democracy. Despite his intention, the liberal, whether classical or modern, remains subjectivistic because of his false theory of reality.

Educational Authority

To view the educational enterprise as a corporate act grounded in nature, that is, as objectively necessitated by the requirements placed upon man in a world capable of responding to his attempts to order it, is to suggest that education is autonomous and speaks in its own name. Its will must be done for life to be right. Therefore, educators are not businessmen speaking for their private right, but professional agents speaking on behalf of objective authority. Not educators as such, but education requires more school buildings, classroom space, laboratories, libraries, personnel, etc., in precisely the same sense that industry requires its materials and personnel if its act is to be brought to completion and complement the acts of other corporate agencies. Education's authority does not derive from any person or collectivity of persons acting as a causal mechanism from without, but from its objective end revealed in the order of fact there before men's eyes. The school system and the world in which it has its place are no mere mental phenomena to be made over into anything or nothing at all. Education, through the form it has taken, is a reality in its own right and the authority of education is the logic which best defines both its static and dynamic tendencies. Said another way, its authority is superindividual in precisely the same sense that scientific authority is superindividual. Neither science nor education has an organic reference to particular scientists or educators, but rather to the body of logically validated categories which most adequately characterizes the object of study and concomitantly defines the capacities necessary for a scientist or educator.

The control of education is public and educators speak on behalf of public authority, but the meaning of "public" in corporate theory is supremely important here. As we have seen, Jordan asserts that the great problem of politics is to make control public, that is, impersonal. Public control in this sense is to be distinguished from public control interpreted as the rule of all. From Jordan's point of view, the latter might more accurately be called social control, in accordance with the distinction between the corporate or cultural theory and the social point of

view. "Public" for Jordan does not mean "all of us," and consequently public control does not mean control by the people as
a whole. Subjectivity is not escaped when control is shifted from
one, few, or many to all. Control by one, few, many, or all is
still personal in the sense that natural persons provide the principle of the act in question. To make control social, therefore,
does not involve a change in the principle of control, for it leaves
the natural person at the center of things, whereas Jordan's
Copernican Revolution makes corporate person that center. Jordan expresses the fundamental ideas of the corporate conception
in different ways. When he asserts that control must be impersonal, he intends to deny the natural person as a principle of
social organization. Another way of stating this is to stipulate
that control should indeed be personal, but to insist that the institutional or corporate person is what is meant. What is required
is an understanding of the act, its object, and the conditions of
its fulfillment. It is the responsibility of politics to provide the
conditions of the fulfillment of the educational act, as well as to
harmonize education with the other acts comprising the whole.

The idea of external authority is foreign to the corporate
theory, is, in fact, the very thing it negates; what it asserts is
the autonomy of the act, of the institution. Again, Jordan here
makes different uses of language to express a common idea.
Either he says that authority must be eliminated in a rational
system of politics and law, or that it must be made impersonal.
The latter term, as indicated above, means that authority inheres
in the act itself, in the corporate person, by virtue of the object
of the act. Each act as a form of the good possesses authority
in its cultural function. Rights are not imputed, assigned, or
delegated to the act; they belong to it. Its rights derive from the
object that it contemplates as a good in the whole good; hence
rights are not individual or social but cultural. In the sense that
the state is the state of culture, the ultimate moral object, the
state itself is the source of rights.

Right . . . has a social origin only when society is interpreted in
terms of other than individual or group relations or interests. For
this interpretation is isolationist in its tendency and thus subjective
as long as social interpretation is based either upon the nature of the
individual or the group . . . the conception of group has added
nothing to the conception of individual. The subjectivism of individualism cannot be avoided by appeal to the group. . . . It is also in this

sense that it is true that rights originate from the power or authority of the state, that they are created by positive law, and their incidence upon persons dependent upon the will of the state. These propositions are true in so far as they imply that the state is the *status* of institutions of fact. As such it is the ground of the opportunities to those forms of action which are calculated to result in satisfactory ends. The state is therefore that larger person which represents the principle of order which holds persons and things and actions to unified effort in the interest of large ends. It is the unity of institutions. But if it be objected that these ends are always the ends of individual persons, the reply is that they are so, but in the sense only that individual persons must be component and competent elements within the state, that a state is not an abstraction that exists apart from or over and above individuals. The ends embraced in the ideal constitution of the state then are the ends of individuals, but they are those ends as become universal. Also, the individuals of which the state is composed are not all natural persons. The consequence is therefore that the state is a *state of fact* and differs from other states of fact or situations involving thought and action and things only in that it is more compendiously inclusive of detail than others and is thus more broadly universal as a principle of unity. . . . The state is an institution of precisely the same principle as the natural person or any individuality within the series whose limits are the natural person and the state. . . . Rights are then 'derived' from the state in the sense that they have no meaning apart from the principle of individuation which makes the state a person along with other institutions.[28]

There is no question here of subjugation by the state; the one thing to be avoided at all costs is the idea of domination. Art, education, religion, industry, every institution, must be publicized, and this means that each must be politicized; none should be removed from the political sphere or the state. Institutions must be pervaded by politics to guide them toward their public ends, and to keep them allied with other institutions in forming the whole does not mean destroying their autonomy; it means giving the various acts their head, while fitting each of their ends into the End; hence they do not negate each other. Jordan says that in this permitting of the act to be itself lies the real worth of the idea of laissez faire. Freedom as objective requires access to the means necessary for the attainment of the end. The responsibility of politics is to provide these conditions.

When these considerations are directed to academic freedom, it is seen that the rights of the school and of its agents, all those participating in its act, are not derived from society, if that be taken as the whole of men, but from the state in the sense already indicated. Once again, rights are not social but cultural in origin, and they are sustained by the political act of furthering and harmonizing all the acts of the state. Education makes its demands and justifies them by speaking in its own name and on its own behalf. To be sure, these claims must be weighed in relation to the needs and resources of the whole. There can be no individualism with respect to institutions either. Each institution must be considered as a whole or unity within the larger whole or unity of unities, just as each organ of the body must be studied as a functional whole related to other organs and to the organism in order to understand its place. So conceived, the authority of the organ is clarified and men of knowledge are enabled to promote its function.

Conclusion

On the positive side, Jordan's contribution to the problem of educational authority lies essentially in his insight into the nature of the constitution of modern society as corporate. His identification of status or property and contract with objectified and objectifying will, based upon an underlying theory of individuality, provides an objective ground for authority, and suggests an education which is tied to the structure of society rather than to interests or other subjective phenomena. As Cairns in his examination of legal theory has concluded, the interest theory of the state is invalid and must be replaced by an institutional theory.[29] Jordan provides such a theory; he attempts to avoid the errors of the institutionalisms that have subjugated rather than freed man. If education is to be based upon objective authority and constructed in accordance with the constitution, if it is to provide the intelligence to sustain, maintain, and extend culture, it must rest upon cultural rather than social foundations.

CHAPTER 9
THE NATURE AND CONDITIONS
OF THE EDUCATIONAL ACT

Introduction

In the world ordered upon the principle of justice, a world where each corporate act is so instituted as to sustain and develop the others, the educational act is effective, for education depends upon a world that concurs in its purpose. The corporate world is responsible for education's materials, as well as for the mind set of the child. Industry, government, family, church, recreation, art, instituted media of communication, the state of international relations, etc., must be so ordered as to expedite the educational act, just as the act must be of such a nature as to sustain the institutional complex of which it is a vital part. The concrete effectiveness of education depends upon the quality of the corporate complex in which it exists. The corporate world is virtue and mind made real, so that the principles of education, as of law and ethics, are based upon philosophic insight into the nature of this world. Without knowledge of culture, of objective mind, the mental training of students as a deliberate enterprise is left to chance.

Education, when it is regulated by an understanding of the action life of men, is based upon objective principle, objective because the principle expresses a state of affairs not dependent upon the psychology of the knowing subject or upon the psychology of a group or a nation. Like the laws of science, cultural principle either reveals this objective reference or it is meaningless, e.g., the "principle" that education may be anything which the individual, group, or society wishes to make of it. Education, as grounded upon objective authority, is founded in the corporate make-up of the state, the state being the synthesis of the various forms of action which constitute it.

Although in his discussion of education Jordan does not mention Aristotle, his agreement that education must accord with the constitution of the state is clear. Education, then, cannot succeed unless it is based upon knowledge of the nature of cultural reality. If a theory of the state misconceives the state's constitution, its educational concept must fail and thus fail the state. Jordan believes that the decline of culture under the influence of subjectivity is nowhere more apparent or calamitous than in education. Education, as well as the other forms of mind, must be rescued from the control of private interest and the business "mind," and the autonomy of the cultural establishment must be recognized and advanced; but this requires that all human acts and the objects in which they issue be moralized by being made thoroughly public. If education is not to be reduced to propaganda, it must be objective; it must conform with an objective or corporate theory of society.

The End of Education

"If our first obligation is to know, then the development and cultivation of intelligence is our most important moral function." [1] Indeed, elsewhere Jordan has put this responsibility even more strongly by making it man's first, last, and only obligation. Intelligence is the special capacity of the natural person needed to complement the acting or working capacity of the institution.

Intelligence, comprehension, the act in which thought integrates itself, knowing in its universal form, is . . . the highest function of the individual. But an active function or capacity is what is meant by virtue. Intelligence is then, as knowledge, the summation of all virtue and the totality of his obligation for the human individual. The first and highest, and at the last, the only, obligation of the individual is the obligation to know. [2]

It is not surprising, therefore, that Jordan calls education the most important of the worlds in which the individual lives, for it is the means to his moral achievement and, as such, is itself a moral function. Education opens the good life to the individual, and it provides that life with the intellectually competent individuals it needs. To the gift of nature, it adds the gift of culture; it controls the things of nature and culture in the interest of producing intellectually fit persons. Education, when it is functioning properly, enables the individual to acquire intelligence and thus to see things in their true value.

The life for which it [education] should prepare is that which adds to natural existence the abundance of the cultural, which enables us to see in the good person the good world. The latter is nothing more or less than the orderly whole of all the activities and objects necessary to sustain the act by which it is created. It is this act which is the end, the ultimate object, the good which morality contemplates.[3]

Man's obligation to know is at once his obligation to himself and to culture or the state. Jordan believes that the corporate conception eliminates the false question of how to build the social out of the individual. Once we abandon atomism and grant that human nature is cultural nature, the false opposition between individual and society or between individual and state disappears. For corporatism, the injunction "to thine own self be true" is identical with being true to the state. The state is the individual writ large; it is what the individual means. Jordan believes that obligation is always due to the corporate person, and this conception is consistent with the view that the corporate person, rather than the natural person, taken singly or collectively, is the basic concept of ethics, politics, and law. As moral-political, the obligation to know is the public function, since its reference is not back to the actor or agent but outward to the whole of culture which it maintains and extends.

Stated negatively, the ultimate end of education is not defined by the needs or wants of the natural individual, or group, or society conceived as the group of groups, or by a mystical God viewed as a spiritualized abstraction whose will may be as arbitrary and lawless as that of any despot. The ultimate end of education is the moral world, and this is the state, for the state, *when it is truly a state,* is a moral enterprise. It is not the whole of the empirical "state" described by political "science" which is to be sustained, but only that in it which is of value in the sense of being constructive of the action life of man. Since the state is not an abstraction but the whole of its institutions, the specific ends of education have concrete or objective existence in the corporate activities of human life, from which they are derived and which they sustain and advance. The task of education is to bring the mind of the student to a critical awareness of the instituted acts of human life—the family, industry, education, religion, art, politics, science, recreation, etc. All the acts and objects of value which require understanding in terms of their historical development, current status, and future tendencies, provide the concrete ends of life with which the mind of the student is to be connected, and the making of these connections is the development of intelligence.

The special cultural function which education performs is to infuse the corporate complex with intelligence, i.e., with men who think and know. Institutions can do but cannot see; men can see but cannot do. Man's special function, his moral-political obligation, is to know, and education fulfills its moral-political obligation in developing intelligent men, an intelligent citizenry. Not only is education the primary means by which persons of the highest intelligence are discovered and prepared for the legislative office, and thus an agency through which law is made as rational as possible, but along with administration it is also an instrument by which the law is promulgated, that is, by which the law as an embodiment of the highest intelligence is made effective in the minds of the citizenry.[4]

The intelligent mind, the goal of education, is not an abstract container of ideas. The mind is itself developed through action in the world and is known as intelligent because of the difference it creates in its objective circumstance. It makes a difference in the world because it possesses a peculiarly important faculty; intelligence goes beyond the presented data to ideal constructs, and ideal constructs specify or at least imply the active relationship to the world which is to be taken by the knowing person. Moreover, intelligence and will are not separate for Jordan because will is will only when it is rational; thus for will to effect itself in the world in the form of an object, it must incorporate sound ideas. Nor is intelligence separate from feeling, since how the individual feels, the emotional quality of his experience when looking at a painting or listening to music, depends upon knowledge; and reciprocally the feelings themselves, as they give body to idea, impel the knower toward action. Jordan insists on this point:

The effort to divide the educative process into education of the intelligence, of the will, of 'character,' and of the emotions is misleading, therefore; the 'mental function' to be educated is the intelligence as the unity of mind or the common cognitive thread which runs through all manifestations of mind.[5]

Intelligence is the subject's harmonious and developed unity of feeling (the "organic receptivity" or sensitivity to the environing world), willing (the active tendencies of the organism), and thinking (logical formulation, experimentation, and reflection upon ideas), through which he sustains an active relationship to the world.

Jordan describes knowledge as essentially imaginative and projective rather than simply theoretical; it is not only of things as they are but as they might be.[6] Knowledge is closely related to action; it is the projected ideal that calls forth action for its realization. The break between existence and value, between what is and what ought be, is the reason for action. Intelligence, then, knows what is and suggests what ought to be, and it determines the means for bringing the latter into being. This is true whether one speaks of the piece of wood as it is, containing the possibility of a bookcase whose design controls the action to be undertaken, or whether one refers to the broadest political considerations.

There is no disjunction between the development of intellect and of will. "All will is rational, and all reason is volition in the sense that it intends ultimately to impress its form upon the face of things." [7] Consequently, it is false to separate the education of the intellect from that of the will or of "character." Jordan's description of the educational function as the work of producing intellectually competent persons should be interpreted within his conception of the mind as a corporate phenomenon, involving the world of objects as its content and using that world as the means for its objectification and realization. The intelligence which is to be educated is the cognitive unity of all aspects of mind, and the individual's obligation to know is his obligation to maintain this cognitive unity of being amid the changes which take place in his world.[8] To "know thyself" is to know all one's capacities and to see, even to make, one's self whole, which is possible only through the intellect. "Personality in this connection is nothing more than the organic unity of all the physical and the mental functions, as effected and maintained by intelligence." [9] The intelligent man whom education is to produce is thus the whole person, not an isolated intellect, "the person conceived as complete in himself but as being so through the fact that he is, when we think of him in terms of mind and capacity, the synthesis of his objective circumstance, which his own inner unity represents." [10]

Jordan defines personality or the self as active; in fact, persons and things are implicates of action, not the other way around. Action is the fundamental concept; person and thing are derivative. The act joins person and world, and in and through action the mind is made up as well as objectified. Mind is of and in the world. A moral situation is one in which the whole self as integrated is centered upon an act issuing in a moral object.

This pulling myself together and directing myself to some end is my *act*, by which I mean to alter not only the world but also myself and to state the altered world and the altered self as a new synthesis. An act points in two directions, and a perfect act is a relation of analogical identity between two objects that are both ends. That is, the 'subject,' or person in terms of mental capacities, and the world manifesting itself as quality, are superseded and transformed into the objective or corporate person; this corporate person has the same moral status as any natural person, except that it possesses more powers and capacities and is hence able to attain ends that are beyond the reach of the 'natural' person. These ends are moral objects, and are the proper content of politics.[11]

An integrated personality depends upon an integrated world, and it is the task of politics to effect the world of acts and objects as objective mind.[12] Said somewhat differently, the "subjective" mind of the natural person is continuous with the "objective" mind of the corporate or institutional person; or more simply, the unity of individual minds is founded upon the unity of culture which is the state. If it is the function of education to develop the intelligence as the factor effecting the unity of the individual, it will still be dependent upon politics to supply wholeness to the corporate system. Ultimately, an adequate education is possible only in an ordered world; the confusion within and between nations, i.e., in the state of objective mind, will result in a corresponding confusion in individuals. A shattered world shatters individuals.

Policy: Speculation, Administration, and Adjudication

One of the difficulties in the teaching-learning process is the deadening influence of administration, which impedes the vitality, spontaneity, and free curiosity of the teacher and learner in pursuing their common objective. Jordan generally regards administration as an unfortunate influence on education because of its authoritarian manifestations, and he calls for the demobilization of education in order to get rid of its top-heavy burden. While he explicitly consigns to educational administration the relatively minor task of caring for the externals—equipment, supplies, and the like [13]—quite another and more important function may be inferred from his description of administration at the constitutional level. If the assumption may validly be made that the speculative, administrative, and judicial functions are required not only at the interinstitutional level but at the intrainstitutional level as well, then a function for educational executive officers is suggested.

Jordan's discussion in his *Theory of Legislation* of administration as an aspect of the legislative process has significant implications for the administration of education. In terms of this discussion, educational administration would neither be discarded nor confined to minor tasks, but would be a highly important part of the educational institution. Nevertheless, it would not be charged with the responsibility for making policy. It is the usurpation of the policy-making function that makes administration a general obstruction to the educational act; moreover, this authoritarianism in administration is not inherent in the function but is a perversion of it.[14] If educational administration is to function similarly to administration at the constitutional level, its province must be experimentation in the application of policy.

Jordan holds that the concept of the administrative autonomy of the corporate person furnishes the new political and legal principle which contrasts to the older doctrines of dictatorship or representation.[15] He suggests that institutions develop their own momentum; they exhibit a spontaneity and growth which, while needing the guidance of human intelligence, must nevertheless not be dominated. We must discard the view that institutions have to be bossed; rather they run themselves. Acts are autonomous, and they and their objects need to be understood rather than subjected.

An act implies an object and . . . the kind of object determines the nature of the act; in fact, the act is precisely what, when realized is the object, the object is the act as objectified. This principle determines the type of process involved in education, since the process of learning is an act. Then it is true that the type of person demanded by morality should determine the educative process as to both form and content.

. . . Then if the acts of the educative process are to be determined by the nature of the object to be produced, the acts of the learner cannot be dictated by the teacher. Hence the teacher is not a boss, and the educative process has no need of directors, supervisors, principals, etc. . . . The principle is that the educative process is a system of acts determined only by the nature of the objects which they contemplate, and any interference in the action is a perversion of education as a function in the good life. The problem of education as a moral question is to find the nature of the object which the educative process is to produce and to suggest the type of organization for education that will best fit into the good life.[16]

Education must get rid of bosses, whether they be teachers or administrators or, for that matter, students. When a student's interests dominate education, there is again a loss of the freedom necessary to the educational process, which is then reduced merely to satisfying the student, and this leads to the incorporation of trivia in the curriculum. Another result of following the interests of students, parents, and pressure groups often is to eliminate intellectual education in favor of vocational training, which serves neither the individual nor culture.[17] It sacrifices the whole man as a cultural person to the part man as technical, and this is the destruction of the moral man. The specialization of his action as a result of vocational training divests it of moral qualities, precisely because it has lost its reference to the whole which is the end of action. Thus the individual neglects the development of his capacities as a whole and specializes in one, that which will bring him his living. His real education is then reduced to the chance bits he picks up from the world around him, while his formal education is largely confined to "practical" concerns. Jordan's criticism here is that such a view destroys both the individual and the educational institution, for both should be dedicated to the development of the whole man as fit to abide in and to extend the world of action, the state. He and his education become commercialized, devoid of morality. Education must choose between the development of persons who have a special capacity for sale and those who understand and use their capacities as creative instruments of culture. Referring to education as it is now conducted, Jordan says:

We do not aim at producing moral persons but human machines; not agents capable of complete acts but 'agents' who sell themselves as implements which repeat a movement indefinitely. We do not produce a man whose whole act creates a house but a salesman who puts together building material for sale. Morality requires that education produce men who can build houses that can take their place in a beautiful and happy city, not that will stand up until they can be sold. The act is whole and right only when its object is capable of becoming a part of the end. This is the principle by which we judge every act.[18]

If dictation must not come from within the institution, neither must it come from without, whether from interest groups or from the people as a whole. Education must free itself from tyranny both within and without. The nature of its object determines the conditions which the act requires for its fulfillment. The relationships of persons, such as teachers and students, to each other, as well as to the cultural objects which provide the medium or material of education, are set and settled by that object. Sovereignty provides no principle of organization. Jordan is, of course, not arguing against organization as such; he does not believe that organization in itself is necessarily tyrannical, but he says that the principle of educational organization today is fallacious and denies freedom. It would contradict fundamental corporate conceptions to oppose organization as such; organs are necessary if the purpose of education is to be realized. In fact, Jordan believes that the problem of organization is the most urgent one facing education today.[19] The difficulty with school organizations today is that, lacking principle, they have become either coercive power structures forcing decisions upon a rebellious or passive staff, or discussion groups unable to make intelligent decisions because principle is presumed to derive from the group per se. In both cases there is a failure to recognize principle inherent in the corporate structure, which is the objective ground for the policy-making process.

Understanding of the corporate act, and of the corporate world in which it takes place, is the concrete basis for educational administration. The administrator must have knowledge of and be sensitive to the ongoing requirements of the good life, as well as to the special function of the educational agency, so that the educational act may be guided more effectively. In executing educational policy the administrator is sensitive, therefore, to *ideas* from two areas. On the one hand, the over-all tasks of education are formulated speculatively by the policy-making body of legislators, whose task is to fit the educational act and its growth tendencies into the corporate world in such a way that it will complement and be constructive of the family, church, industry, etc. Corporate persons and their purposes are the "publics" he attends to in implementing policy, and not groups and their interests. The object at all levels of legislative activity is to convert private advantage into public function; therefore, it is only for pedagogical reasons and for the practical purpose of immediate implementation of the educational act that he studies and deals with interest groups. Owing to unfortunate historical accidents, these are the dominant contemporary "realities" of the social "order." The challenge of the administrator's work on this level lies in the effort to put into practice broad policy by co-ordinating the work of his educational agency with the other activities of the community (local, state, national, and international) that have a bearing upon the performance of the educational function.

One of the chief problems of educational organization and policy-making today, apart from the crucial matter of failing to understand clearly the ends of education, is how to provide the material means for the success of the teaching-learning process. In any corporate activity the materials must be adapted to the needs of the act, not the act to the materials, such materials as may be available on a catch-as-catch-can basis. The ability of economic organizations to control the political process to their own advantage, and the concomitant failure of the legislative body to make comprehensive policy for the industrial act, has meant that the requirements of education, as well as of family life, art, religion, etc., have been overlooked or granted only token recognition. The impotence of the administration of educational agencies, and of the disrespect for teachers in general, is a direct result of the effective control of the political order by business and the planless but at times deliberate starvation of education by business. In our life business calls the tune to which cultural agencies abjectly dance.

The second source of educational policy, which when sound is principled by the first source, develops out of the active functioning of the staff in carrying out the educational tasks. Like the citizen on the constitutional level, as the most active doers, teachers are the direct makers of policy and are in the best position to know what is educationally needed. Special problems may arise because of the background of the pupils entering the school system or because of new methods; skills and knowledge may be developed which require new materials or new space and time arrangements in order to improve the educational process. All the policies made within the educational establishment, such as curriculum planning, the criteria of competency for staff members, the specific types of materials needed, etc., are developed out of deliberation as a result of the staff's direct experience of the teaching-learning process, and these become the specific responsibilities of the administrator to implement; or he may bring them back to the legislative body as new facts to be the basis for further acts of policy-making. For example, if new materials are required, recourse may be needed to the industrial order, and this the educational administrator is himself powerless to effect.

For the above reasons Jordan asserts that the making of policy by administrators is a clear usurpation of function. What is required of the administrator is the necessary intelligence to confirm the policy which has emerged from the ongoing activities of the educational process, and the executive ability to implement it. He neither makes nor creates over-all or specific policy, but as the overseer of the whole he tries to fit the varied activities of the organization together so that they do not impede one another. The policy body within the institution consists of the corporate doings of the institutional person, expressed by the relevant faculty in terms of specific formulations and plans. Guided by the larger and more comprehensive statements of policy formulated by the speculative group of the legislature, the faculty as a whole or through policy-making committees, depending upon the size of the school, and in consultation with students and others affected, depending upon the nature of the problem, develops a balanced plan of educational activities. Administration is the mediatory function; through its access to and communication with both policy-making levels, it expedites policy and sees that the policy created on the constitutional level and on the intrainstitutional level is consistent, and it implements the resultant policy. The right of the administrator is to be the intelligent medium of communication and execution of the policy-making bodies. This suggests that since the administrator is the agent of two complementary policy-making bodies, either one has the right to remove him for just cause. While the employment rights of the administrator are often overly fragile and ought to be strengthened if he is to do a forthright job, machinery should be available on the constitutional level and the intra-institutional level to review policy and hear the charges that may be brought against a faculty member by either level or both. This means some form of a judicial body.

On the constitutional level adjudication is performed by professional judicial bodies, although they are impeded by the present inadequacies of legal theory and antiquated mechanics of operation. Nevertheless, there is at least recourse to a public adjudicative body, which through its very existence often prevents unlawful acts of policy-making and administration. Adjudicative machinery on the intrainstitutional level is conspicuous by its absence or its impotence, since even when such machinery does exist, it is the administrator who often performs the judicial review or who directly or indirectly controls the reviewing board. This is as much an administrative usurpation of power as the typical administrative domination over policy-making. Since most of the problems faced by men occur on the intrainstitutional level, within the body of the immediate corporate agency whose function they are effecting, the general lack of machinery with power to declare uninstitutional the policy-making of the staff, and/or the executions of the administrator, creates a vacuum inevitably filled by the authoritarianism of the administrators or the staff policy-makers. Since policy is always experimental, and faculty and administrators may err, an independent judicial body on the intrainstitutional level is required to judge the policy experiment. The presence of such a body, independent of both the administration and the policy-makers, would also help to prevent abuses from occurring or to resolve them expeditiously, without anyone needing to make his case a *cause célèbre* in order to have a judicial hearing at all. As a reasonable procedure in the selection of the judicial body, a special committee of the staff might select a number of men for this position, and, after consultation with the administration whose co-operation and advice should be sought, the staff as a whole should have the opportunity to discuss with the appropriate committee and administrative personnel the qualifications of the individuals chosen for the judicial function. More important than the specific details of selection are the criteria to be applied in the choice and the administrative safeguards established to enable the judicial group to enjoy independence of judgment. The appointments made to the federal bench and to the Supreme Court provide some guidance here for the answer to both problems. The individuals selected should be of obvious maturity and balanced temperament, should possess traits of "high-mindedness" as displayed through their manifest concern with problems of principle, and should have been with the organization long enough to become familiar with the variety of its activities and problems. The administrative safeguards established should appropriately safeguard the employment rights of the judicial group, just as all functional members of a corporate body from the "lowest" to the "highest" must have their right to function formally defined; the judicial group must be immune from the coercion of the administrative and policy-making bodies, and thus free to adjudicate on the basis of principle. The corporate structure is not a check and balance of powers that are assumed to be in opposition to each other, but a separation and distinction of interrelated functions so that they may be more effectively performed.

In summary, then, the administrator is not a boss over his faculty hirelings, for the administrative act is so organized in terms of selection, policy-making, and judicial machinery that few authoritarians would obtain executive posts and those that did could be dealt with promptly. The administrator is, instead, an intelligent mediator between the legislative body and the teaching and research staff, between the good of the whole state and the good of the educational function. His constructive function is to expedite the policy of the former, which is, however, not arbitrary but based upon the requirements of the latter. Nevertheless, it must be borne in mind that owing to the realities of any act that takes place in the world and the unanticipated problems which it may face, administration cannot and should not slavishly follow the educational policies developed by policy-making bodies. For the shifts in course that it may take administration must have objective, concrete grounds to which it can point with justification. Similarly, the legislative body cannot and should not unthinkingly follow the new requirements of the educational act as they may be presented by educational administration, for the latter needs to be fitted within the whole of acts. However, where the legislative body denies the claims of education, reasons must be provided based upon the good of the state, of the whole instituted world of human acts, or the denial will be unconstitutional.

Wisdom is in the world when administrative agencies are principled by the whole good and soundly ordered within. Only then can they function intelligently.

Content

The content of education is the world of culture, the world of objectified and objectifying value. The content of education is the corporate world, for the corporate world is objective mind and the student develops a mind as he is related to it. The mind that does not include more than its own biopsychological processes is psychotic, defective, or animal. Growth in knowledge of the world is growth in the mind of the student. Now the specific meaning and application of this insight derived from Jordan must be developed from the contributions of philosophy and psychology. The crucial philosophic task is to provide the concepts through which culture is made intelligible, that is, to develop the objective principles or categories through which we may identify objects of value, and it is upon the development of such principles that the determination of educational content depends. However, not only does virtually the whole of modern philosophy ignore this task, but it is precisely the very possibility of developing objective criteria of value which modern philosophy proudly negates. This is, perhaps, the basic explanation why so much of the content in education today is based upon little more than the whims of teachers or pressure groups rather than on careful thought.

Psychology, on the other hand, because it conceives its task as locating the "causes" of behavior, has fragmented the unity of mind into an anarchic aggregation of mental factors; or, viewing science as a rigorous attempt to reduce its object of study into ultimately simple elements, it has found the neuron and the cortex and the synapse and the reflex instead of mind; or, under the influence of Darwinian biology, it has found an organismic or instrumental mind, the "mind" of needs and wants and self-referent problem-solving. However, mind is a unity of affective-conative-cognitive capacities, or it is not mind. Mind conceived as distinct and separate capacities (factors) to be exercised or developed is a false conception, for an atomistic mind is the negation of its own meaning. The conception of a network of stimulus-response patterns mechanizes mind and fails to explain or to provide a basis for developing its creative capacities. As controlled by needs and wants, thinking collapses, since mind is their helpless tool. Finally, when mind is thought of as a means to self-advantage, as if it and culture were separate and distinct, and as if culture were something to be exploited by the keen "brains" of the individual on his own behalf, then mind is equated with animal cunning. The ground of mind is culture, and the individual proves that he has a mind when he minds its ground; if this were not the case, the educational attempt to develop mind would be irrational and destructive.

The two great weaknesses in the determination of content for the school system are based, then, upon two catastrophic intellectual failures, the philosophic failure to define objective mind (culture) and a concomitant psychological failure to understand subjective mind. In the corporate view of objective mind, each institution is a type of mind because it is the realization of ideas, and it is also creative of ideas through its organization of the action life of the individual. The mind of man typically represents the quality of the institutional order, so that whether or not it is made deliberate content for education, each institution, the state as a whole, is mind-forming in terms of its effects upon the individual. In this basic sense the subjective mind of the individual is corporate, representing an individuated unity and outgrowth of the corporate world. From a more immediate pedagogical standpoint, the mind of the individual is corporate in another sense: it is not only integrally related to the world as an outgrowth of and contributor to the cultural medium, but it is also integrally related to the biopsychological corpus of the individual. The very fact of a biopsychological corpus means that, in common with all organismic life, mind has feeling and activity for its basic structural components. Feeling is related to mind-development in the dual sense of sensitivity, or the more or less passive receptiveness to stimuli, and of the impulsion to action and thought. Withdrawing one's hand from the hot stove is a sign of nascent intelligence. The flexibility of movement pattern in the organism is largely determined through its structure, and since the development and understanding of ideas are dependent both upon the possibility of acting and the carrying out of plans of action, the biopsychological organism as a whole is involved in mind-development. The development of the active thinking processes of mind, which seems almost to be an activity apart from the affective and volitional impulses of the individual, does take on a relatively independent course of its own, but when this occurs it is the proof of thought's unity with the feeling and will. The unified ordering of the biopsychological bases of mind is the foundation for flights of the mind into the highest realm of ideas, just as the mechanical order of the automobile is the largely unperceived background for the plans of the motorist. The ideas of the individual are not *caused* by his organism but are *grounded* upon it as a necessary condition of thought, just as the car does not do the driver's thinking and yet is the underlying basis for his making and effecting plans as a motorist.

Jordan's corporate theory attempts to fill the gaps in the objective understanding of culture and the psychology of mind. The former has been the major point of this study and its significance for educational content seems obvious; we have briefly discussed the latter to suggest the inadequacies of current theory. However, the relationship of content to the mental development of the student cannot be conceived abstractly, since the level of the school is organically related to a level of mental development; therefore, this point will be specifically developed in the next chapter in the section on "Applications to the School." The three basic principles involved in the organization of mind will be taken up in the following section on method.

Method

Jordan's educational method, which in its larger meaning is identical with the method of political control or order, is predicated upon his view of the organically interrelated mind-object, for, from the point of view of the subject, mind is objectified or realizes itself through action in an object, while from the point of view of the object, it is objective mind. His three principles of mental organization, upon which educational method is grounded, are based upon this relationship. They are as follows: (1) *"Mind always acts through its body and is known only in and through its actions."* (2) *". . . Mind always acts as a whole or as a unity and is known only as such."* (3) *". . . Mind, as essentially active, completes itself or makes itself up in the objects of the external or practical world and is controlled only through the manipulation of the objects of the practical world."* [20]

We understand the first principle to mean that educational method utilizes the active energies of the organism in relating it to the objective circumstance about it, the materials of education in and through which the mind of the learner takes on its form and realizes itself. To develop his mind and to demonstrate that he has one, the student must develop a competent body, trained in the disciplined response to his ideas. It is for this reason that training in physical agility, strength, and skills in general is one and the same with enlarging the student's mental capacities. Thus, the development and realization of intelligence is fundamentally predicated upon an educational method infused by the idea of work, not in the negative sense of monotonous drudgery to be ended as soon as possible, but in its positive meaning as the disciplined attention and application needed to attain anything of value. The physical health and vitality of the organism is a basic precondition for the development of mind.

The second principle means that in the normal active functioning of mind no single part ever operates to the exclusion of other components or capacities of mind. In the active situation, when mind is cognizing something, whether a physical object or a logical object, thinking, willing, and feeling are all present.

When the mind acts, it is the whole mind that acts and never a part of it. Every object which I know is, in the completest case, a point around which all the activity of my whole mind centers. It is this fact of the reference of all aspects of the mind to an object whenever any one aspect refers to the object, that is the secret of the organization of the mind.[21]

It is this which also explains why physical education is related to mind, insofar as we conceive of mind as the unity of all the active traits of the organism, since through the organization of physical activities the organism's traits of will receive encouragement and expression. The development of will, in the individual as in the world, depends upon an organic capacity to do. Moreover, a rightly ordered physical education may encourage the development of such active attitudes toward life as endurance, strength, courage, self-confidence, and "good sportsmanship," the last being a capacity for honor and integrity in playing the game (life), without which achievement would have no meaning. The quality of physical education and the quality of mind are integrally related.

This principle that mind *always acts as a whole or as a unity and is known only as such* clearly implies that educational method extends beyond the immediate teacher-student relationship; it must comprise *the whole of activities with which the educational program is involved.* The balanced, temperate mind of the student is directly related to the balanced, temperate activities to which he is exposed. The overemphasis placed upon competitive sports by schools develops minds whose thinking, feeling, and willing are directed toward basketball and football, and as a result the history or mathematics teacher is impotent before such minds, no matter what psychological tools he has acquired in his methods courses. The objective order of the curriculum is the basic method through which the student's mind takes on form and content.

Jordan says of the third principle of his general method, "This is the fundamental *educational* law or principle, and it governs all the growth aspects of human activity." [22] It is here that the fundamental importance of the curriculum may be clearly seen, since the mind is qualitatively shaped through the environing object system in which it has its active relations. Ideas, feelings, and will energies are reached and molded through the nature and order of the materials made accessible to the student, and what he wills to do and learn, the way in which he feels, depends upon the design of his active relationships to the objects of education. For this reason the curriculum, as the objective design of the intelligence to be achieved in students, is ultimately a political and ethical problem. Political order is involved because the type of mind produced inevitably bears upon the instituted life of man; the student's developed intelligence must be such that it is capable of objectification, of realization in objects that have a constructive bearing within the cultural whole.

If mind is an active integration of the object world within

which it functions, then the teacher cannot know the child merely, for this would be a contradiction in terms. To know the child, the student at any level, the teacher must know objects. Knowledge of the educative management of the child involves much more than knowledge of Freudian "adjustment mechanisms"; the teacher must know culture. Said another way, mind is not already packaged in the child, needing only a methodological hocus-pocus to bring it out of the student's biopsychological innards; mind is in the objects of culture. Therefore, the first requirement of method is that the teacher himself be a cultured person. He must be a man of wide knowledge, capable of a sensitive and refined discrimination of the materials which best serve the end of developing the student's mind to its highest capacity.

From the above principles of mind it logically follows "that the approach to any special field of study is a matter of acquaintance of the student with the object-system peculiar to that field," [23] e.g., art objects develop aesthetic minds, mathematical objects mathematical minds, etc. However, just as the nature of the object-system introduced is ultimately an ethical and political problem, the particular method or mode of its introduction is also at bottom a political and ethical problem. For example, so far as the use of fear in pedagogical method makes the student more readily accessible to control by external authority, it must be proscribed as a principle, and this would be true even if it were experimentally verifiable that through the use of fear students learn more quickly and more adequately retain what they learn. Civilization requires individuals who know no such fear, who dare to innovate and think creatively, who act and are not moved by causal forces external to them. Since method is ultimately an ethical and political problem, its determination is the responsibility of philosophy. The contribution of psychology, which has nothing whatever to do with the determination of desirable educational outcomes, is the knowledge of how best to expedite the student's coming to terms with the object systems; and here are considered such matters as sequential order, repetition, style of communication, and the appropriate exposure of students to educational materials at all developmental levels of the organism.

Freedom

There are perhaps three major meanings to the concept of freedom in education. First, education must have access to all the means necessary to its function, for without such access freedom remains a vaporish phenomenon, without much importance. Without school buildings, equipment, personnel, etc., education is not free to carry out its responsibilities. A second meaning of the concept of freedom, which has already been touched upon, is that there is no place in education for control by external authority over the teacher-learner relationship. The authoritarianism of administration is an abuse of its function; its proper function, as we have said, is the facilitation and implementation of policy, but not the making of policy itself. Within the educational process a third significant meaning of freedom is that all those engaged in the process must be free from the distractions which prevent their minds from concentrating on the object of education.

But the largest point of meaning of freedom in connection with education is what is called freedom of mind from the annoyances which hinder concentration. The worst enemy of education is the distraction of mind caused by poverty, insecurity, disease, etc., and by athletics and other irrational 'social' functions. No one who is hungry, or in fear of losing his job, or sick, or on the team, is in condition to do intellectual work.[24]

The student who is thinking about how much money his education will earn or what prestige it will bring cannot get an education.

Similar considerations extend to teachers. The poor salaries of the teaching profession may cause teachers to worry about financial problems or to work simultaneously at other jobs, so that they are mentally and physically exhausted and in no condition to teach.

The implication is that the freedom of the teaching-learning process requires a rightly organized corporate order as well as a rightly organized education. The responsibility for this organization belongs to politics, which is charged with the obligation to look after the total order of life. It is of interest to note that in assessing the educational theory of the past few centuries, in his famous chapter on the democratic conception in education, Dewey states that the individualistic ideal of the eighteenth century lacked the means of its fulfillment, a deficiency overcome by the institutional idealism of the nineteenth century but accompanied unfortunately by a subordination of the individual to the state. He asks whether it is possible for the state to assume responsibility for the conduct of education without destroying freedom.[25] Yet Dewey and the modern liberal generally, in education as well as in other spheres, conceive a positive role for the state, in contrast to individualism. On this point Dewey is at one with the institutional idealist and with Jordan's corporatism. He does not believe that freedom can be won apart from social control, though he is at pains to distinguish between the type of control associated with institutional idealism, with its concomitant subjugation of the individual, and the democratic type.

Concerned as he is with the danger to freedom, the modern liberal is not anti-institutionalist. On a score of most significant points, deducible from different assumptions about the nature of individuality, he is at odds with the classical liberal. He certainly does not take the view that what is private is good and what is public is evil, or the position that that government is best which governs least. In fact, he finds no necessary opposition, as does the classical liberal, between freedom and law, planning, social control, organization, order, or institution. His view is identified with a positive conception of the relation of these to each other. Freedom itself must be institutionalized. Dewey calls for the institutionalization of the method of intelligence as itself essential to freedom. Institutionalization of the goods of life is necessary for their universalization or socialization.[26] Publicization is thus needed, but usually the modern liberal will not go all the way; he retains vestiges of varying degrees of the private. Like his predecessor the classical liberal, he also fears institutions and the state. He is concerned about the dangers of the subordination of the individual to the institution or to the state. He is a professed institutionalist in part, while he criticizes institutional idealism. Institutions we must have, but they must constantly be watched if liberty, which is attainable only in and through them, is not to be destroyed.

While modern liberals differ among themselves with respect to the extent of the sphere of the state, they nevertheless agree that the negative state of atomism is inadequate. Generally, they will not go so far as to say that all institutions should be public and that there should not be, for example, any private schools. Often, too, they are advocates of an economy which would include both private and public enterprise, but evidently more of the latter than is the case now. Perhaps their position is best described as mixed and dual, whether in reference to the economy, to education, or to some other institution, but they do not want to continue "the mixture as before." They call for greater socialization of property, of medicine, etc. Nevertheless, they would still limit public enterprise; they would not give it a monopoly. While granting that values must be institutionalized or embodied, modern liberals generally stop short of making institutions completely public and hold to the necessity of preserving an area for the private institution for the sake of freedom. Their arguments against public monopoly may be illustrated by their comments on the educational enterprise, which is presumably in this respect similar to other institutions. Their chief argument against a single public school system is that it would bring about the danger of state monopoly. Freedom requires the dual or mixed system; a single system is inherently tyrannical. The state is needed to assure universal access to such a form of the good as education, yet it must be checked by contending private institutions. While the modern liberal then recognizes that the attainment of ends cannot be achieved except through institutions, he still wishes to preserve the dual system and to maintain what Jordan calls a contradiction in terms, private institutions. If we return to Dewey's question of whether the state can maintain the necessary agencies for education and maintain freedom at the same time, Jordan's answer is fully positive, while the modern liberal makes reservations and qualifications. However, it is false to believe that freedom requires private institutions divorced from the state. Quite the contrary, thorough publicization or politicization of all institutions is needed if freedom is to be a reality. Only by full publicization, the task of politics, can we achieve the wholeness of the good life through education, industry, etc. The state is the state of culture.

Public Purpose

The development of intelligence through the school system requires that education be motivated by public purpose, and this means that it must be supported by public funds and that the legislative process must make it an object of constructive thought. Public purpose, the import and significance of education as evaluated by the cultural order, may be seen objectively in the nature of the building, the grounds of the school, etc. These convey the public spirit of the enterprise. If schooling is an important life endeavor, then this importance is best expressed in the layout and beauty of the property system of the school, and the objective place of its personnel in community life. Teachers also need the means to a good life, and the child is hard put to understand the public purpose of education when he attends a broken-down school staffed by dispirited teachers who are economically squeezed and otherwise restricted in their activities in the community.

However, Jordan means more than this. Public purpose is "the public motive . . . [and] the motive of the whole good which we have seen is the heart of the meaning of morality," [27] and this must suffuse the educational program. The relationship of intelligence to the principling of education by the whole good is revealed in the fact that the intelligent mind, as distinguished from one that is sheer impulse, acts so as to perpetuate the public life men have erected. Intelligence is a quality of an act, and not an abstract quotient attached to an individual; public purpose must imbue the act.

So-called public institutions may be infested with the virus of privacy, and private institutions may be public-spirited. This, however, is an accident. The interest in private advantage needs to be systematically eliminated from the school. That which is public is accessible to scrutiny and may be rationally guided. That which is private tends to keep itself hidden, and what cannot tolerate free and open examination cannot be good. Every aspect of the educational enterprise must be able to stand up and prove itself as a contribution to the public life.

The most fundamental criticism Jordan makes of contemporary

life is that public functions have been expropriated by private interest; therein lies the immorality of modern society. On the positive side, therefore, the one great need is the thorough publicization or republicization of these functions, and this is also the means to their rationalization. Moralization means publicization; hence, far from keeping the various institutional acts out of politics, or keeping politics out of the acts, institutions are the content of politics and it is essential that politics incorporate them all in the whole good, i.e., in the moral polity which is the state. Politics supplies the wholeness of the good life.[28] Every institution must be fully public in character; a private institution is a contradiction in terms.

When these principles are applied to the specific institution of education, it follows that if education is to be free, free from private interest and free to achieve a cultural end, it must be public and so must the control necessary to attain this freedom. Since it is necessary to render public all the typic acts of man, there can be no thought here of keeping education out of politics or politics out of education. Politics moralizes rather than demoralizes. Education is a constituent institution of the state and requires the appropriation of its act to those of other institutions in a harmonious whole through political guidance. Freedom will not, therefore, be won by keeping education out of politics: this can only succeed in placing or keeping education in the control of private interest.

The Support and Control of Education

The meaning of Jordan's corporatism in connection with a number of the most important questions of educational philosophy has already been explored fairly extensively in the discussion of educational authority, and policy formation, execution, and review, and content, method, and freedom. Although his position bears upon every philosophical question facing education, no attempt will be made to deal with every one or with any one intensively. Two current areas of controversy, however, have been selected for discussion: the support and control of education, and religion and education. Discussion of these will be limited to brief accounts sufficient to indicate the basic direction of Jordan's thought.

Corporate theory advocates federal aid for and the federal control of all institutions, and consequently of and for education. Ultimately, it looks to world as well as to national order, and correspondingly to support and control at that level. Institutions draw upon the world for their materials, and their acts in turn affect the quality of world culture; Jordan's proposals in ethics, politics, and law extend, therefore, to world organization. The fundamental meaning of corporatism lies in its conception of mind or will as embodied; this means that great ideas require great objects for their objectification or realization, objects which, when institutionalized, become permanent features of the good life and provide in their growth the dynamic for progressive expansion of that life. Present society, as corporate, is characterized by this progressive realization of more comprehensive purposes, larger than those ever before consciously attained by man,[29] often evolving in spite of him and involving, in any case, elements of chance and indirection as aspects of the corporate will.

Freedom to achieve an object demands an organization commensurate with the task of reaching the highest relevant level of culture possible and in making the object accessible to as many as possible. Moral polity is world polity. Individualism cannot be sustained at any level, whether it be that of the natural person, of national institutions, or of the national state. The moral law necessitates the world state, for the essence of freedom is cultural, not national, in nature. Such an organization may already be apparent in a rudimentary way in the United Nations and in such agencies, for example, as the World Health Organization, and in education, the United Nations Educational, Scientific, and Cultural Organization. Presumably, corporatism implies not only world institutions, a world state, and world government, but also personnel organizations within such institutions. One may infer that each institutional act should have its professors organized on an international scale, and in education the elements of the idea are present in the World Organization of the Teaching Profession.

Religion and Education

In the corporate view, religion is not a private affair but a public one, as are all the typic acts of life. The issue of the relationship of politics and religion cannot, in corporate theory, be considered in terms either of the separation of church and state, or in terms of the domination of one by the other. The world of faith is a public world, and as such its act constitutes part of the content of politics, as do each of the various acts.[30] Similarly, if religion itself is to be moralized, like every institution it requires publicization. Furthermore, as with all other institutions, the freedom of religion rests in its publicness, and politics is the good provider that is responsible for the conditions necessary to realize the religious object.

Since religion is a public act, the education it imparts is also public. All institutions are public acts and hence educative. Jordan's politics maintains that there is no such reality as a private institution; hence neither the church nor its schools are private. The publicization of religion means that there can be no separate so-called private system of parochial schools, while it suggests further that religion is part of the subject matter of education as it is of ethics. In the corporate view there can be but one public system of schools, for which all the institutions of culture are the central subject matter. To the question of whether or not religion should be taught in the public schools, the implication of Jordan's theory is "yes," if it be qualified by his criticism of existing forms of religion and the requirement that corporate religion replace their deficiencies.[31] If the assumed universal word of God is contradictory or foolish, He is not worthy of respect, so that scholarly attention to the philosophical problems of religion is required. The unity of mind that education proposes, and the settling of the problems it now faces regarding the relationship of religion to education, requires that religions become Religion.

Since religion produces concrete effects in the world and is a practical institution in the same sense as any other, it requires public support and public control of its administration and policy-making, in the sense previously indicated, if it is not to remain subject to business or other forms of interest and power motives. The control is undertaken on behalf of a cultural end, for public authority is necessary to assure each of the institutional acts their autonomy in realizing their objects and in order to provide support in terms of necessary persons and property. Since, in terms of current controversy, corporatism implies federal aid for and federal control of religion, then the exercise of legitimate authority requires legislators who are competent to deal with questions of religion.

Universality

While universal education under democracy has not secured the political blessings hoped from it, the trouble does not lie with universal education. The real meaning of the democratic insistence upon universal education, according to Jordan, is that the accomplishment of large, public ends requires the development of an intelligent citizenry, but he adds that subjective theories of society and education cannot meet this responsibility. Under other auspices, however, quite different results can be obtained. Corporate society must sustain and be sustained by universal education, whose aim is to develop the intellectual competence of every individual to the fullest.

Culture is not the prerogative of a few, nor can the state, considered as the cultural whole, develop unless the intelligence of every individual is adequately nurtured. To make culture public or political is to universalize it, to make it the medium of every individual's life. The crucial aspect of the corporate view of the universality of the good is that culture in all its forms— religion, art, etc.—should be available to all. Education must then be universal in the sense that, as one of these goods, it must be freely and fully accessible to all. From Jordan's theory it can be inferred that the school cannot be a social-class institution in any sense, neither in terms of its enrollment nor as the promulgator of class values. Class can be said either to have nothing to do with culture or to be detrimental to it. The school does not exist to promote interests, whether those of a social class or of any other group. Class legislation is the negation of law, and when the school operates as a class institution, it promulgates not the law but interest, and is therefore subjective. If law is to become operative in the intelligence of men, institutions must be cultural. The schools promulgate the law when education is cultural. When true to its nature education is of, by, and for culture.

Universal education involves much more than the establishment of schools for everybody. Every influence on the individual, within and outside the school, must be cultural, must attest the highest level of culture attainable. Since every institution is an active form of mind and is therefore an educational medium in its own right, *the fuller meaning of universal education is to be found in the demand that all the influences which make the man must be cultural—religion, art, industry, recreation, etc.— and his entire environment then must be pervaded by objects of value.*[32] Moral law demands the individual who is all that he can be living in a world that is all that it can be, or simply a cultural person living in a cultural world. The person must have full and free access to culture or objective mind if he is to be all that he can be, to develop all the potentialities of his own mind. In order to satisfy this requirement culture must be developed as fully as possible and given a permanent place in the world through institutionalization. The state, i.e., the status of institutions or of culture, is this opportunity. Politics has this responsibility: to sustain in enduring form all the various institutions, thus assuring that the entire medium of the individual will be cultural throughout and that every influence upon him will be such as to develop his character. If this is to be the human condition and the educational condition, institutions must be rid of their present irrationalities and appropriated to their individuated purposes and to each other. Politics looks to this order of the whole; and that state which is a harmony of objective virtues embodied in institutions is the just state or the moral polity. In such a state every individual and every institution is doing what he or it is best fitted to do, and the effort of each is joined to the efforts of all. An important inference from Jordan's theory, then, is that the state is the educator of man, but that only a just state can justly or truly educate.

Conclusion

Although education is the most important of the worlds of the individual, the cultural whole "makes the man"; consequently the state is the pedagogical state, the great educator. Education as a specific institution can make its contribution in developing the intelligence of man only if the state affords it a high level of culture and cultural objects as the medium of its act. Education does not create these objects; it discovers them in the whole of culture. Without them it is helpless. Jordan feels that modern culture has fallen to a very low estate through the failure of the state as the corporate embodiment of culture, and the inference is that politics has not given education what it needs in order to carry on its function. The irrational character of modern institutions has denied the individual the material means to his fullest development. The state of culture is the state of freedom in the sense that it creates opportunity for purposeful action; the lack of a cultural state is a denial of human personality. Despite great technological advances, gains in political and legal freedom, and growth in religion and aesthetics, Jordan believes that modern man has less access to cultural substance than his predecessors.[33] Man does not know how to use the leisure that he enjoys, and if he does, he must seclude himself from the crudity of the values all about him. The possibilities exist for great cultural development, but the institutions are often lacking or have been perverted from their function.

The state must advance culture in all its forms, and education depends upon the advance for the realization of its object. Consequently, when the state promotes art, religion, etc., it is thereby already promoting education, apart from its direct appropriation of objects to the school. State financial support for the school is only an element in the total responsibility of the state for education. In the larger sense, the maintenance, extension, and order of culture are the fundamental obligations of the state to education.

CHAPTER 10
THE EDUCATIONAL PROFESSION
AND THE SCHOOL

The Profession of Education

According to Jordan the educational profession offers the last hope for the survival of culture. He believes that almost all the professions have capitulated to business, and that the forms of culture which they profess are now dominated by interest. The professions themselves have become business-minded, says Jordan, and this is equivalent to saying that they have lost their minds, because mind is cultural and is related to ends and not to advantage. A business mind is a contradiction in terms. A profession that is business-minded is not a profession, since it ceases to profess culture. Jordan declares that the choice is between business and culture, interest and mind. Either the public be damned or business be damned. Although almost all the professions have yielded their autonomy to business, the teaching profession yet remains resistant, at least to some extent, and therefore constitutes the last stronghold of culture.[1] The destiny of mankind rests on the outcome of the struggle between the teaching profession, which represents mind and culture, and the businessman. In institutional terms the struggle is between education and business. Business currently stands committed to the *status quo* and the way of the fathers; it is conservative, even reactionary, because this is now in its interest. Education desires the transformation of things as they are to what they should be. Business wants safety and security, but education seeks adventure.[2] Jordan's characterization might be put another way: business is not action, but education is; and all action is adventure because the outcome can never be known fully in advance. It is necessarily in the nature of experiment.

The teacher is not, of course, the only one involved in the educational process, and obviously he is not the only one who has even a direct stake in its cultural outcome. Jordan decries the fact that the student, "once the most significant person in all humanity," is now an automaton, an appendage of the business machine no longer requiring mind or character. Jordan finds students scarcely educable because they have business minds. The fault is not theirs. They cannot develop minds except in a thoroughly cultural atmosphere, whereas society is now permeated by the business spirit and a cultural education is thought to be impractical. What is taken to be practical is the specialty that will earn a living, not what will build a way of life. If culture is to be saved, not only must the teacher be an agent of culture, but the student must once more be restored to his former status as the most important person in all humanity. The future of culture, its very survival, rests upon the capacity of education and its professors to be true to their public or corporate nature.

Several important inferences apply to the professions generally as well as to the educational profession. What a profession professes is a form of culture, the object intended by the individuated act.[3] All who engage in the act, whatever their part, profess this object. In the case of education this object is an intelligent person, and this is what is professed by all the participants in the process: teachers, students, administrators, etc. In this sense they are all professors of education. Academic freedom is sustained when the persons and things necessary to the act are present, the right kinds and amounts at the right times in the right places in right relations. The freedom of the teaching-learning process rests upon these conditions, which the state must assure within the limits of the resources available. Consequently the inference is obvious that whenever any of these are lacking, a violation of education and of academic freedom has occurred, and the profession, as it is broadly conceived here, justifies its complaint on the ground that the educational object cannot be attained. The appeal is simply to the object of the act and to the lack of the conditions necessary to its realization. Sufficient numbers and kinds of classrooms, adequate remuneration for teachers so that they may maintain themselves professionally, purchase the books they need, continue their education, etc.—these, as well as an atmosphere which permits the free play of inquiry, are all pertinent to academic freedom.

The autonomy of the institution is the source of the autonomy of its professors. The ground of the educational profession is the object which the act of education projects. The profession rests its rights and obligations in the nature of the act or office of education. The authority that educators exercise is not derived from themselves or from others, not even from all others (the people as a whole), but from their office: that is, it is ex officio, and all educators are public officers. Consequently there is no such thing as a professional interest or any concern with what accrues to the private advantage of a group. Interest and right stand opposed to each other. On the basis of Jordan's theory, the educational profession cannot become one more interest group with its private ends opposed to those of other interest groups. Interest groups have no legitimate status or being as such. So far as groups are legitimate at all, they have public status in relation to an end, not private status in relation to an interest; "for interests there is neither substance nor law, neither reality nor value." [4] Group is not a principle but requires one to sustain it. Positively stated, every group professes a good rather than an interest. Hence, like the institutions they administer, professions are public. This distinction, however, is not meant to refer to the professions narrowly conceived; rather, all forms of work are professions in this sense, but then all workers are public workers and all profess the good in individuated ways. Those who man the various offices of culture are public officers. Thus the distinction between private and public workers is removed, and the person who teaches in a so-called private school is no less a public professor or professor of the public than one who teaches in a public school.

Another important consideration here concerns the distinction between private workers and public servants. Jordan is sharply critical of the servant idea, indicating that no man is a servant, whatever his sphere of work. The master-servant relationship is invalid, whether the master be the lord of the land or the public considered as the whole of citizens. Men do not work against each other for themselves, nor do they work for others, either in an altruistic sense or in the sense of working for masters, but rather they work with each other for things. [5] Hence each of the actors engaged in the act, educational or other, bears this co-operative, mutually sustaining relationship to others, and the work of each is individuated within the institution-building act, ultimately the state-building Act. Teachers, then, are neither private nor public servants, but like all men are public agents within the meaning Jordan gives to "public."

The examination of any act reveals its public character. There is no such thing as a private act, whatever the law at present says to the contrary. The law is unfaithful to the fact, and is therefore itself illegal. Every act, whether called private or public, draws from and affects the whole and has reference to the world, not merely back to itself. The measure of the moral quality of the act is found in its outward reference or influence on the whole, in whether or not it sustains that whole, the system of acts, so that further acts may be continuously undertaken and their ends effected. Jordan maintains that objective ethics rests on this criterion, while subjective ethics uses the measure of backward reference to the actor.[6] The act must be seen in its reach, which includes but is not confined to the immediate particular. Its scope is the whole. This "wholism" is what atomism ignores, and its portrait of the private character of most of life is false to the facts of life. The act's the thing, and its public character or public personality must be retained, preserved, and, in modern times, restored.

There is no such thing, then, as a private institution, and with respect to education this means that there is no such thing as a private school, parochial or otherwise. The profession cannot be broken up into private and public school teachers. Jordan rejects the idea that freedom is best assured by a combination of public and private enterprise, whatever the sphere involved. The atomist or classical liberal hopes to retain as large a measure of the private as possible: "that government is best which governs not at all" or "that government is best which governs least." Jordan indicates that this entails as a logical and inevitable outcome the substitution of private for public government. The modern liberal wants a mixed economy, mixed education, etc., in the sense that he would combine both private and public elements but would particularly emphasize the latter. According to Jordan, the mixed system is a mixed-up system and denies rather than insures freedom, whether reference is to the economy, to education, or to any other act. Many advocates of a mixed system believe it to be the only way of insuring experimentation in education, but public authority in no sense precludes this, as witness the operation of many public agencies today. Rather it is a faulty political theory and a faulty understanding of the constitution of the state and the role of government which is at bottom responsible for this recommendation by modern liberals. Jordan maintains that the essence of politics and the public life is their experimental character. The implication is that there is no reason to believe that only "private institutions" can have such a character, a point developed in Chapter 8, "The Authority of Education"; quite the contrary, the private motive, since it is incapable of reduction to law, cannot be free. On the other hand, there is no reason to believe that public enterprise must operate under the dead hand of fixity and uniformity. These statements apply to all acts; consequently the public school can be and must be experimental and open, and only such a school, and such institutions generally, are consistent with a free society. An experimental politics requires a purposive experimentalism throughout the whole cultural complex, including education, the whole experimental apparatus to be continuously sustained by the state. In this view, there is no antithesis between a single public system of education and freedom, but rather the direct implication that the two go hand in hand.

Applications to the School

THE ELEMENTARY AND SECONDARY SCHOOL

The effectiveness of the public school program is contingent upon the nature of the child when he reaches the age at which the common school largely takes control of his education. The child's nature has already been shaped for better or worse by the cultural medium in which it has taken form. This is inevitable and explains the attention paid by discerning educators to problems of housing, race relations, the adequate institutionalization of health, family income, etc. The corporate world must be rightly ordered as a precondition to the effective performance of the duties of the common school, and of course this applies to higher education as well. While this is a political problem, those concerned with education must also understand that the full development of the student is predicated upon a wholesome world.

There must be present to every child, as the medium in which he grows up, an atmosphere of culture that will stimulate his curiosity about significant things and tax his intelligence to its last ounce of energy. The world must be peopled with persons whose every suggestion is toward the cultivation of the inquiring mind.[7]

Otherwise the public school has a struggle on its hands in which the energies of both pupils and teachers are exhausted. The educable child is physically competent and comes from an environmental atmosphere in which sound habits and active attitudes toward his world have already been established. For such a child, whose feeling tone has been positively formed, the elementary school is the promise of his continued growth.

At the lower grade levels of the public school, feeling is the largest and dominant factor in the student's mental organization, although it is present also even in the most rarified abstractions of the speculative mind. For Jordan, feeling and intelligence are not antithetical, since feeling leads to the withdrawal of one's hand from the fire and to at least the germ of an idea about the meaning of fire in relation to the organism. Moreover, a fact often noted by experienced teachers is the real difference in intelligence between the student who intellectually knows and the one who has a "feel" for the subject. It is the latter whose intelligence makes an active difference in the world; obviously this biopsychological capacity of the organism, the total complex of its "organic receptivity" called feeling, is matter to be sensitively formed in the school. To say that it is material to be *formed* suggests that, left alone or left to its own inner movements as they push the organism hither and yon, feeling is of relatively little educative value. In working upon the biopsychological capacities of the individual, education has a *rational* role —it is the objective form of the wisdom of man designing feeling so that it has a nisus toward value.

Since feeling may, when unformed and amorphous, attach to anything at all, the educational process at the lower levels strives to connect feeling with objects of value, and this connection itself is established in the elementary school through the medium of feeling. Feeling, on its objective side, i.e., considered as an objective fact rather than merely as the subjective property of the organism, is the quality of an object, its qualities referring to the relations in which it stands. To comprehend the qualities of an object, to view this house in its design, its symmetry of proportion or harmony as it stands in relation to other objects about it (the shrubbery, the trees, the flower garden, other houses, etc.), is to experience, subjectively speaking, a "feel" for it. To have a "feel" for something is to perceive the sense of the whole in which the object stands; that is to say, my feelings are not imposed upon the object, but an object, when seen whole, determines the feelings I ought to have toward it. The most complete object, the object in which every element acts upon every other to create a whole of meaning, is the aesthetic object; therefore, as a whole of qualities, the aesthetic object is the most perfect form of objective feeling. Then the medium of early education is art, the forming of the child's relatively amorphous feelings on the design of the harmony and truth present in the most perfect forms of art. Through objective feeling—art—the child's subjective feelings, his sensibilities, are qualitatively affected; through the medium of feeling art conceptualizes the realities of life, thus making the real available to experience. The feelings of children are to be attached to, or formed by, the best qualities of the world about them.

In school the child should be led to develop his physical form through the dance, through music to develop sensitivity to the audible rhythms of the world, through painting to learn to appreciate and create visual beauty, through literature to learn the grace of language and a feeling for the truth and beauty of poetic substance. This education is much more than aesthetic education as ordinarily understood, for art in its highest reaches, according to Jordan, always asserts some truth to be found in the universe. What is of real beauty must be true and good as well, so that aesthetic education is at one with religious or moral education. To learn to desire consistency, harmony, and proportion in all things is to learn the criteria for truth, goodness, and beauty. When the child is introduced to the finest qualitative features of the world, he is being related to God, not God the mystical abstraction, but God as the good objectified in the world—culture. These imaginative and ideal pictures, made real in art and given the form of beauty, give men powerful incentives to seek the good life not yet realized, for the spirit of the student becomes akin to the artist—imperfection anywhere is intolerable.

Familiarity with nature is important, since it is a storehouse of materials for aesthetic education as well as a feature of any good which may become real. In early education it is the wonder, beauty, order, and mystery of nature which is to be imparted, rather than the cold and colorless abstractions of science. While the relation of cultural to scientific-technological education is a difficult one, for the elementary and secondary school at least the pre-eminence of the first is a necessity. The student must be humanized—he must be sensitized to the qualitative dimensions of his world—and here the importance of cultural education is seen as superseding, although not opposed to, technical competence. Since advanced scientific achievement frequently ensues from a sound beginning in the public school, this problem is one which educators must resolve; but in working out this relationship the important point for educators to bear in mind is that the technical man and the practical man are not to be identified. The technical man is interested in a *result* to be achieved in some narrowly abstract and isolated situation; the practical man is concerned with "the relations which the abstract result stands in to other facts," [8] i.e., its place in an *end*. The technical man saves money in his operation of a hospital or a school; the practical man asks whether the economy of operation has helped or hindered the health of patients or the education of students. For the same reason vocational education is to be done away with wherever possible, or minimized as part of the educational program of the common school, since it tends to have a narrowing influence upon the mind of the learner. Vocational education "is not education but training; not an appeal to spontaneous curiosity but an attempt to deaden this curiosity in the interest of routine." [9]

Physical education and sports, as we indicated in the section on "Method," have a definite place in education, but only when this place is understood to be the development of physical capabilities for a cultural purpose. The ability to carry out intellectual tasks, to study effectively, to implement ideas, is intimately related to physical vitality and physical skills. Physical competence is a necessary ingredient to the will components of mind in the sense that it is always required in the activities of the organism. Moreover, physical traits are not merely biological, but biopsychological, since the feelings and ideas of the organism are necessarily brought into play. For example, to learn physical

endurance, perseverance, and the pleasure of exerting oneself
strenuously in gymnastics and athletics is one and the same with
becoming psychologically "toughened up," and is the basis of a
virile, vigorous relationship to life. It was precisely this assumption which underlay the Spartan regime of military recruits, although excesses of basic training are not required to achieve the
purposes of a rational education. Physical education and sports
activities have a moral or cultural purpose in the school system,
since they bring into play important biopsychological characteristics of the student, and hence all students are the proper subjects of the physical education and sports programs of the
school. If this is the proper emphasis, then the school's focus
of attention today upon competitive sports and a tiny elite of
athletes, and its concomitant failure to give sports a proper place
in the program of character development, constitutes an overemphasis upon physical education. In the decent school system
a mindless athlete can be neither a justifiable educational product
nor a hero for the student body.

Since the relating of the child's active nature to objects of
historical and contemporary worth depends upon the maintenance and development of physical competency, upon the skills
with which he handles objects, upon the encouragement of his
free curiosity or play with things in the environment, upon the
development of reading, writing, and mathematical skills, all
these factors must be considered in drawing up the curriculum.
It has been frequently noted that young children readily develop a "feel" for foreign languages, and competency in a foreign
language is a significant extension of the individual's relations
to the world; therefore, foreign languages may be suitable subjects for the grade-school curriculum. The principle which should
govern the selection of content for the school is that mental
growth is the same as the growth of active relations to the world.
Nothing cosmic is foreign to the educational enterprise; the alien
is that which has no value wherever it may be found.

The good to be celebrated by public-school education is the
institutional world of man. The feelings and active tendencies
formed in the young on behalf of the ends of life are the basis
for a life that is moral, cultural, and practical, a life in which
all individuals partake of and contribute to the good. In song
and story and drama, in all the forms of art, the ideals of a fine

family life, the universal ideas of religion, such as the blessings of peace and the brotherhood of man, the ideal of clean and honest government, the creativity of work, etc., are to be celebrated as the values of human experience which must be achieved ever more completely. So far as early education is truly effective, physical education and aesthetic education co-operate in the unified development of strength of body and sensitivity of heart for the achievement of ends.

To the extent that early education depends upon art as its vehicle, the logic of man's life is of far greater moment than literal accuracy. The apocryphal story of George Washington and the cherry tree is a case in point. For the education of the child, whether or not this incident ever occurred is a trivial consideration, but of great consequence is the value of the imaginative picture presented; for so far as the child's feelings are caught up in an ideal of honesty and integrity in social relations, and so far as these virtues make for social peace and an ordered life in which men together may achieve objectives, then the story is both a logical truth in aesthetic form and as a result, an educative experience. That George Washington was an American is incidental. It is honesty and integrity that are of value; they do not get their value from George Washington either as such or as an American. In the later stages of common-school education the intellectual and cognitive elements of educative content, and elementary understandings of the why and wherefore of institutional life, begin to assert themselves and should be as fully developed as the capacities of the students permit. Nevertheless, probably feeling more than reason will continue to be dominant in the secondary school, although the nascent reasoning process should be encouraged to the fullest extent possible. In any case, intelligence and feeling are not opposed to one another. Intelligence connects with, or has its base in, a mind made sensitive to a world of meaning and value, and the point at which a transition may be effectively made from the more primitive feeling to the higher processes of conceptualization is a matter for careful experimental determination.

The best teacher, from the earliest grades on, is more than an agent of the biopsychological organism, considered as complete in itself or formed entirely through social interactions. In the fullest sense of the term, the teacher is an agent of culture and must be capable of the most refined appreciations and sensitive discriminations. He is a person who can make distinctions of value, who can see in an object its implication to a wholesome mind, and in a detail the universal which it represents. The teacher is in his way the true artist of Plato:

> We would not have our guardians grow up amid images of moral deformity, as in some noxious pasture, and there browse and feed upon many a baneful herb and flower day by day, little by little, until they silently gather a festering mass of corruption in their own soul. Let us rather search for artists who are gifted to discern the true nature of the beautiful and graceful; then will our youth dwell in a land of health, amid fair sights and sounds, and receive the good in everything; and beauty, the effluence of fair works, shall flow into the eye and ear, like a health-giving breeze from a purer region, and insensibly draw the soul from earliest years into likeness and sympathy with the beauty of reason.[10]

The teacher is himself a finely educated man, and the heart of his educational program is effected through the liberal arts college.

THE COLLEGE OF LIBERAL ARTS AND SCIENCES

Just as the corporate structure is the basis in mechanism upon which spontaneity of thought depends, and as nature is the basis of culture, so the habituation of the physical-affective sensibility of the student is the foundation upon which intelligence is further developed; "and when reason comes," as Plato says, "he will recognize and salute the friend with whom his education has made him long familiar." [11] College is the place where the student's intellectual understanding is the focus of attention, and where his reasoning ability is brought to as high a point of perfection as his nature and previous training allow. Whereas in the common school the attempt has been made to educate all men, the college admits only those who are fit for further education. No one knows who these students will be, for the test is not their money, their class or caste status, but their demonstrable educational capacity. "Students" are to be scrupulously eliminated whenever it can be determined that the applicant is barren of curiosity and is interested in college only as a hunting ground for a mate, as a means of getting ahead, acquiring social prestige, and other irrelevancies. In the pursuit of its purpose, educational authority is autonomous in its right to develop the standards which college students must meet and to make the selection upon this basis. Man's corporate world requires the development of a highly intelligent body of men, and the specialized organ for this development is the college.

The type of moralized or practical intelligence which Jordan would develop, and which we are identifying as the special province of the college, is discussed fully in his *Theory of Legislation*, particularly in the last three chapters, "Legislation as Speculation," "Legislation as Administration or Social Experimentation," and "The Judicial Process and Its Relation to Policy and Administration." This is the type of mind, previously discussed in Chapter 5 of this book, which is the end of the college program and to which the college program must adjust itself. Through the legislative intelligence man *minds* the corporate order; therefore, the college develops the legislative intelligence and implants it in a body of men who have respect for ideas and the facts of life. If these public-spirited minds are to be educated so as to man the corporate structure, then the object of study is necessarily the instituted world of man.

The individual's political or public obligation is fulfilled when he devotes his intellectual energies to the task of thinking the order of the cultural life. But as all thought is mediated to mind in and through specific objects, that is, objects which incorporate the species of the real, the individual's political thought must find its characteristic objects in which to embody and render permanent the forms of its organization. These specific objects are the institutional means through which the individual's various activities work themselves out in objective forms. What the individual thinks *about* as he thinks politically is, then, the various corporate instruments through which his personal 'interests' are expressed and objectified and thus made public. He thinks about the institutions of government, education, industry, art, recreation, and the order of his thought upon these objects, formulated under law, constitutes the *state* to which his ultimate allegiance is due. The order of these objects is the constitution of his life.[12]

In the fact that the constitution has both stable and dynamic elements resides the authority of education to continuously reinterpret itself and the political order. In fact, Jordan asserts that the school "should be continuously examining the grounds upon which the organization of life rests and suggesting new principles as the changed conditions of life demand them."[13] This view he contrasts with the present situation, in which generally the school, at virtually all levels, merely adopts the attitudes, beliefs, and methods of the existing social structure. Jordan conceives experimentation as the method of politics, as the method, in fact, by which all knowledge is gained,[14] and this implies an experimental education. It is an experimental society that Jordan envisages, and such a society requires institutional and natural persons who, as cultural agents, embody the capacity for experiment. The open society requires open minds; this places upon education the obligation to produce men who possess open minds.

If Jordan seems both to affirm and deny the place of intelligence in the ordering of public affairs, this does not mean that he is simply contradicting himself. Perhaps Jordan's whole effort in ethics, politics, and law has been to rationalize these realms and the practical life as a whole. Yet, if one accepts Jordan's statements literally, the contradiction seems to exist. For example, he says that it is only a myth that the state rests upon the education and intelligence of the people as a whole.[15] On the other hand, he states that the principle of legislation is intelligence.[16] What he is trying to do here is to avoid the conception that politics rests upon an intelligent man, class, or people as a whole. The principle is intelligence, not persons. It is worth stating again that Jordan always looks away from individuals, one or many, to find the ground of politics and law. Legislation itself deals with ends, not with men. Ends and intelligence rather than men furnish principle. Democracy has held that a people can act intelligently; Jordan suggests that the real significance of this belief, which "represents an obscured vision of the truth," is "that the order of life in its highest corporate form is intelligible but it [the democratic ideal] fails dismally in discovering any of the essential principles of that intelligibility." [17] Subjectivity destroys intelligibility, and cultural reality along with it, by making the external world a creature of the knowing mind. Intelligent action rests upon a world assumed to be objectively intelligible in nature. Jordan seeks a government of law rather than of men, of reason rather than of persons, of philosophy rather than of philosopher-kings. Men are to conceive themselves in their political function as agents of principle, just as the physicist is an agent of his science.

If the system of legislation is to be rational, then education is a requisite. Culture cannot be sustained and extended unless the educational institution fulfills its function. The school affords the opportunity for the development of individuals in relation to the offices of life. This does not mean technical or vocational training, but rather a cultural education which will enable every individual to make the most of himself as a person, that is, as a cultural being. Jordan's statement that the state does not rest upon the intelligence or education of the people does not mean, then, that the people should be unintelligent or uneducated. The accomplishment of large public purposes requires an intelligent citizenry, and this is the genuine meaning of the democratic insistence upon universal education. Although Jordan believes that it is more than coincidence that along with universal education has come the greatest irresponsibility in government and political affairs, the blame cannot be imputed to universal education as such, but rather to the fact that it has been pervaded by subjectivity. Jordan wants every individual to be educated to the fullness of his stature, whatever his native capacities. In fact, one of the standing and most devastating criticisms of contemporary society is that it fails to do this, since it discriminates on the basis of race, class, sex, and the like. Jordan affirms universal education as necessary to the good life, to the just state, and to the moral law which calls for the union of nature and culture in the development of an individual who will be all that he can be in a world that is all that it can be.[18]

There can be no doubt that Jordan seeks a rational state where intelligence lives in every corner of men's lives and their social order; "the good life presupposes intelligence at every point and in every relation of the life of the person." [19] This applies to the institutional person as well as to the natural person. To be human is to lead an intelligent life; to be a state is to embody wisdom in all the spheres of human endeavor, in every institution and in their unity. Wisdom must be embodied in the world; intelligence in the minds of men is not enough. Rational man and rational society are the aims. The task of education is to give culture the intellectually competent individuals it needs. While, therefore, Jordan derides the conception that the political system rests upon the education and intelligence of a people *in itself*, since intelligence must have the corporate reality as its object, and while he asserts that education had best be ignored in the construction of a rational system of legislation, he insists upon the absolute necessity of the fullest instrumentation and operation of intelligence in "private" and public affairs; for this to be possible, not only a competently ordered world but a competent educational institution is essential. Jordan then means to affirm the importance of intelligence and education in relation to ethics, politics, and legislation.

The liberally educated college graduate is educated on behalf of disinterested public service. The broadening of his mind should not be, as it is at present, the largely accidental accumulation of a smattering of knowledge in unrelated courses, but the systematic study of the corporate world whose important decision-making offices he is to man and mind. The point is that effective cultural thought, without which man's life becomes chaos, involves much more than reliance upon an abstract ratiocinative method, but has a specifiable object, the institutions of life. These institutions—government, education, religion, industry, property, art, recreation, family, etc.—and their interpersonal relations are the grounds of life, and the grounds of life must be carefully investigated in college in relation to their historic development, their present organization, and their active tendencies. After having acquired some ideas about the nature and interrelations of the several institutions, thought must turn to the consideration of the directions in which they ought to move and to the problems which must be overcome.

The entire program should be based upon a comprehensive study of the ideas of philosophy, with special attention to logic and metaphysics, the logic of ground and implication. Through the critical use of ground and implication man can build a world in idea and fact. The logic of ground and implication is in contradistinction to the logic of cause and inference, which only shatters the world into elements, thereby eliminating the possibility of knowledge. The logic of Jordan has reality as the subject of every proposition, other than purely formal ones, and hence is directly allied with metaphysics. Studies of logic-metaphysics are the foundations of the other parts of the curriculum, the sciences and humanities. In contrast to the disjointed studies which presently comprise the program of liberal education, the curriculum implied in Jordan's thought is integrated through the unity of nature and culture in the state, the synthesis of institutions, and by the unity of the disciplines which provide knowledge of that corporate world. The structure of society and a valid theory of reality and knowledge are the basis of the unified education whose end is the intelligent person. Thus the intelligent man will know the corporate ground upon which he stands, and as a result he will be infused with statesmanlike spirit and purpose.

The liberally educated man who is capable of responsible public service has acquired the ability to take a synoptic view of life, to think life on the whole, so that its details may assume the meaning proper to them. Upon this base, specialized professional training in teaching, law, medicine, the ministry, industrial management, etc., should be organized. While specialized knowledge is important, it must be grounded upon a moral and political base, in order that the specialized function may be understood and exercised in its right relation to the whole.

The requirement that the teacher, as an exemplar for our youth, be first, last, and always a liberally educated man, a person of advanced cultural attainments, may well require an extension of the period devoted to teacher training. The master's degree, for example, might be the prerequisite for the teaching certificate in the public schools. The specialized education of the teacher probably ought to deal with the following areas: (1) The organization and problems of the profession of education as it is and ought to be in contemporary life. (2) History, philosophy, and interinstitutional relations as these have influenced education, and the influence education has had and should have upon the state. (3) Knowledge of the best materials available, of the modes of communicating, and of the specialized skills and content of the elementary and secondary school, as well as practice in the application of such learning. The elementary teacher ought already to have skill in the techniques of the arts, as well as knowledge of their content, and these should be developed further in advanced courses. Ideally, the elementary school teacher ought to be able to help beginning students of all the arts in the technical development of their skills, and ought to have special knowledge of one, so that the more precocious student may be more fully developed. This special competency in some subject and technique would be a more important requirement for the teacher on the secondary school level, for on this level a beginning can be made in helping the student to understand intellectually the institutional nature of his world and the challenge it presents to the development of his highest capacities and energies; here, too, the opportunity arises to acquaint him with the techniques and abstractions of science. (4) Instruction and practice in the content and methods of educational experimentation leading toward the end of developing a flexible and open approach to the art of communication, broadly understood as the use of language and other systems of symbols, the personality style of the teacher, and the objective structuring of the physical circumstances of the learner. While the preceding applies largely to the common-school teacher, it may be apropos to suggest that the college and university teacher ought also to be educated along the lines of points one, two, and four. Since he is chosen for college and university work on the basis of his scholarly competence and is presumed to be a leader in his particular field, professional educators have nothing to suggest to him in connection with point three. Moreover, since there is also no way of knowing in advance which students will become scholars, the intellectual identification of the scholar with the profession of education, his acquaintance with its problems, and his sensitivity to problems involving his own pedagogical skills might more realistically be effected through working out special "on the job" opportunities for him. Whatever specialty he professes, he is also a professor of education and should be aware of its historical, philosophical, methodological, and practical problems. That is, he has the right to speak as an educator, as well as an obligation to know what he is talking about.

A liberal education of the type here envisioned as essential to specialized training need not in itself require more time than the present program, since many of the present duplications, irrelevancies, and trivialities could be eliminated. Nevertheless, when one considers the length of time involved in developing the highly educated, technically oriented skills required in such professions as medicine and the natural sciences, there are real difficulties in the way of introducing a full liberal education as the base for such narrowly proficient minds. The development of these highly specialized intelligences, so necessary to culture, might be frustrated by requiring a liberal education first. However, certain courses could be taken concomitantly, as at present, and especially important subjects might be those dealing with the history and nature of institutional development, a critical investigation of philosophies of science, and the nature and content of aesthetic experience. Moreover, with the development of rational institutions this problem might decline in importance from the point of view of the public, since a more sound institutional order would serve culturally to objectify or moralize the technical work of medicine and science and help to redeem their status as honorable professions in the life of men. As a further consequence the need for the more sensitive scientists and doctors to exhort their professional brethren to be good men would be reduced considerably.

To maintain the body as a fit instrument for intellectual work, the college should, within the limits of a given student's physical endowment, aim to develop in him the highest degree of health, a body full of vigor, one which would be a model of grace in all its movements, ready and able to do the bidding of the mind. The active, responsible life that lies ahead requires toughness of body as well as of mind and spirit, a physique that can withstand hardships and can perform demanding, exacting tasks with the necessary energy and precision. Control and discipline of the body is essential, not only so that the body can execute the mind's ideas, but for the sake of the control and discipline of the mind itself. Soundness of body, mind, and feeling depends upon the proper integration of intellectual and physical exertion.

Although the intellectual character of the college today has been subverted by intercollegiate sports and has brought moral degradation to college administrators, faculty, and students, there is nothing, of course, inherently evil in sports as such. No doubt coaches are right when, in the present state of affairs, they say their job is to win games, not to develop character, or when they joke that character-building is the excuse for a losing season. Nevertheless, there is truth in the ancient insight that games and sports can build character; however, this means that a reorganized program is needed, and the stadia and sports palaces will have to serve new purposes or come down. The intellectual spirit of college life must take precedence over the sports mania.

THE UNIVERSITY

The university is the home of thought in its most abstruse forms. For all the fields of scholarly endeavor it is the place where the boundaries of knowledge are pushed to their limit, where creative thinking and the interchange and critical discussion of ideas in all the arts and sciences is carried on with vigor and devotion. It is the institution which develops to the fullest extent the intellective or ideational aspect of the student's nature, in order that he may more competently perform his practical and/or theoretical activities. For this purpose the university selects from the college those students and faculty members of the highest demonstrated competence in their respective fields of study, and it performs its function by encouraging their continued growth in the development of systematic skills in speculation and reflection by means of research and experimentation. Experimentation and research, which are too often thought of as exclusively empirical in nature, may be carried on through following out the logic of ideas, as in mathematics and theoretical physics and the examination of philosophical systems, and need not require any other laboratory but the mind in its attempt to build a unified whole of thought. This is not to imply that flights of thought and the concrete world are distinct and separate, for it is the assumed relatedness or intelligibility of things in the world which is the ground for the connexity and order of the system thought builds.

Although the natural sciences in themselves deal with abstract and amoral objects, the bare bones of the universe, the pursuit of the natural sciences is a cultural pursuit, since moral thought erects its temple of value with the sinews of technology. A better world can be the *objective* end for man because science has made this possible in fact. At the university the advanced theoretical work performed in the natural and cultural sciences and the humanities serves as a feeding ground of ideas for the colleges, the public schools, industry, the arts, recreation, the church, indeed, for the whole process of legislation. The liberally educated and public-spirited men who are in positions of responsibility within the corporate life of civilization are men of thought themselves, who have in their education developed a love for truth and a proficiency in distinguishing the better from the worse idea, and they are therefore a fertile soil upon which the ideas elaborated in the university may fall. These ideas are experimentally validated through their wholesome influence upon the observed growth of corporate enterprise. In this way intelligence sustains the world of which it is the logical formulation, recreates it as an ordered whole, and makes possible the achievements of men in all their activities. The university is both the source of the ideas upon which the government of the world depends and, in close collaboration with the college, the educator of the men who will qualify for the chief positions within the technical and cultural institutions of the world.

For the individual, "education [is] culturally perhaps the most important of the 'worlds' into which the person is born and in which he lives his life," [20] and for the world, as Whitehead has said in a statement with which Jordan's thought is in harmony,

the task of a University is the creation of the future, so far as rational thought, and civilized modes of appreciation, can affect the issue. The future is big with every possibility of achievement and of tragedy.[21]

The creation of the future, if there is to be one, has fallen, however, to the so-called practical men—"politicians," businessmen, and militarists—rather than to the university. While there are a number of reasons why human destiny lies in the hands of the least qualified, those whose every act destroys culture, part of the blame lies within the university itself. The very disciplines which might be expected to develop the ideas that would "keep man's corporate head on straight" have declined this responsibility. Philosophy has gone analytic, claiming that it is no part of the philosophic office to declare moral ideals or to design the state of culture. Social science, in the name of objectivity, has confined its mission to describing the facts of life in society without evaluating them. Nowhere in the university is there a professional search for the knowledge that is most important to man. The university is no longer concerned in any significant way with ideals.

If the university is to do anything to build a future that will be one of achievement rather than tragedy, it must return to the quest for ideas. The crucial part of that quest is to define the categories of cultural reality, which at present are tragically lacking. This is a task for logic and metaphysics. Logical constructs shape the world in idea or as ideal, and the real is ideal, i.e., the use of logical constructs is the only way to determine the status of facts *in reality*. The very empiricism of social science is self-defeating, for its insistence upon sticking to the facts and only the facts has made it simple-minded. The result is that social science cannot tell the meaning, in terms of the quality of life and culture, of such facts as it has. For example, modern political science, observing the widespread struggle for power, takes power "politics" to be political reality, and hence, for all the asserted gains of the discipline and despite its active involvement in problems of government, is no farther along in political theory than Thrasymachus.

Politics must be philosophical to be politics at all. Only by going beyond the empirical to the realm of ideas is knowledge of political reality attainable. For the comprehension of the institutional structure and the direction it may and should take, empiricism, which, for example, reports and classifies various constitutions, has little to offer. Knowledge of the universal is necessary, knowledge of the idea or the constitution which is the genus of the types.[22]

Although Jordan did not complete his work in metaphysics, in *The Aesthetic Object* he attempted to develop constructs which would define that entity which he regarded as the archetype of value objects. These constructs he did not regard as final but as suggestive. Believing that natural science had achieved a considerable degree of success in developing the categories of existence, he tried analogously to develop the categories of value. In opposition to the subjectivity of current belief, Jordan held that value is real and that it is the imperative task of philosophy to produce the constructs of value by which that reality can be known, known as truly and fully as any object of natural science. The objectivity of value is fact, as real a fact as any other, even more real, if anything, than the facts of science, which are abstract by their very nature. The urgent task of the university is to develop the categories of all the realms of value and to formulate an ethics, politics, law, and aesthetics founded, as Jordan believed, upon the corporate theory of individuality as the metaphysics which best interprets the world of nature and culture.

Adult Education

If the obligation of man is to know, then education is his lifelong career. The objective of adult education is to continue throughout life the career begun in childhood and advanced in adolescence. The development of man's intelligence ends only with incapacity or death. The pursuit of knowledge is inevitably ever-continuing, since the conditions and objects for the realization of ends change and will go on changing rapidly. To realize the ideal, the eternal human act, there must be a ceaseless education which will instill the vision of what ought be under the conditions that are, and develop in man the desire and the knowledge to attain the highest state of culture possible.

As with the child, so with the man: education must be universal, both in the sense that it must be available to everyone in accordance with his capacity and in the sense that every influence which plays upon the individual must be of the best possible quality. If the state is truly cultural, then man in his everyday round of activities will meet goodness, truth, and beauty everywhere. By its very existence the state of culture will constitute an all-pervasive adult education working deeply into the intelligence and character of men. Thus the educative formation of the individual through the positive influence of his milieu will continue the training begun in childhood without interruption.

The legislator oversees and harmonizes the whole of culture; hence the legislative act, as constructive of a world which man experiences in the daily round of his activities, is indirectly but fundamentally educative. Indirectly, the advance of the whole of culture, brought about in part through the role of intelligence in guiding the corporate will, provides the universal adult education already mentioned. Directly, it is the responsibility of the legislator to teach the people the nature of the state as a stable and dynamic whole of acts or institutions, and the place of each of these parts in constituting the whole. Not only is this a responsibility at the political or interinstitutional level, but it is one which must be fulfilled within each organ of culture, e.g., industry, as well as within each of the various industries and within each of the particular branches of each of the industries. To say that the worker must know his job means that he must be not only technically proficient but also morally competent: that is, he must know what kind of world he is building with his every act. A tool and die maker in an automobile plant, for example, must be a good man both in the quality of the work he does and in the political sense that he comprehends the rela-

tionship of his work to that of others in his particular plant, in
the automobile industry, in industry as a whole, and the place
of industry as an institution in relation to other institutions in
constituting the whole of institutions or the state. This is the
knowledge that it is the obligation of each individual to possess
so far as it lies within his capacity to do so. The technical man
is incorporated in the moral-political man. Vocation is not to be
conceived narrowly, for it is not only to his job in the usual sense
that man is called, but to the vocation of man, that is, his calling
is to be a whole man, a citizen. To impart the education appropriate to him is the responsibility in individuated ways of
every institution. These various forms and degrees of knowledge,
then, may be provided for individuals through an education in
which all institutions participate, each having particular educative functions and the state having the function not only of inter-
weaving all institutional acts but also of educating men in the
appreciation and understanding of the way in which these institutions constitute the state. Thus there would be education at
the political or interinstitutional level concerned with a knowledge of the relations of institutions to each other, and at the
intrainstitutional level with a knowledge of the relations within
particular institutions. Education is a responsibility of legislators
at both these levels.

Since the function of legislation is to sustain and continuously
to develop the state as the realization of culture, law by its very
nature provides universal education, because it assures the highest quality of culture currently possible as the constant environment of every individual, young or old. Institutions, as guided
in their growth by intelligence, provide the constitution or constitutional law of society, and are thus the living law of our
lives, inevitably imparting an education to all. The law is worthy
of the respect of men and commands their obedience because it
is rational and enacts justice. Because it is just, the law is binding, and men, in living by the law, are at the same time being
educated. Men become good, educated in virtue, by participating in institutional acts. The state simply by virtue of what it is,
the whole of acts or the status of culture, is a pedagogical state.
In all that it is and does it influences the development of men.
This informal or indirect education is the most powerful education of all, developing moral ways of thinking, feeling, and

willing as concomitants of normal life activities. Right habits are thus developed either consciously or unconsciously.

The law needs to be promulgated: that is, the highest intelligence, that of the speculative body, needs to be made effective in the minds of the citizens. This is achieved objectively through the act of administration, by which the ideas developed in speculation are put into practice as far as possible. When they become in this way a part of culture, these ideas take hold of men in the manner already described as indirect education. Full promulgation, however, requires a direct appeal to the minds of men. Depending upon the various capacities of citizens, this education would be aesthetic for some and ideative for others. It has already been indicated that part of this education would take place on the job, or perhaps more accurately in connection with the job, but a variety of institutions would be used. Aesthetic education could be provided through religious rites and civic convocations, as well as through the various arts—literature, drama, painting, music, and dance. However, the form and content of the mass media in particular would need to be radically redesigned in order to perform educational functions, as contrasted with their present purposes. They would have nothing to sell, no businessmen to reckon with, no propaganda to spread; therefore, reaching a mass audience would not be a virtue in itself. Their form and content would be determined by the aim of enlightenment for particular groups. As aesthetic education, their moralized task would be to bring citizens to appreciate the problems of the state and the need for certain political policies. Through the use of dramatic and imaginative forms, men can feel the need for more and better schools, for the Saint Lawrence Seaway, for international amity, and for world organizations to achieve such ends as health, better agriculture, etc. What some can sense, other citizens will be able to understand, and correspondingly theirs should also be an education of understanding, an education of ideas. Even when the same agencies are used for this latter group—media such as television, radio, etc.—the quality of the programs would be primarily intellectual in character. The BBC Third Program is an example of the type. So, too, with periodicals, movies, and other forms of education.

Using such instruments the legislator, at both the political and the intrainstitutional level, may inform the people of particular laws and the need for their enactment. After policy has been formulated rationally and disinterestedly, it is the task of the legislator to persuade men of the justice of the law. The free man must be persuaded, and true persuasion is neither sophistry nor coercion but the education appropriate to the development and sustenance of an enlightened citizenry. The legislative body could perform this educational function in ways already cited as well as in others, such as public discussion, the issuance of state-of-the-union messages, the declaration of preambles to the laws, etc.

It has already been pointed out that the worker will receive part of his adult education in connection with his job training in its technical aspects as well as in its broader implications for society. However, there is another aspect of adult education related to work, a most important one, that has not yet been discussed. The worker may be educated about his job and its relations to the larger world, but he is also educated in a most significant way *by* his job, the very character of the work done and the object it produces. Any act educates man, and since work is perhaps the primary activity of man, the education it gives is of great importance. One of the most significant forms of adult education is to be found in the organization of work. In that organization lies a set of values, a system of human relations bound together in the construction of objects as ends. The first requirement of work is that it produce an object which is not only technically good but is created and distributed through processes that are moral throughout. In the production of an object under these circumstances, both man and culture are created, but here our concern will be confined to the worker directly engaged in making the product. If each institution produces the object which is its end, each worker will be educated both by the process and by the product itself.

So far as possible work must sustain not only physical health but the mind and sensibility of the worker. Students of the factory system have criticized it because it places serious obstacles in the way of attaining these desiderata, regardless of the auspices under which work is conducted. While this is an important problem, no attempt will be made to deal with it here. Instead, attention will be given to a problem that does not lie in the nature of industrial work as such, but in the motive that currently underlies it: private profit and power. It is the business domination of work that largely accounts for the deterioration of objects and the degradation of the men who produce and distribute them. In the existing state of affairs, laborers and managers, both considered as workers, find a false set of values established by the business system, which by its very nature has concern neither for objects nor for persons. Shoddy objects will be made if they are profitable; well-made objects if they are profitable. In neither case is there concern for objects as such. Neither labor nor management feels a responsibility for the quality of objects or for the appropriate quantity of objects. When unions make their demands, they seldom if ever consider the quality of the objects that are being produced nor the ends to which they will be put. The very *raison d'être* for labor and management is not considered important by either group. Workers are as business-minded as business itself.

To work for private gain, rather than for an object as end, is itself degrading to workers, who then literally become wage slaves, and it distorts or perverts the object for which presumably the work should have been undertaken in the first place. What has been said is as true of professional as of unprofessional workers and objects. A writer recently questioned about what she had meant by a puzzling story which had received wide acclaim, answered that she had meant to make money by it. The complaints mount against the increasingly business-minded doctors who have one eye on health and the other on the till. Like other professionals, doctors are becoming single-minded, but unfortunately not in the direction of the true object of their profession, health, but in the wrong direction, so that theirs has been called "the doctor business." Meanwhile business is business, and the potential educational revolution offered by the printing press and television, for example, is suppressed by the business mind. Following the logic of the idea of business to its correct conclusion, a book publisher recently stated his hostility to the development of paperback books, quality or otherwise, saying that he had to sell five paperbacks to equal the profit of one hard-cover book. A television producer, who is regarded as having successfully wed culture and commerce, pointed with pride to the fact that the highly worth-while program he designed was able to sell paper towels, aluminum, and a number of other products. Evidently culture had made good after all, had shown that it was of value, was even worthy to be "sponsored" by business, as though culture needed sponsors and was nothing on its own. To the business mind, of course, culture can be justified only if it is good business. Business society turns values upside down: business becomes the measure of culture, rather than culture the measure of business, so that business society fills men with false values and inescapably miseducates them. Both men and things are valued solely in terms of how much they will bring on the market. Put negatively, what men learn is that no significance is to be attached to work and objects in terms of their value as culture and for the development of human beings. Since the nature of the object produced is not considered important, then with only a few restrictions, any and all objects that can be sold will be made. Hence a large part of the wealth and energy of our economy, the use of our natural and human resources, is devoted to the production of objects of little or no earthly good, and not surprisingly, of positively harmful "goods."

As a matter of fact, the economy of the United States is geared more closely to nonessential goods and services than is the economy of any other major country. Since economists, like other people, disagree on what is essential, their estimates of the expenditures for essential and nonessential items vary a great deal. Nevertheless, while granting the extreme flexibility of the criterion of essentiality, most economists would probably place the total expenditures for nonessential items at from fifty to ninety per cent of the nation's total expenditures. . . . From 1939 to 1955, expenditures for education declined from about three to one and one-half per cent of the national income; during the same period, there were substantial increases in both the total national income and in the percentage of the national income expended for nonessential items.[23]

Another writer has said:

Though we are rich in many futile things, such as over-horsepowered automobiles, we are still poor in schools and hospitals and in facilities for the care of the aged and mentally defective. This will not change under automation. We shall dump our precious resources at one end of an automatic machine, only to get, at the other, all the whitewalled tires that underpaid and undertrained school teachers need to ride on to their firetrap schools.[24]

A well-known social scientist put the matter this way:

We have reached an era of 'private opulence and public squalor.' Our vital need is not for more and more consumer goods supplied by private enterprise, but for a wide range of social 'goods' that can be created only in the public sector. . . . While we have been saturating ourselves with fintail cars, motels, movies, juke boxes, outboard motors, cosmetics, Miami Beach, Las Vegas, filter-tips, quiz programs and comics, we have neglected education, health research, urban redevelopment, river pollution, parks and public beaches, airports, flood control, hospitals, conservation—a host of social services essential to the national well being and to the individual enjoyment of our personal wealth.[25]

Meanwhile the needless work goes on, and the needed work remains undone. A recent example of our vast squandering of resources was the expenditure of a quarter of a billion dollars to add an unneeded "new" car to the world, so that a particular motor company might have a competitive line at every price level. In view of the urgent necessity for more schools, hospitals, and so forth, cited above, such a car was about the last thing needed in the world; in fact, it was not needed at all. Yet under the business system of values, the only fault to be found with the motor company in producing the car was that it had made a mistaken prophecy: it thought that the car would sell and the car did not. There was nothing wrong in its great effort to put and push such a car on the market, to use the labors of great numbers of workers and also huge amounts of natural resources; this was not only a perfectly legitimate enterprise, but in fact the very theory of the free enterprise system applauds such an effort. The only failure was a failure to know the market, not a failure in wisdom regarding the ends of life. The very nature of wisdom is falsely conceived by the business system, and from that system the worker learns the false idea that what is rational is what sells.

Under the sponsorship of business, work for the production of consumer goods will be largely misdirected; nevertheless, objects of cultural value will be made, if only because it happens now and then that it is profitable to make them. When, however, work is dominated by the military motive, as it is at present in our war economy, the production of cultural objects will be something more in the nature of a miracle. War is the complete contradiction of work, both in itself and in the activities which go into producing matériel. Work for war is work against work. Work constructs culture; war destroys it. The complete perversion of work is readily seen when scientists, technologists, and other workers, who in a sane world would be devoting their efforts to constructive ends, turn instead to the task of making The Perfect Bomb, which as a cartoonist logician said would be completely clean and utterly destructive. Other scientists and their fellow workers are engaged in the development of intercontinental ballistic missiles of ever-greater range and deadly accuracy; chemists perfect nerve and other gases intended to destroy or incapacitate persons; still others work at the job of destroying crops and livestock, while numbers of biologists turn their minds and hands to the creation of catastrophic diseases, man-made epidemics, and other horrors. Our scientists "create," and workers on the line help produce the deadly objects of their creation. The war effort employs increasingly greater numbers of our best minds in this complete inversion of work. Persons who normally would be engaged in valuable pursuits, and who in the process would become moral men, have been turned into satanic agents, literally doing the work of the devil. The use for military purposes of human energies, skills, and knowledge destroys morality. Intelligence is thus turned against itself; work of all kinds is turned against itself under such auspices; and as work goes under, men go under with it. In these circumstances, every technical gain is a moral loss. Tolstoy wrote:

If the arrangement of society is bad [as ours is], and a small number of people have power over the majority and oppress it, every victory over Nature will inevitably serve only to increase that power and that oppression. This is what is actually happening.[26]

Since Tolstoy's time our victories over Nature have been incredible, but our moral insight is still deficient, so that much more recently, in a world hardly imaginable to Tolstoy, Bertrand Russell said:

Broadly speaking we are in the middle of a race between human skill as to means and human folly as to ends. Given sufficient folly as to ends, every increase in the skill required to achieve them is to the bad. The human race has survived hitherto owing to ignorance and incompetence, but given knowledge and competence combined with folly, there can be no certainty of survival. Knowledge is power, but it is power for evil as much as for good. It follows that, unless men increase in wisdom as much as in knowledge, increase of knowledge will be increase of sorrow.[27]

The economy threatens to become a permanent war economy, one whose chief effort will be the production of military goods by business. So committed is work to military purposes that an economist has said that "a large-scale shift away from armaments will require almost a revolution in our economic concepts." The prosperity of the economy during war and the recurrence of recessions and depressions during peace would seem in itself to argue for a permanent war economy, regardless of the international situation. The economy is so bound to war that the prospect of peace makes workers, whether classified as labor or management, shudder. War is thus a blessing, peace a curse. There is talk of peace threatening to break out, of peace scares, with occasional reassurances from the national administration that our economy is as sound in times of peace as in times of war. There is great fear that should peace come, profits will go down or disappear and unemployment will again grow, so that tense international relations seem necessary in order that men may survive and prosper. The production of guns becomes essential for the production of butter. A criminologist once pointed out that if crime stopped, millions of people would be thrown out of jobs. The logic of a world gone mad is that evil must be sustained or men will have no work to do in the world.

Between the aims of business and the military, most of the work in our society is accounted for. Unfortunately, war and business on the one hand, and education on the other, do not and cannot mix. They are miswork and miseducation, both in the values they establish in society as a whole and in their influence on the objects and persons directly involved in production. Work must produce both true objects and men. The fundamental criticism of our economic system is that it is concerned with neither. Business and war exist for the purposes of profit and power. Work should be the production and distribution of significant objects, the moral responsibility for which falls upon all those engaged in the activity. In the production and distribution of cultural objects men would create themselves as well as a world of culture. True education is the concomitant of true work.

Popular belief is close to the fact in regarding present-day work as slavery, something that must be done against the individual's will, the doing of which violates human personality. Work means dying a little every day, and living begins only when workday ends. Leisure is considered free time for the worker to do with as he wills, time when he can become and be himself. Then he wears no man's collar, unless it be his own. In short, labor is slavery, leisure freedom. This view of leisure is mis-guided, however, for, in the first instance, present-day leisure is little if any less enslaving than labor. There are a number of reasons for this, among them again the values which hold men's minds in thrall and curse both their working and their sup-posedly free time. Time is not free unless men know how to use it; if they engage in activities which are worthless, they can hardly be said to have been liberated by leisure. Secondly, leisure is continuous with work and cannot escape the effects of work. The ruinous character of work unfits a man for the proper use of his leisure. When work is maddening or deadening, leisure will not be temperate or wholesome. The drunkenness, gambling, sexual promiscuity, and the like which mark the leisure of soldiers, or their plain apathy, are the natural aftermath of military work. So, too, with the army of workers stupefied or crazed by their jobs and further stupefied or crazed by their leisure. The man who leaves work wild-eyed or dead-eyed cannot be expected suddenly to spring back to the life of a normal human being. The nature of leisure cannot be separated from the nature of the work which precedes it, and the work itself is inevitably affected by the hangover, in more than one sense perhaps, of misspent leisure. When leisure does not refresh and recreate the worker, he is not ready to go back to work. Thirdly, the leisure of man has turned out to be another profitable, growing market. Since busi-ness is no more concerned in this sphere with educative influences than in any other, men will be sold whatever it is profitable for them to be sold. Business falsifies whatever it touches, and it will only be an accident if its effect on leisure is beneficial. The com-mercialization of leisure has led to the careful cultivation of so-ciety's tastes by those who have something to sell; an outstanding example is the low level of television programs. At present work has little or no meaning, and neither does leisure. Instead of making the man, labor and leisure deform him.

There is, however, a general fallacy in the popularly held no-tion that work by its very nature is degrading, for life without work would be meaningless. There would be no self. True work is the very realization of man and the development of personality. If man is stultified by work and cannot find himself in it, this does not mean that work is inherently destructive of man, but that, as it is known today, it is not true work. When work is right, a man will lose himself in it, in the good sense of that phrase, and in being so lost will be found. Since work is perhaps the salient act of man, through true work man does find himself. As an act of such import, work is the making of man when it is right, the breaking of him when it is wrong. Workers are now lost souls because of their work and motivations, whereas they should gain their souls through their labors. Souls destroyed by work and its miseducative effects cannot be saved by religion or by anything else. The purpose of leisure is not to repair what work has destroyed, which it cannot do in any case. Under business conditions it can only reinforce the debilitating effects begun by a mode of labor that is falsely organized and motivated.

As our current notion of the true nature of work is erroneous, so, too, must be our idea of the nature of leisure. Leisure is thought of as freedom, and freedom is conceived negatively as an escape from work, the opposite of work. Leisure means getting away from it all, not so that we will come back renewed, but ideally to stay away from it all for good. If work is doing, then leisure is not doing. It is life as passive—inaction or antiaction. Given our choice, presumably we would not work; the life of leisure is the good life, and the good life is doing nothing. What we want to do when we have the time is nothing. As Jordan says, we do not know what to do with our leisure. Time hangs heavy on our hands; it is something to be killed before it kills us. Men off the job are bored to death, except where the undeveloped nature of their tastes allows them to be titillated by the current offerings in television and to be engrossed with spectator sports.

To be sure, a man must have "time for himself," but how is this to be conceived? If the life of work is organized rightly, then work is already time to himself, since it is the worker's self which is in the making, being realized on the job. Leisure, then, would simply be another extension of that time. All time ought to be time for the individual, whether at work or at leisure. Furthermore, the conception of leisure as simply time away from action is not adequate. In place of the idea that leisure is inaction or antiaction, leisure should be viewed as action also. Leisure is not the opposite of labor, but is legitimately conceived as time for another kind of work. Not only could work be gratifying in a properly ordered society, but leisure as the pursuit of other activities could also be gratifying. The man who works in a laboratory as his regular job can well become a worker at a number of other occupations, so that his "free" time is well occupied. His on-the-job and off-the-job activities can both be work, though of different kinds and perhaps of different degrees of intensity. However, often leisure can be as intense as labor. The worker can work just as hard and as much at one activity as at another. Leisure may be rightfully conceived as getting away from it all, if that serves as recreation or re-creation in order to bring the worker back to work renewed and ready to go. The individual may then feel like a new man, prepared once more for his regular job.

Leisure may also be play. For that matter, so may work itself, depending upon its character, and perhaps all work should have certain aspects of play. This is necessary if only to avoid the deadliness of all work and no play, but play itself can include work. In short, as work itself may combine work and play, so may leisure. Leisure need not be solely play, any more than work need exclude play. That work and play must be opposites, rather than distinctions within action, is false. For example, the play of imagination, the entertaining of new ideas, the playing with things—these constitute an important form of play which ought to be present in all work, as it is in art. Such play itself may be considered a most creative kind of work. Play in the popular sense of the term, incorporating games, sports, horsing around, and sheer fun, while not considered work, constitutes a kind of action which, like all action, is formative or recreative of the individual in its own distinctive way, thereby lightening and enriching life. The rhythm of life demands a proper order of work, play, and rest for the continuous making and rebirth of man.

For the adult, perhaps even more for him than for the young, physical exercise must be an important part of life. The worker whose job is largely physical may satisfy many of the needs of the body through his work, although even he may need further exercise of a different nature than that provided by the job. For the worker whose occupation does not require much use of the body, it is essential that exercise be provided. For all individuals, whatever their occupation, exercise must be part of the rhythm of their lives. The forms such exercise may take are many, as are the places where they may be provided. For example, there could be on-the-job arrangements with plants, office buildings, and the like, providing gymnasia, playing fields, and other means of exercise, depending upon the kind of work, its location, and other factors. There could be gymnastic centers in areas where there are large numbers of workers. Communities could also provide, as they do now to greater or lesser extent, facilities in schools, and could set up other buildings and fields. Homes could incorporate whatever equipment and space may be necessary, both indoors and outdoors. The bodily needs of the adult could then be cared for at or near work, as well as at or near home. The range of possibilities is great, and there is no necessity here to name others. What is important is that the body properly nurtured in the earlier years be looked after throughout life and that men have ready access to means for maintaining and further developing the body as well as the mind.

Our ideas of labor and leisure and their relationship must be transformed if they are to be the kind of education that they should be and can be. Rightfully, work and leisure both play distinctive parts in developing man, each of them in itself and the two in harmony constituting a highly significant education. There is no need to oppose one to the other nor to divide men into two groups, the working class and the leisure class, the domain of culture belonging only to the latter. Correspondingly, workers need not be given an illiberal education, while only men of leisure receive a liberal education. Science and technology have, on the one hand, made it possible for the young to be freed from working in the economy so that they may work as students to develop their intelligence, and on the other hand, have enabled working adults to spend far less time on the job and far more time in adult education conceived as the further growth of their own intellect. If adults have not taken nearly as much advantage of the opportunity offered them as they should have, the reasons for this have already been discussed and all of them are remediable. At the same time, it should be noted that, despite the overwhelming devotion of mass leisure to trivia, there has also been a considerable development of intellectual interests among large numbers of people, as indicated by sales of quality paperbacks, higher aesthetic tastes evidenced by attendance at concerts, art exhibits, greater participation in creative activities, etc. In the Age of Leisure, which is to a considerable extent already here and is bound to expand, men may actually work harder, even longer than they have before, but what they work at and for will be significantly different. In fact, so different will this work and its purpose be that it may eventually produce a higher type of human being than was ever possible before. The Age of Leisure can well be and ought to be an age of work in which man and objects will be revolutionized by the higher quality of culture created. Man's dream has not been to be unemployed but to be freed from a kind of work that demeans him in order to pursue a kind that exalts him. What needs to be done is to make work itself a cultural activity as far as possible and to open up the world of value from early years throughout life to all who can take advantage of the opportunity. Then, indeed, labor and leisure will both be enveloped in culture, and the individual engaged now in one and now in the other will at all times be in close touch with activities of value. The reformation of work and leisure, in conception and organization, is the prerequisite for the continuance of education from childhood and adolescence into adulthood, a prerequisite to the kind of adult education that will permit the mature individual to develop continuously according to his capacities.

Justice and the moral law require that every individual do what he can do best. Education is one of the most important agencies in selecting and developing persons according to their native capacities. Inevitably errors will be made for a variety of reasons—chance, accident, the late maturing of some individuals, or a lack of knowledge regarding the best ways of choosing and nurturing individuals. Souls will be lost and culture will be something less than it could be because of such mistakes. Adult education, then, has as a continuing responsibility the salvation of such souls, turning them to their proper vocation in both the narrower and the broader sense of that word. The formal educational system and the work agencies must constantly evaluate persons, so that lives will take their proper direction and in order to "recover" those who for one reason or another have been misdirected. All agencies involving adults must be alert to the need for finding such individuals and guiding them back into the appropriate educational system or vocation or both, as the case may be. It is the obligation of every institution to see to it that man takes his proper place in the world and to correct whatever errors have been made in this respect. "Salvation," the salvaging of individuals, is an important function of adult education.

Self-education may also have a more significant meaning than it does at present. Too often now it means that a man who was prevented from receiving a formal education manages nevertheless to read and observe and think. In a rational society the educational system, along with other agencies of culture, would seek to eliminate as far as possible the necessity for this kind of chance self-education by providing education for all, regardless of race, sex, etc. Self-education would not then be conceived, as it often is now, as an education that the individual has obtained all by himself. This is the counterpart of the notion of the self-made man, and is just as false to the fact. In the true sense of the term, self-education would identify the cultivation of the individual with institutions, not as an attribute he obtained despite them or apart from them and through great personal sacrifice, and it would involve choices made by a mature and continuously maturing individual among the various and plentiful cultural possibilities afforded by institutions. Having had a good education in his earlier years, an adult would be a mature individual who could go his own way, choose his own reading, listening, studying, etc., and continue his growth as an intelligent man. Such a man may be trusted to make these decisions, the decisions suited to a free man made free through liberal education.

Then in older age we might expect to have the men of mature intelligence whom age can only produce when education has been right throughout life. Given such an education, growing old need not mean growing conservative and rigid; instead, it should mean acquiring greater insight and opening new worlds. Science promises to give a longer life and a more healthy one, thus extending the time in which the individual may acquire wisdom and helping him to retain the youthful energies and enthusiasms with which to act upon ideas. We may then have large numbers of the aged who are vigorous thinkers and doers. The ideas of age and the energies of youth may to some extent be joined, indeed a happy combination. For the mature reflections of the elders there can be no substitute. Sages are not and cannot be young men. Child prodigies may occur in chess, mathematics, music, and other fields, but not in knowledge of the meaning of life or the affairs of state. Only the man long educated in ideas and experience can be wise. The folly of youth can be lessened but not altogether escaped; it is the unavoidable product of necessarily limited experience. What can be done through right education, the education of a cultural world, is to assure so far as possible right opinion in the young and highly developed intelligence in the mature. Then the insanity of a society which exalts youth beyond all possible justification and has little patience with or use for human beings even in their forties, let alone their later years, will become apparent. The wisdom of the elders, which has sometimes been worshiped as fact when it was nonexistent, or regarded as myth because age was thought necessarily to be out of step with contemporary realities, would then become a fact, worthy of reverence. Not only would this be true of the citizen but of the elder statesman too. All too frequently now there are seated in political office men of age but no wisdom. In a rational society we would have men whose age meant wisdom, and the ideal of the elder statesman, so long cherished, would be realized. Age would come to be respected for the knowledge that only adults can have. The young would then also have a model toward which to aspire. If youth does not respect its elders now, there may be good reason for this attitude. The world they never made, but which their elders did make, is not one worthy of respect. Youth can be expected to behave sensibly in the world which genuinely reveals the wisdom of their fathers.

Through education man is called to his true work, the vocation of man, i.e., building the ideal world. What education seeks to produce is the universal man—universal because he thinks, feels, and acts as a citizen of the world, and is finely developed culturally as well as in his special work. In former days world citizenship was only an idea; the conditions for making it a reality were lacking. Then one might have possessed the state of mind of a world citizen, but one could scarcely perform the act of world citizenship. Today, of course, such action is both possible and absolutely necessary. Despite obstacles of many kinds, this action is nevertheless taking place, furnishing thereby a good example of the workings of corporate will, which to some extent is having its way despite the "will" of men to the contrary. Both within and without the United Nations, corporate bodies providing industrial, religious, educational, and health services are transcending the limitations of nationalism, and culture is being enacted despite power "politics." Culture, whether in the form of science or any other endeavor, can be no respecter of national boundaries. In all its aspects culture is the universal language of man, one that all men within the limits of their individual capacities can understand, on whatever bit of earth they happen to live. Education is slowly coming alive to its responsibilities in using culture wherever it may be found in order to develop intelligent men, and in recognizing that intelligent men will be world-minded men—world-minded because the world is their oyster and because they seek through their intelligence to bring the entire world to as high a level of culture as possible. Colleges and universities are becoming more world-minded in the kind of liberal education they give to all citizens and in training professional workers whose dedication to their profession includes also the desire to use their abilities wherever the world may require them. Curricula have been organized such as "Engineering Education for International Service," which includes along with regular engineering courses such subjects as foreign languages and the study of various foreign cultures. In addition, a growing number of universities are directly engaged overseas in offering programs of technical assistance, establishing schools at all levels, preparing statesmen, etc. If earlier education has been successful, the individual will have a world cultural outlook to which later education, including adult education, will add what is fitting for the years of maturity.

Given the possibilities of time and means now available to man, he can, as he never could before, create a world of culture, and in so doing he can create himself as the highest type of man the world has ever seen, the man of universal culture.

Education and Contemporary "Reality"

The dominant element of contemporary "reality" in the Western world is business, a system of relationships organized for the purpose of achieving profit and power. However, education cannot follow the business reality, since to do so would be to negate its own function. Business and education have no organic relationship to each other. Education avows its purpose as the development of the broadest, most comprehensive, public-spirited intelligence, whose thinking, feeling, and willing capacities have been sensitized to, and brought into unity with, the world in its meaning and value. Business, which is to be distinguished from industry, is interest and has no cultural end or purpose. Business is driven by advantage; it sensitizes the individual to his own interest and makes him a narrow, self-centered animal, cunning in the ways and means of attaining his advantage against the world which sustains him. Education carries out its function and sustains the corporate world; business follows interest and subverts the state. Business hampers education at every turn, for it is corrosive of all the institutions from which education draws its content and the individual his physical-emotive-intellective sustenance. The church, industry, recreation, health, family, art, politics, the mass media of communication, etc., have all been coarsened and subverted from the attainment of objectives, from their proper ending in objects of value, by the business mechanism. This world is a jungle in which education fights for its very survival, the prey of every competing interest whose eye it catches. In such a world, such a jungle, what does education do?

Jordan suggests what his answer might be in his article dealing with "The Role of Philosophy in Social Crisis." There he points out:

The role of philosophy in time of crisis is the same as its role at any other time. A crisis only emphasizes the practical aspect of philosophy. Its normal function is to keep humanity's corporate head on straight. To perform this function it operates to maintain systems of critically clarified basic ideas.[28]

The role of education in a business world is the performance of its universal task, the development of intelligence in man through relating his capabilities to the world of value. Its ability to function at all is predicated upon the fact that interest has not altogether destroyed culture, that meaning and value still exist with which it may connect. In a communist society education has the right, if not the obligation, to relate the minds of students to such materials as the George Washington story about the cherry tree and to Abraham Lincoln and his freeing of the slaves in order to effect its end. Similarly, in a business society education must work toward a state of affairs in which teachers may in safety communicate the sensitivity of Karl Marx to the oppression and exploitation of man by man as he found it in life and tried to overcome it. Moreover, education in any society can benefit from ideas drawn from the life of Christ and other great religious leaders who stood for the brotherliness of men in a world governed by peace and justice. In the very affirmation of its autonomy, the expression of its institutional obligation, education combats business, or interest in any guise. "Enlightened" business knows this and thus attempts to retain and strengthen its strangle hold over the entire educational process. When education does what it can to develop men of intelligence, men of character and principle who reflectively and experimentally concern themselves with the institutional world created within the historic process, and when it exerts its claim to all the cultural materials needed to perform its function, the business "intellect" is exposed for the diseased mind that it is. Indeed, in this sense the development of autonomy in every institution which performs its function and claims the objective means to do so is in itself destructive of business.

Moreover, we believe it to be consistent with Jordan's view and his positivistic insistence on coming to grips with the facts as they are that the institution of education must come to terms with the business principle by exposing its nature, just as in communist society the special task and rightful obligation of educators is to expose the collectivistic notions of communism. In the public school this can be done on the level of feeling, e.g., through being clear about the larger meaning of the character of Scrooge, and on the level of intellect for those capable of carrying the argument further. The fully developed intelligence possesses critical insight into the nature of culture, and this clearly means a knowledge of what his life may be up against, as well as what it is for.

To develop this critical intelligence, academic freedom and the security of educators on every level of the school system must be strengthened, positively through the right of educators to obtain and use any material which is of educative value and through their economic right to sustain themselves and their families, and negatively through their protection from external coercion by sound tenure provisions. That is, educational courage needs to be institutionalized. Educators must be able fearlessly to sustain their vision of achievement, for as Bertrand Russell poetically proclaims:

No institution inspired by fear can further life. Hope, not fear, is the creative principle in human affairs. All that has made man great has sprung from the attempt to secure what is good, not from the struggle to avert what was thought evil. It is because modern education is so seldom inspired by a great hope that it so seldom achieves a great result. The wish to preserve the past rather than the hope of creating the future dominates the minds of those who control the teaching of the young. Education should not aim at a passive awareness of dead facts, but at an activity directed towards the world that our efforts are to create. It should be inspired, not by a regretful hankering after the extinct beauties of Greece and the Renaissance, but by a shining vision of the society that is to be, of the triumphs that thought will achieve in the time to come, and of the ever-widening horizon of man's survey over the universe. Those who are taught in this spirit will be filled with life and hope and joy, able to bear their part in bringing to mankind a future less somber than the past, with faith in the glory that human effort can create.[29]

It is culture, the state of life ever to be more fully attained, which is Jordan's reply to William James's plea that men develop a "moral equivalent for war," the hope he suggests as inspiration for education in all its reaches.

Yet educators have themselves been institutionalized: in their own process of acculturation to the structure of fact in their world they have adjusted themselves to the business atmosphere. Many are its passive, unwitting defenders, where they are not its active protagonists. Public-school teachers infest the colleges and universities during the summer, inspired by the hope of a salary increase when, after having served their time, they return to their jobs. Deans and presidents of colleges become overjoyed when the advertising arm of business informs them that it will publicize their needs, so that they may be kept victims of the dole system of support: "enlightened" business knows that education maintained by charity under private auspices is good business. From the lowest to the highest levels educators have become, for the most part unawares, the unwitting tools of business, so that they do not even know enough to stand on their own feet on behalf of Education, a public endeavor of the highest value which merits its claim to the utmost in public support. The public-private issue is a smoke screen for the continued dominance of private interest in education, when the only "interest" education ever has is the whole good, of which it is a profoundly important organ.

In the last analysis, how can educators know the facts of life when philosophers do not know them? The tragedy of education, as of all our institutions, is that philosophers have not kept "humanity's corporate head on straight." Thus men have been busy—busy disordering the whole of life which sustains them—and crisis has come. Jordan states the difficulty with perfect clarity:

When crisis is upon us it is too late. There is nothing that philosophy can do. The philosopher's sin lies in the fact that for the last three hundred years he has done nothing in the way of redefining the systems of practical principles or of adapting them to the changed conditions of life. And this during a period when the conditions of human existence perhaps shifted more than in any other equal period in its history. By way of atonement for this negligence he might now try to anticipate an end of the present crisis, by attempting to construct valid principles on the ground of existing facts for a possible future—if there is to be any future after the carnage is over.[30]

Such hope as still persists in the affairs of mankind lies in the growth of a philosophic grasp of life which will succeed in ordering man's world in peace and justice. In the writers' view, Jordan's corporate theory is a capable and constructive philosophic attempt to provide such a moral and objective base for a sounder education and a better world.

NOTES

NOTES TO INTRODUCTION

1 Peyton Richter, "An Interview with Jordan" (unpublished manuscript), March 30, 1952.
2 W. H. Werkmeister, *A History of Philosophical Ideas in America* (New York: The Ronald Press Company, 1949), p. vi.
3 Morton White, *The Age of Analysis* (New York: The New American Library of World Literature, Inc., 1955), Preface, unpaged.
4 Mortimer Adler, "God and the Professors," *Pragmatism and American Culture*, ed. Gail Kennedy (Boston: D. C. Heath and Company, 1950), pp. 67–76. This paper was originally given before the conference on Science, Philosophy, and Religion in Their Relation to the Democratic Way of Life in 1940.
5 Everett Hall, "Metaphysics," *Twentieth Century Philosophy*, ed. Dagobert D. Runes (New York: Philosophical Library, 1943), p. 147.
6 Robert M. Hutchins, *The Higher Learning in America* (New Haven: Yale University Press, 1936), pp. 97–99.
7 Sidney Hook, "The Nature of General Education," *General Education in Transition*, ed. H. T. Morse (Minneapolis: The University of Minnesota Press, 1951), pp. 68–69.
8 John Brubacher, *Modern Philosophies of Education* (New York: McGraw-Hill Book Company, Inc., 1950), p. 24.
9 Max H. Fisch, Preface, E. Jordan, *Metaphysics* (Evanston: Principia Press of Illinois, 1956), p. xiv.
10 Eugene O. Golob, *The "Isms": A History and Evaluation* (New York: Harper and Brothers, 1954), p. 542.
11 Ralph H. Bowen, *German Theories of the Corporative State* (New York: McGraw-Hill Book Company, Inc., 1947), pp. 12–13.
12 *Ibid.*, pp. 15–16.
13 John Dewey, *Individualism Old and New* (London: George Allen and Unwin, Ltd., 1931), pp. 36–37.
14 *Ibid.*, p. 37.
15 *Ibid.*, p. 43.
16 *Ibid.*, p. 47.
17 *Ibid.*
18 *Ibid.*, p. 49.
19 Since for Jordan the true state is the state of culture, the narrow meaning often given to politics does not apply to his position,

and it is correct in discussing his theory to ally the philosophy of politics and the philosophy of culture.

20 Theodore Brameld, "The Philosophy of Education as Philosophy of Politics," *School and Society,* LXVIII (1948), p. 329.

21 Hook, *op. cit.,* p. 75.

22 Alexander Meiklejohn, *Education Between Two Worlds* (New York: Harper and Brothers, 1942), p. 267.

23 Sidney Hook, *Education for Modern Man* (New York: The Dial Press, 1956), pp. 41–47.

24 There are two schools of thought which bear this name. For the purposes of this essay social reconstructionism will refer to the theory of Dewey and his followers.

25 Cf. "Corporate versus Modern Liberal Educational Theory" in Chapter 8.

NOTES TO CHAPTER 1

1 For a direct statement of Jordan's theory of action, see Chapter 2, "The Analysis of Action," and Chapter 3, "Implications of the Facts of Action," in Jordan's *The Good Life* (Chicago: University of Chicago Press, 1949). However, this work in its entirety may properly be viewed as an extended discussion of the active life, man's life as corporate or cultural.

2 *Ibid.,* p. 18.

3 *Ibid.,* p. 24.

4 *Ibid.,* p. 264.

5 *Ibid.,* p. 154.

6 *Ibid.,* p. 54.

7 *Ibid.,* p. 18.

8 *Ibid.,* p. 227.

9 *Ibid.,* p. 115.

10 E. Jordan, *The Life of Mind* (Indianapolis: Charles W. Laut and Co., 1925), pp. 309–12.

11 *The Good Life,* p. 18.

12 *Ibid.,* p. 40.

13 *Ibid.,* p. 249.

14 *Ibid.,* p. 251.

15 *Ibid.,* pp. 252–53.

16 *Ibid.,* pp. 253–54.

17 *Ibid.,* p. 254.

18 *Ibid.,* p. 84.

19 *Ibid.,* p. 254.

20 *Ibid.,* p. 34.

21 *Ibid.,* p. 37.

22 *Ibid.,* p. 40.

23 *Ibid.,* p. 39.

24 *The Life of Mind,* pp. 313–14.

25 *The Good Life,* p. 263.

26 *The Life of Mind,* pp. 317–18.

27 E. Jordan, *Business Be Damned* (New York: Henry Schuman, Inc., 1952), pp. 192–93. Hereafter referred to as *Business*.

28 *Ibid.*, pp. 193–94.

29 It is in this sense that it is the logical rather than the mystical judgment which merges mind with the world. The development of the concepts and skills of physics or carpentry to that extent unites the individual with his world, but the more sensitively he judges, and the more inclusive his concepts, the more he has made of the world a home.

30 E. Jordan, *Metaphysics* (Evanston, Illinois: Principia Press of Illinois, 1956), pp. 120–21.

31 Ruth Benedict, *Patterns of Culture* (New York: Penguin Books, Inc., 1946), p. 19. Originally published by Houghton-Mifflin Company.

32 E. Jordan, "Possession and Individuality," *Philosophical Review*, XXXI (1922), p. 371.

33 *Business*, p. 209.

34 The body of means appropriated to a common life end which man has erected in the process of carrying out his purposes Jordan calls an "institution"; it is the act instituted, physically ordered into the world. Specific individuals within the institutional type he calls "corporate persons." (See *The Good Life*, p. 85.) But Jordan does not mean that institution *and* corporate person exist as two separate types; rather they are variations in the degree form of a common type. The institution is the most comprehensive or inclusive individuality (we are here anticipating the theory of individuality developed in the next chapter) typifying and principling a certain class of corporate persons. Industry is an institution; United States Steel and General Motors are each corporate persons of the industrial type.

On the other hand, Jordan also uses the term corporate in its basic meaning as "bodied," and when used in this sense *corporate* becomes the widest term. Corporate society fundamentally means society as having a physical body, the basic components of which are institutional persons. Even the natural individual may be viewed as corporate in the sense of having a body, but the degree to which the person is bodied is the significant and distinguishing characteristic in our general use of the term *corporate*. It is this more comprehensive body which gives special significance to the institution and corporation. The basic use of the concepts *institution* and *corporate* will be to designate an organization of individuals and materials directed toward the realization of an end.

35 *Business*, p. 205.

36 *Ibid.*

37 E. Jordan, *Forms of Individuality* (Indianapolis: Progress Publishing Co., 1927), pp. 400–401. Hereafter referred to as *Forms*.

38 *Ibid.*, p. 419.

39 *Ibid.*, p. 328.

40 E. Jordan, *Theory of Legislation* (Chicago: The University of Chicago Press, 1952), pp. 313–14. This is a reprinting, with new prefatory remarks by Jordan, of the edition originally issued by the Principia Press, 1930. Hereafter referred to as *Theory*.
41 *The Good Life,* p. 255.

NOTES TO CHAPTER 2

1 "The Definition of Individuality," *Philosophical Review,* XXX (1921), p. 566.
2 *Forms,* p. 137.
3 "The Definition of Individuality," p. 567.
4 *Ibid.,* pp. 568–69.
5 *Ibid.,* p. 570.
6 *Forms,* pp. 94–102.
7 *Ibid.,* p. 94.
8 *Forms,* p. 96; "The Definition of Individuality," p. 570.
9 *Forms,* p. 95.
10 "The Definition of Individuality," p. 570.
11 *Forms,* p. 101.
12 *Ibid.,* p. 102.
13 *Ibid.,* p. 96.
14 "The Definition of Individuality," pp. 570–71.
15 *Forms,* p. 43.
16 *Ibid.,* pp. 64–65.
17 *Ibid.,* pp. 43–44.
18 *Ibid.,* p. 131.
19 *Ibid.,* p. 133.
20 "The Definition of Individuality," pp. 571–72.
21 *Ibid.*
22 *Ibid.,* pp. 572–73.
23 *Forms,* p. 137.
24 *Ibid.*
25 *Ibid.,* p. 107.
26 *Ibid.,* pp. 107–8.
27 *Ibid.,* p. 108.
28 *Ibid.,* pp. 79–81.
29 *Ibid.,* p. 109.
30 *Ibid.,* p. 153.
31 *Ibid.,* pp. 51 ff.
32 *Ibid.,* p. 77.
33 *Ibid.,* p. 79.
34 *Ibid.,* pp. 134–35.
35 *Ibid.,* p. 134.
36 *Ibid.,* p. 135.
37 *Ibid.,* p. 38.
38 *The Aesthetic Object* (Bloomington, Indiana: The Principia Press, Inc., 1937), pp. 21–22.
39 *Ibid.*

40 *Ibid.,* p. 219.
41 *Forms,* pp. 61–62.
42 *Ibid.,* p. 81.
43 *Ibid.,* pp. 137–38.
44 *Ibid.,* p. 198.
45 *Ibid.,* p. 210.
46 *Ibid.,* p. 207.
47 *Ibid.,* p. 213.
48 *Ibid.,* p. 212.
49 *Ibid.,* p. 224.
50 *Ibid.,* p. 213.
51 *Ibid.,* p. 223.
52 *Ibid.,* pp. 215–16.
53 *Ibid.,* p. 226.
54 *Ibid.*
55 *Ibid.,* p. 191.
56 *Ibid.,* p. 193.

NOTES TO CHAPTER 3

1 *The Good Life,* p. 308.
2 *Forms,* p. 236.
3 *The Good Life,* p. 308.
4 *Ibid.,* p. 309.
5 *Ibid.*
6 *Forms,* p. 197.
7 *The Aesthetic Object,* pp. 58–60.
8 *Forms,* pp. 60–61.
9 *Ibid.,* pp. 224–25.
10 *Ibid.,* pp. 225–26.
11 *Ibid.,* p. 233.
12 *Ibid.,* p. 234.
13 *Theory,* p. 86.
14 *Forms,* p. 108.
15 *Theory,* p. 82.
16 *Ibid.,* p. 84.
17 *Forms,* p. 148.
18 *Ibid.,* pp. 246–48.
19 Jordan remarks on the conflict within Aristotle between the conservative view of the state as natural and fixed and the progressive, experimental conception involving man in the task of re-creating and revolutionizing the state.
20 *Forms,* pp. 248–50.
21 *Ibid.,* pp. 250–51.
22 *Ibid.,* pp. 252–55.
23 *Ibid.,* pp. 253–54.
24 *Ibid.,* p. 253.
25 *Ibid.,* p. 258.
26 *Ibid.,* p. 256.

27 *Ibid.*, p. 258.
28 *Ibid.*, pp. 258–59.
29 *Ibid.*, p. 274.
30 *Ibid.*, p. 170.
31 *Ibid.*, p. 261.
32 *Ibid.*, p. 263.
33 *The Good Life*, pp. 144–45.
34 *Ibid.*, pp. 437–38.
35 *Ibid.*, pp. 436–37.
36 Richter, *op. cit.*
37 *Forms*, p. 243.
38 *Ibid.*, p. 327.
39 *Theory*, p. 85.
40 *Forms*, p. 328.
41 *Ibid.*, pp. 80–81.
42 *Ibid.*, p. 241.
43 *Theory*, p. 8.
44 *Forms*, pp. 63–64.
45 *Ibid.*, p. 167.
46 *Forms*, p. 308.
47 Reprinted by permission of the publishers, Abelard-Schuman Limited, from *Business Be Damned* by Elijah Jordan, © 1952, p. 243.
48 *Forms*, p. 275.
49 *Ibid.*, p. 311.
50 *Ibid.*, p. 309.
51 *The Good Life*, p. 436.
52 There is little question about the close relation between Plato and Jordan, both in terms of the critical period in the history of their respective civilizations in which their thought matured and their philosophic positions. While he is critical of certain aspects of Plato's thought, Jordan considers Plato *the philosopher* and believes that modern thinkers must return to him for insight into life problems and for positive suggestions as to how to move on. To call attention to the closeness of their positions is to run the risk of identifying Jordan with fascism, since, "as everyone knows," Plato was a fascist. For example, Edward O. Sisson, in his presidential address to the Pacific Division of the American Philosophical Association in 1930, said: "I have earnestly reconsidered that original philosophical charter of fascism—a noble and austere doctrine indeed, but fascism—Plato's *Republic*, the beauty and surpassing genius of which has made it, I think, one of the most dangerous items in the education of the western world." ("Human Nature and the Present Crisis," *Philosophical Review*, XLIX [1940], p. 143.) That certain negative elements in Plato are being identified with the whole of Plato seems obvious to the writers, who believe that Plato's central effort is to get away from a force principle of societal order and to develop a state principled by

justice where ideas rule and not men. This is no place to defend Plato from accusations of fascism or communism but merely to suggest caution in dismissing Plato or Jordan in this manner. Not even John Dewey is immune from such charges made by serious scholars. Frank Knight, in his article on "Pragmatism and Social Action" (*International Journal of Ethics*, XLVI [1935–36], pp. 232–33; published by the University of Chicago Press), scores Dewey's appeal to "education" as the heart of a program of social action. "As usual," Knight acidly comments, "nothing is said about who is to do the educating of 'society.' Presumably 'we' are to do it—we reformers, saviors of society. This throws us squarely into communistic, or possibly fascistic theory, the antithesis of democracy, of freedom and of any liberalism. It is to be noted especially that there is no approach to agreement among the reformers themselves, and the first, and perhaps the main, task of 'me and my gang' would be to suppress a vast congeries of competing aspirants for the same role."

53 Reprinted by permission of the publishers, Abelard-Schuman Limited, from *Business Be Damned* by Elijah Jordan, © 1952, p. 252.
54 *The Good Life*, pp. 64–65.
55 *Forms*, p. 402.

NOTES TO CHAPTER 4

1 *The Good Life*, pp. 80–81.
2 *Ibid.*, p. 82.
3 *Forms*, p. vi.
4 *The Good Life*, p. 438.
5 *Ibid.*, p. 229.
6 *Ibid.*
7 *The Life of Mind*, p. 249.
8 *The Good Life*, p. 275.
9 *Ibid.*, p. 279.
10 *Ibid.*, p. 280.
11 *Ibid.*, p. 286.
12 *Ibid.*, pp. 282–83.
13 *Ibid.*, p. 274.
14 *Ibid.*, p. 291.
15 *Ibid.*, pp. 291–92.
16 *Business*, pp. 252–53.
17 *Ibid.*, pp. 260–67.
18 A fuller discussion of education will be found in Chapters 8–10, but it may be helpful to make in this context a few points of a general nature.
19 *The Good Life*, p. 302.
20 *Ibid.*, p. 303.
21 *Ibid.*, pp. 303–4.
22 *Ibid.*, p. 311.

23 *Ibid.*, p. 313.
24 *The Life of Mind*, p. 53.
25 *The Good Life*, p. 314.
26 *Ibid.*, p. 317.
27 *Ibid.*, p. 336.
28 *Ibid.*, pp. 336–37. On the other hand, in *The Aesthetic Object* the entire meaning of Jordan's effort, which the writers take to be his real meaning, is to make logic basic to the comprehension of beauty. In *The Aesthetic Object*, p. 219, he writes: "Beauty then is the objectivity of a system of categories, and is experienced as the quality (beautiful) of an object, which quality appears in experience as the analogue of the object's constitution, and cannot be known by direct intuition. What we call beauty, then, in terms of the qualities of objects, is the constitutional system of categories by which the object is determined, as that system is analogously imaged to us, or symbolized to us, as color, form, etc., in perception. And it is only as the history of past experience furnishes us with this categorical system that beauty has meaning for us; not that the categories will be known as such in the case of every individual who experiences beauty, but they are there by implication and in some form, otherwise there would be no experience of beauty, since they are precisely the conditions of the existence of the experience." Then perhaps Jordan's intention in his discussion of the institution of art is to convey a profound and significant effect that beauty has upon men with reference to its influence upon action life, that through its peculiar impact upon the sensibilities it convinces them of the true and the good. The selling and advertising arm of business, that stronghold of "practical" men, is, of course, intensely aware of this influence conveyed by things of beauty, and in its own interest exploits all of the arts and the physical beauty of men and women. While beauty is its own justification and fulfills its function through its existence, its appropriate (moral and cultural) use, as exemplified by religion, is on behalf of public ends.
29 *Ibid.*, p. 333.
30 *Ibid.*, p. 337.
31 *Ibid.*, p. 339.
32 *Ibid.*
33 *Ibid.*, pp. 339–41.
34 *Ibid.*, pp. 351–56.
35 *Ibid.*, p. 347.

NOTES TO CHAPTER 5

1 *Theory*, p. 328.
2 *Ibid.*, p. 324.
3 *The Good Life*, p. 24.
4 E. Jordan, "The Structure of Society," *Ethics*, LV (1945), p. 81.
5 *Theory*, p. 354.

6 *Ibid.,* p. 345.
7 *Ibid.,* p. 333.
8 *Ibid.,* p. 359.
9 *Ibid.,* pp. 359–60.
10 *Ibid.,* pp. 345 and 429.
11 *Ibid.,* p. 385.
12 *Ibid.,* pp. 426–27.
13 E. Jordan, "The Role of Philosophy in Social Crisis," *Ethics* (University of Chicago Press), LI (1941), pp. 384–85. What are our purposes? In this connection it may be noteworthy that it has taken the challenge from Communism to bring this question into focus, and that curiously two years elapsed before President Eisenhower established his special committee to help American democracy formulate its purposes.
14 *Theory,* p. 325.
15 E. Jordan, "The False Principle of Liberalism," *Ethics,* XLVI (1936), p. 285.
16 *Theory,* p. 24.
17 *Ibid.,* p. 25.
18 *Ibid.,* p. 33.
19 *Ibid.*
20 *Ibid.,* p. 336.
21 *The Aesthetic Object,* p. 213.
22 *Theory,* p. 338.
23 *Ibid.,* p. 307.
24 *Ibid.,* p. 432.
25 *Ibid.,* pp. 369–70.
26 *Ibid.,* p. 351.
27 *Ibid.,* p. 336.
28 *Ibid.,* p. 345.
29 *Ibid.,* pp. 367–69.
30 *Ibid.,* p. 338.
31 *Ibid.*
32 *Ibid.,* p. 339.
33 *Ibid.,* pp. 371–72.
34 *Ibid.,* pp. 377–78.
35 *Ibid.,* pp. 373–74.
36 *Ibid.,* p. 454.
37 *Ibid.,* pp. 386–87.
38 *Ibid.,* p. 416.
39 *Ibid.,* p. 383.
40 *Ibid.,* p. 384.
41 *Ibid.,* p. 394.
42 *Ibid.,* p. 396.
43 *Ibid.,* pp. 405–6.
44 *Ibid.,* p. 386.
45 *Ibid.,* p. 421.
46 *Ibid.,* p. 429.

47 *Ibid.*, pp. 429–30.
48 *Ibid.*, p. 422.
49 *Ibid.*, p. 386.
50 *Ibid.*, p. 456.
51 *Ibid.*, pp. 439–40.
52 *Ibid.*, p. 151.
53 *Ibid.*, p. 479.
54 *Ibid.*, p. 478.
55 *Ibid.*, p. 479.
56 *Ibid.*, p. 442.
57 *Ibid.*, pp. 147–48.
58 *Ibid.*, pp. 153–54.
59 *Ibid.*, p. 154.
60 *Ibid.*, p. 455.
61 *Ibid.*, p. 457.
62 *Ibid.*, p. 444.
63 *Ibid.*, p. 450.
64 *Ibid.*, p. 442.
65 *Ibid.*, p. 443.
66 *Ibid.*, p. 476.

NOTES TO CHAPTER 6

1 *The Good Life*, pp. 378–79.
2 *Ibid.*, p. 378.
3 *Ibid.*, p. 393.
4 *Ibid.*, pp. 395–96.
5 *Ibid.*, p. 403.
6 *Ibid.*, p. 405.
7 *Ibid.*
8 *Ibid.*, pp. 406–7.
9 *Ibid.*, p. 408.
10 *Ibid.*
11 *Ibid.*, pp. 410–13.
12 *Ibid.*, p. 414.
13 *Ibid.*, pp. 415–16.
14 *Ibid.*, pp. 416–17.
15 *Ibid.*, pp. 423–24.
16 *Ibid.*, p. 418.

NOTES TO CHAPTER 7

1 *Theory*, p. 7.
2 *Forms*, p. 40.
3 "The Role of Philosophy in Social Crisis," p. 381.
4 *Forms*, p. 108.
5 *Ibid.*, p. 97.
6 *Ibid.*, p. 249.
7 *The Good Life*, pp. 351 ff.
8 *Theory*, p. 85.

9 *Forms,* p. 223.
10 Thomas M. Haynes, "Institutional Theories of Law: Hauriou and Jordan," unpublished dissertation, University of Illinois (1949), p. 3.
11 Herbert Schneider in review of *The Good Life* (*The Journal of Philosophy,* XLVII [1950], p. 389).
12 An extended development of this thesis is given by Karl Popper, *The Open Society and Its Enemies* (London: George Routledge and Sons, 1945).
13 Max Fisch, *Classic American Philosophers* (New York: Appleton-Century-Crofts, Inc., 1951), p. 36.
14 Haynes, *op. cit.,* p. 30.
15 *Forms,* p. 222.
16 *Ibid.,* p. 274.
17 "The Role of Philosophy in Social Crisis," p. 381.
18 *The Good Life,* p. 351.
19 *Ibid.,* p. 420.
20 *Ibid.*
21 *Ibid.,* pp. 420–21.
22 E. E. Cummings is responsible for this phrase.
23 The discussion of Jordan's corporatism and democracy is confined to the briefest of statements, partially because his criticism of democracy has been given at some length in Chapter 5 and is elaborated further in the chapters on education which follow, especially in Chapter 8.
24 John Dewey, *Logic* (New York: Henry Holt and Company, 1938), pp. 518–19.
25 John Dewey in Paul Arthur Schilpp, ed., *The Philosophy of John Dewey* (New York: Tudor Publishing Company, 1951), p. 544.
26 John Dewey, *Experience and Education* (New York: The Macmillan Company, 1938), pp. v–vi.
27 Haynes, *op. cit.,* p. 167.
28 *Forms,* p. 27.
29 *The Good Life,* p. 338.

NOTES TO CHAPTER 8

1 See the section on "The Growth of Mind and Will" in Chapter 3.
2 "The Structure of Society," p. 85.
3 *Forms,* p. 328.
4 *The Good Life,* p. 144.
5 Two schools of educational thought bear this name. The first, inaugurated by Dewey and developed by his followers, is exemplified in such writings as B. Othanel Smith, William O. Stanley, and J. Harlan Shores, *Fundamentals of Curriculum Development* (Yonkers, New York: World Book Company, 1950; revised edition, 1957). Theodore Brameld heads the other school whose position is described in his *Patterns of Educational Philosophy* (Yonkers, New York: World Book Company, 1950; revised in two volumes,

Philosophies of Education in Cultural Perspective and *Toward a Reconstructed Philosophy of Education* [New York: The Dryden Press, 1955, 1956]). The similarities and differences between the two theories are not of concern here. Our analysis is confined to the first position, which is the more clear-cut elaboration of the social point of view.

6 The modern liberal in educational philosophy tends to identify "corporate" with "group"; thus Stanley characterizes contemporary society as a multigroup society.

7 Smith, Stanley, Shores, *op. cit.*, p. 194.

8 William O. Stanley, *Education and Social Integration* (New York: Teachers College, Columbia University, 1953), p. 1.

9 *Ibid.*, pp. 8–9.

10 *Ibid.*, p. 7.

11 *Ibid.*, pp. 10–11.

12 *Ibid.*, p. 12.

13 *Ibid.*

14 *The Good Life*, p. 139.

15 *The Aesthetic Object*, pp. 22–23.

16 Stanley, *op. cit.*, p. 246.

17 Stanley's conception of publics and the public follows the theory set out by Dewey in his major political work, *The Public and Its Problems*. A public comes into being when the consequences of action involve persons beyond those directly engaged in the act, and affect them to such an extent that it is necessary to provide systematic regulation of these consequences. In the creation of such regulatory agencies, a public becomes organized into a state. (*Op. cit.*, p. 39 *passim.*) For a sharp criticism of Dewey's political philosophy as an interest or pressure group theory of the state leading to disastrous results for education, a criticism which is in fundamental agreement with our evaluation of Stanley's position, see Alexander Meiklejohn, *Education Between Two Worlds* (New York: Harper and Brothers, 1942). Meiklejohn says, "The pragmatic account of intelligence, as here given (*The Public and Its Problems*), robs it of all objectivity, all disinterestedness. What it offers us is not a state. It is a shifting, whirling collocation of pressure groups, of factions, of parties, in the baser sense of that term. Government becomes, not a unified attempt at freedom and justice, but a miscellaneous collection of 'interested' activities, each of which is directed toward the welfare of some individual or private group." Though Dewey talks much about unity, The Great Community, shared interest, and the like, according to Meiklejohn, "the logic of his argument is driving irresistibly in the opposite direction. It is that pluralistic logic which has tended to make of our American scheme of government nothing more than the competitive clash of 'pressure groups,' each fighting for its own hand. Each such group, as it is affected by the consequences of the actions of other groups, rushes to its own defense. The body

politic becomes, therefore, not an organic unity of sympathy and solidarity, as Rousseau would make it, not an agency for taking counsel together, for establishing disinterested and objective judgment. It is a bedlam of privately warring factions. The method of inquiry into consequences, as Dewey uses it or fails to use it, does not, and cannot, give an adequate theory of political life. In a world gone mad with self-interest, it provides no sanity. It does not unite men in the common search for justice, for objectivity, for disinterestedness. It splits them asunder into groups, between which such terms as 'discriminating criticism,' 'intelligent method,' or 'a conscious criterion' can have no meaning whatever. In such a world there is nothing 'objective' to teach." (*Education Between Two Worlds*, pp. 178 and 180–81.)

18 John Dewey, *Democracy and Education* (New York: The Macmillan Company, 1916), p. 117.

19 R. B. Raup, G. E. Axtelle, K. D. Benne, and B. O. Smith, *The Improvement of Practical Intelligence* (New York: Harper and Brothers, 1950), p. 217.

20 Stanley, *op. cit.*, p. 226.

21 *Ibid.*

22 *Ibid.*, pp. 256–57.

23 *Democracy and Education*, p. 59.

24 *Experience and Education*, pp. vi and 115.

25 Alfred North Whitehead, *Adventure of Ideas* (Cambridge: Cambridge University Press, 1933), p. 68.

26 *The Good Life*, p. 306.

27 *Ibid.*

28 *Forms*, pp. 286–87.

29 Huntington Cairns, *Legal Philosophy from Plato to Hegel* (Baltimore: The Johns Hopkins Press, 1949), p. 331.

NOTES TO CHAPTER 9

1 *The Good Life*, p. 301.

2 *Ibid.*, pp. 242–43.

3 *Ibid.*, p. 313.

4 *Theory*, pp. 387–88.

5 *The Good Life*, pp. 303–4.

6 *Ibid.*, p. 302.

7 *Ibid.*, p. 241.

8 *Ibid.*, p. 304.

9 *Ibid.*, p. 240.

10 *Ibid.*, p. 303.

11 *Ibid.*, pp. 240–41.

12 The adjective might be omitted before both "personality" and "world" since they are such entities only to the extent that they are unities or wholes. A disintegrated personality or a disintegrated world would be the elimination of each rather than a form of each.

13 *The Good Life*, p. 355.

14 *Ibid.,* p. 368.
15 *Theory,* p. 33.
16 *The Good Life,* pp. 354–55.
17 *Ibid.,* pp. 305 and 313.
18 *Ibid.,* p. 312.
19 *Ibid.,* p. 355.
20 These maxims of method are stated in Jordan's early work on psychology, *The Life of Mind,* pp. 4–5, and in his work on ethics, *The Good Life,* pp. 308–9. Ethical control is not imposed from without, but is built upon understanding the nature of the object to be controlled.
21 *The Good Life,* p. 308.
22 *The Life of Mind,* p. 5.
23 *The Good Life,* p. 310.
24 *Ibid.,* p. 306.
25 *Democracy and Education,* pp. 113–16.
26 John Dewey, *Reconstruction in Philosophy* (New York: The New American Library of World Literature, 1950; original edition published by Henry Holt and Company, 1920), p. 160.
27 *The Good Life,* p. 306.
28 *Ibid.,* p. 357.
29 *Forms,* p. 258.
30 *The Good Life,* p. 314.
31 Cf., for example, *Forms, passim; The Good Life,* pp. 314–23; "The Philosophical Problem of Religion," *Ethics,* LXV (1955), pp. 192–200; "The False Principle of Liberalism," pp. 281–83.
32 *The Good Life,* p. 307.
33 *Ibid.*

NOTES TO CHAPTER 10

1 *Business,* p. 95.
2 *Ibid.,* pp. 94–95.
3 *Ibid.,* p. 65.
4 E. Jordan, "Concerning Philosophy," *Philosophical Review,* L (1943), pp. 114–15.
5 *The Life of Mind,* pp. 302–7.
6 *The Good Life,* p. 445.
7 *Ibid.,* p. 307.
8 *Ibid.,* p. 313.
9 *Ibid.,* p. 305.
10 *The Dialogues of Plato,* Vol. II, trans. by B. Jowett, p. 249.
11 *Ibid.,* p. 250.
12 *Theory,* pp. 228–29.
13 *The Good Life,* p. 311.
14 *Theory,* p. 35.
15 *Ibid.,* p. 336.
16 *Ibid.,* p. 338.
17 *Ibid.,* p. 325.

18 *The Good Life*, p. 59.
19 *Ibid.*, p. 301.
20 *Ibid.*, p. 313. The slight equivocation is unnecessary.
21 F. S. C. Northrop and Mason W. Gross, eds., *Alfred North White-head: An Anthology* (New York: The Macmillan Company, 1953), p. 921. From Alfred North Whitehead, *Modes of Thought*.
22 *Theory*, p. 8.
23 Myron Lieberman, *Education as a Profession* (Englewood Cliffs, New Jersey: Prentice-Hall, Inc., 1956), p. 495.
24 John S. Gambs, in a book review, *The Progressive* (October 1957), p. 38.
25 Stuart Chase, "Peace, It's Terrible," *The Progressive* (January 1960), p. 19.
26 Cited in Aldous Huxley, *Science, Liberty, and Peace* (New York: Harper and Brothers, 1956), p. 1.
27 Bertrand Russell, *The Impact of Science on Society* (New York: Simon and Schuster, 1953), pp. 97–98.
28 "The Role of Philosophy in Social Crisis," p. 379.
29 Bertrand Russell, *Why Men Fight* (New York: The Century Co., 1916), pp. 180–81. Originally published as *Principles of Social Reconstruction* (London: George Allen and Unwin Ltd.).
30 "The Role of Philosophy in Social Crisis," pp. 390–91.